A CHRISTIAN
FOR ALL CHRISTIANS

A CHRISTIAN
FOR
ALL CHRISTIANS

Essays in Honor of
C. S. LEWIS

Edited by
Dr. Andrew Walker *and* Dr. James Patrick

REGNERY GATEWAY
Washington, D.C.

LIBRARY OF CONGRESS CATALOGING-IN-PUBLICATION DATA

A Christian for all Christians : essays in honor of C.S. Lewis /
edited by Andrew Walker and James Patrick.
    p.   cm.
Originally published: London : Hodder and Stoughton, 1990.
Includes bibliographical references and index.
ISBN 0-89526-735-7 (alk. paper)
1. Lewis, C. S. (Clive Staples), 1898–1963. 2. Theology—20th
century. 3. Christianity and literature—History—20th century.
4. Apologetics—History—20th century. I. Lewis, C. S. (Clive
Staples), 1898–1963. II. Walker, Andrew, 1945–   . III. Patrick,
James, 1933–   .
BX4827.L44C48   1992
230'.092—dc20   91-46796
                                                                      CIP

First published in Great Britain by Hodder and Stoughton Limited,
in conjunction with the C.S. Lewis Centre.

Published in the United States by
Regnery Gateway
1130 17th Street, NW
Washington, DC 20036

Distributed to the trade by
National Book Network
4720-A Boston Way
Lanham, MD 20706

Printed on acid free paper

Manufactured in the United States of America

96 95 94 93 92   10 9 8 7 6 5 4 3 2 1

C. S. LEWIS

Jack knew his Master's awesome tenderness
And tongue that slashed through Pharisaic stress.
The willing servant grew more like his Lord:
At once a lover and a genial sword.

       —Sheldon Vanauken

CONTENTS

PREFACE

by Andrew Walker, Director of the C. S. Lewis Centre

The C. S. Lewis Centre for the Study of Religion and Modernity has made it clear, since its inception in 1987, that it is not a C. S. Lewis appreciation society, but a research organisation dedicated to tackling the problems of the modern world in the light of the gospel. To demonstrate our commitment to this programme, we published in 1988, on the twenty-fifth anniversary of Lewis' death, not a book *on* Lewis but one dedicated *to* him. This book, *Different Gospels* (London: Hodder and Stoughton/C. S. Lewis Centre, 1988), was our way of saying to Lewis, 'Though we honour you, and your witness to the gospel, we do not wish to build a shrine to your memory; we wish to try, however inadequately, to continue your work.'

Nevertheless, while we do not wish to idolise Lewis, or join his ever-growing band of hagiographers, we do wish to remember him well. The C. S. Lewis Centre, after all, did not adopt Lewis' name by chance. We chose the name of C. S. Lewis for three specific reasons.

First, we felt that Lewis, perhaps uniquely in the twentieth century, appeals to all those who stand for the common, or foundational, basis of historic Christianity. The concept of 'Mere Christianity', which Lewis takes from Richard Baxter, is certainly not without problems (see James Patrick's 'Lewis and Idealism' in this volume, pp. 156–73), and clearly is not explicit enough for denominational exactitude. However, as a basis for a genuine ecumenism that reflects a 'high' view of Scripture and the doctrines of the ancient creeds and councils of the early church, it has much to recommend it. As the C. S. Lewis Centre says in its promotional literature, the Centre qua research organisation stands for a 'broad trinitarian orthodoxy'. Consequently, the Centre has been able to attract Roman Catholics, Eastern Orthodox, and Protestant Reformed who have come together, with all their unresolved differences, for the sake of the gospel.

Second, Lewis was recognised by us not only as a standard-bearer for historic Christianity, but also as one who 'earnestly contended for the faith' in a post-Enlightenment culture which is, almost by definition, antagonistic to Christian commitments to revelation and tradition. To divide revelation from tradition may be a false dichotomy, but for most supporters of the C. S. Lewis Centre our concern is to recognise, and indeed promote, the richness of our Christian heritage. We are indeed Christians living in the modern world, but we have a history, and we are what we are as Christians because God has acted decisively in history through the incarnation and the death and resurrection of our Lord.

Lewis' historical Christianity, and his conviction that there was a *philosophia perennis* which transcended (but always penetrated) cultures, led him to a critical appraisal of modernity. From his friend and one-time mentor Owen Barfield he learned that there was a 'chronological snobbery' abroad in contemporary society. Moderns find it very difficult to be convinced that anything in the past was superior to present-day thinking. The wisdom of the sages, which Lewis believed was an unchanging *sapientia*, is often given short shrift in modernity. For many of our students in North America and Europe today, old books are old hat.

Lewis spent a great deal of his critical energy in challenging chronological snobbery. If he did not always totally succeed (and Basil Mitchell, in this volume, asks us to remember that Lewis was not a professional philosopher, pp. 10–11, 14–15), neither can it be said that he did not have major successes. In

particular, it is difficult to think of a more brilliant defence of
classicism, in the face of modern subjectivist and relativistic
thought, than his *The Abolition of Man* (London: Collins
Fount, 1978).

We try hard in the C. S. Lewis Centre not to fall into the
reverse trap of Romanticism: rejecting modernity because it
is modern. But we have learned from Lewis not to be afraid to
use the tools of critical analysis (which the modernists among
us value above all else) against modernity itself. As Christians, in the historic tradition, we have adopted a stance
concerning the ideologies and fashions of our contemporary
society not of outright rejection, but of what Lewis called 'a
due agnosticism' (see 'Fern-seed and Elephants' in *Fern-
Seed and Elephants and other essays on Christianity*, ed. W.
Hooper (London: Collins Fount, 1977), p. 122).

If the C. S. Lewis Centre has adopted from Lewis a
critical stance in relation to modern culture – a stance which
is itself rooted in historic Christianity – we have also tried
hard to learn from Lewis the knack of writing for 'every-
man'. This does not mean that we have Lewis' gift of communicating the gospel outside the academy, but it does
mean that we are committed to reaching the intelligent
lay-person with the minimum amount of academic jargon.
This is the third way in which the C. S. Lewis Centre owes a
debt to Lewis.

A Christian for All Christians is, in a small way, an attempt
to repay that debt. There is a time, as we said above, for
remembering, for respect, for love. This does not mean that
we have abandoned our critical judgements, or that all the
people represented in this volume are enamoured with all of
Lewis' life and thought. A great many of us who might call
ourselves 'Lewis buffs' are often more judicious in our evaluation of 'Jack' than A. N. Wilson in his book *C. S. Lewis:
A Biography* (London: Collins, 1990) might lead one to
suppose.

Having said that, as editors, James Patrick and myself
have not insisted on a uniform approach to Lewis. Our

distinguished authors have been free either to defend
Lewis, criticise him, or promote him.

Our aim in this volume has been, first of all, to represent the
full ecumenical depth of Lewis scholarship. Our authors come
from England, Continental Europe, and North America.
They are Catholics, Eastern Orthodox, and Protestants.
Second, we felt that a collection of essays in honour of C. S.
Lewis demanded original material; therefore none of the
essays presented here has appeared in print before. Third,
and most important, *A Christian for All Christians* provides
much information – some of which will be new even to Lewis
aficionados – about the influences on Lewis' life and the
formation of his thought, as well as a critical evaluation of
some of his books and beliefs.

In ordering and arranging the essays in this volume, we
have adopted a 'family resemblance' or 'cluster' approach,
beginning with biography and apologetics, and moving on to
literary and personal influences on Lewis. This focus in its
turn gives way to one on the stories of Lewis, then on his
philosophy and doctrine, and the essays proper end with a
look at Lewis' philosophy of history.

Acknowledgements

We wish to thank Stephen Schofield, editor of the Canadian
C. S. Lewis journal, for his helpfulness during the compilation of this volume. Special thanks go to David Mackinder,
the editorial officer of the C. S. Lewis Centre, for his outstanding contribution in terms of bibliographical research and
the copy-editing of this volume.

INTRODUCTION
James Patrick

On the afternoon of Friday 22 November 1963, Clive Staples
Lewis entered the foothills of the coloured lands and began
the journey towards the centre of the mountains that had
shaped his imagination at least since 1931, when his own
journey from Puritania to the high western hills, allegorised in
The Pilgrim's Regress,[1] had become a Christian quest.
  Lewis died in the house he loved, the Kilns at Headington,
which by then held the memories of a lifetime. The house had
been purchased in 1933 with the legacy that came to the Lewis
brothers, Jack and Warren, at the death of their father Albert
Lewis. Lewis had shared the Kilns with Mrs Moore and her
daughter Maureen until Maureen's marriage in 1941 and Mrs
Moore's death in 1951. When Major Warren Lewis had
retired from active service in 1930, he had moved into the
house with his brother and the Moores, and then from 1956 to
1960 the Kilns saw the unexpected happiness of Jack Lewis
and Joy Davidman, the American poet he had married from
pity who became at last the crowning adventure of his life.
  But in the autumn of 1963 those memories and glories were
past, and Jack Lewis set sail without regret. He had, he told
his brother, finished the work he had been given to do. And
so, C. S. Lewis passed from the church militant and the
university argumentative here on earth into the kingdom of
God's mercy and fruition.

He had finished his work, but readers were hardly finished with Jack Lewis, and after 1963 sales of his books continued to soar, especially in the United States.

The essays that follow are reflections on the meaning of C. S. Lewis after more than twenty-five years. The passing of time inevitably creates a shifting perspective, and Lewis, if his work is to live, can escape the historians no more than any other man whose writing has made his mind a public property. Remarkably, there is still no important revisionist historiography. Questions have been raised about the effects on him of the death of his beloved Joy Davidman, about his interest in Orthodoxy and his relation to the Roman Catholic Church. But these are footnotes; the central themes of Lewis' life's work are as clear after more than twenty-five years as at the time of his death. Each of his apologies rings the changes on the same great themes: the reliability of reason as a guide to God; the pattern of the Christian moral life; the recovery of imagination for Christ; faith as the fruition of desire; and the reliability of the broad and humane Christian tradition.

Yet to enumerate these intellectual contributions – and others could certainly be included – provides no answer to the question: Who was Jack Lewis, the short, stocky man in baggy flannels who became the summary intellect of English-speaking Christendom, and the twentieth-century's most read Christian apologist? He was a great teacher (at least for many), a successful defender of the faith, and a scholar of influence and reputation. But none of these titles captures the significance of his life and work. Perhaps this is because in the most fundamental sense Lewis was the critical link in a tradition of English and European learning which he would have been the first to proclaim greater and more significant than anything he or his friends might think or write. His career was the fulfilment of the English Romantic tradition. The very word Romanticism provokes complex meanings; Lewis himself offered eight definitions of Romanticism in the 1943 Preface to *The Pilgrim's Regress*. But at its root the Romantic movement in England was not a theory or point of view or a single idea, but was at its heart an intellectual campaign for the recovery of the tradition which had formed Europe from St Augustine to Spenser.

Beginning with Coleridge, taking momentum from sources as divergent as Augustus Pugin, Thomas Hill Green, and the *Lux Mundi*[2] authors, there was after 1800 a broad tendency in English letters and scholarship to overcome Hume, Hobbes, Herbert and Wollston by appealing to an older, more deeply rooted tradition which was necessarily Christian. In England access to the tradition rooted in the time before scholasticism was displaced and religion reformed was, especially after the polemics of the Elizabethan reign and the religious tensions of the seventeenth century, difficult and unfashionable. The Middle Ages had been banished from English experience, the 'old, holy doctors' of the first millennium not faring much better than the scholastics. The word 'Gothic' was used by Thomas More in the sixteenth century and by the London diarist John Evelyn in the seventeenth as a pejorative describing the life and art of the Germanic, barbarian, pre-Renaissance civilisation.

Then in the nineteenth century the classic period of Western Christendom came roaring back, borne on the wings of architecture and poetry, then rooted more substantively in theology and philosophy. Oddly, perhaps, this movement was the activity of scholars, poets, and architects, and co-incided with the failure in popular culture of the last living reminiscence of the world of moral discourse presupposed by Shakespeare and Hooker. Since 1500 the dominant English religion had become customary, then conventional, then, by the reign of Victoria, merely aesthetic, so that the sentiments expressed in romantic poetry and Gothic-revival churches were likely to be as progressive as the forms of art and poetry were antique. About 1870 it seemed evident that the native empiricism – Hume perfected by Mill, and Bacon fulfilled by Charles Darwin – would occupy the intellectual terrain unopposed.

Looking back across the nineteenth century, Lewis and his

teachers and friends interpreted the change of mind and heart that took place in English thought and culture about 1830 as a great intellectual divide that separated them from the entire classical, medieval, and Renaissance past. Lewis, Charles Williams, and J. R. R. Tolkien believed that there was more distance between themselves and Jane Austen than between Jane Austen and Plato. Thus they inevitably saw themselves as apostles of tradition, and it was Lewis who succeeded best in rejoining the England of George VI and the National Institute of Co-ordinated Experiments to the world of Macrobius, Dionysius, and Hooker. In his famous Cambridge inaugural lecture, '*De Descriptione Temporum*',[3] Lewis called himself 'old western man', and compared himself to a dinosaur, a rare survival from another age, capable of testifying to a time forgotten by his modern beholders.

C. S. Lewis was the best of the great men born in the twilight of the Victorian age who inspired a kind of second Renaissance, a grand attempt to recover the great tradition regarding things human and divine at a time when it was fading. Lewis sensed himself becoming an alien in a time and place occupied by intellectual and spiritual barbarism. This was the common stance of the great men of the 1930s: T. S. Eliot, Jacques Maritain, Etienne Gilson, R. G. Collingwood, the whole company of Thomist-revival scholars, as well as Owen Barfield and J. R. R. Tolkien. Of this distinguished company none was – as an apologist not simply for past thought, but for the great tradition – as successful as Lewis. One must reach back to G. K. Chesterton, whose work deeply influenced Lewis, to find another apologist as powerful. And the reason for that power was the depth and breadth of the tradition Lewis represented. E. F. Carritt, later Lewis' philosophy tutor and mentor, wrote that when Lewis took the examinations for Oxford in 1916 he was the most widely-read undergraduate Carritt had ever interviewed. This ability to comprehend and mediate the tradition lent Lewis' work its power. Behind the space-fiction trilogy[4] was the immense erudition collected in the lectures that comprise *The Dis-*

carded Image.[5] Behind *The Screwtape Letters*[6] was the entire moral tradition of the Caroline Divines, and behind them Hooker, Aquinas, Augustine and Chrysostom. So the power of Lewis' writing was its ability to capture the very wisdom that first the Enlightenment, and then the new philosophy of his undergraduate days, had rendered obscure; to gather this up that nothing be lost, and to make it the well-spring of his twentieth-century apology. And in that sense Lewis' freshness always strikes one anew. He had few ideas of his own and claimed no originality. But for him knowledge was not simply knowledge of old books. Lewis' learning was rooted in a source that lay beyond libraries and beyond texts. Aquinas and Hooker and Chesterton and George MacDonald were witnesses to Christ, and it was Christ who held Lewis' heart.

If we look for an analogy to his accomplishment, for a figure standing at the end of an age and epitomising it, contemplating on good evidence the extinction of a world he holds dear, but full of faith, we must perhaps look back to the seam that ran between antiquity and the Christian Middle Ages, to Boethius, who, like Lewis, lived in a barbarian time, gathering up the wisdom of the past for Christ, and presented it in ways that made it live beyond the failure of his civilisation. Lewis wrote that to know Boethius was to become a naturalised citizen of the Middle Ages. To know Lewis is to become a citizen of the medieval and Renaissance world in which to be literate was to be Christian.

To the degree that this is Lewis' importance, these interpretive essays in his honour are not only justified but essential, for on this showing C. S. Lewis is an important link in the Christian scholarly tradition, and to revivify his thought through reflection and criticism is to make both Lewis and the great tradition live.

1

REFLECTIONS ON C. S. LEWIS, APOLOGETICS, AND THE MORAL TRADITION

*Basil Mitchell in Conversation
with Andrew Walker*

Andrew Walker: Professor Mitchell, you knew C. S. Lewis and were involved with him in the Oxford University Socratic Club. Can you tell me about the Socratic Club before you became its President when Lewis left for Cambridge in 1954?
Professor Basil Mitchell: Well, before he moved to Cambridge Lewis had been President of the Socratic Club, and a formidable lady called Stella Aldwinckle had been Chairman. I started to go there regularly when I came back from the Navy in 1946.

When Lewis left I became President and Stella Aldwinckle continued as Chairman. And during that period, I think it is fair to say, it was really the liveliest philosophical society in Oxford.
AW: What influence did Lewis have on your generation of Christians? I mean, was he a *major* influence on you?
BM: Undoubtedly. I think he was a major influence on large numbers of people who had been brought up as Christians, who had somewhat drifted away, and who hoped it might be

true but had come to think it probably wasn't; and he, both intellectually and imaginatively, made it seem credible again.

AW: Lewis has sometimes been referred to as 'the apostle to the sceptics'. That might have been true for the decade 1940 to 1950, in which he did a great deal of his apologetical work, but there was a watershed in his output, wasn't there?

In his autobiography *Surprised by Joy*[1] he makes a distinction – and I suppose this is true of the whole of his epistemology – between two ways of knowing. He talks, if I remember rightly, about *savoir* and *connaitre* – and I suppose the imaginative side, the intuitive side of Lewis, became even more apparent in the 1950s when he wrote the children's stories *The Chronicles of Narnia*. And it is the intuitive side, 'Lewis the storyteller', that most people think of today. In 1988, for example, half a million copies were sold of *The Lion, the Witch and the Wardrobe*[2] alone. The apologetical side of him is not so well known, and not so much thought of, but in the 1940s it was Lewis the apologist who was making the play, wasn't it?

BM: Yes, it was.

AW: I suppose that anyone who is an *afficionado* of Lewis, or who is particularly interested in Lewis' apologetical work, remembers the dreaded event of 1948.

In 1948 the Socratic Club held a debate on the subject of naturalism between Lewis and the young Catholic philosopher G. E. M. Anscombe – Elizabeth Anscombe as she is normally known. Now this debate is significant because a number of people thought that Lewis lost it. Whatever is the case, he ceased to engage in much apologetical work from that time until he died in 1963.

You were actually at that particular meeting. Perhaps the chances are you won't remember very much of the actual debate, but what can you remember of the atmosphere and the tension of that time?

BM: I can't remember the debate at all clearly. I don't have the sense that anything decisive happened at that moment, although it is the case, as you say, that from that point onwards Lewis obviously concluded that he wasn't equipped to cope with the professional philosophers.

Perhaps it would be of interest to you if I told you about a sequel to that encounter. John Lucas (a philosophical colleague of mine in Oxford) conceived the idea of having a re-run of the Anscombe–Lewis debate – except that he would undertake to uphold Lewis' side of the argument, and Elizabeth agreed to this. The debate took place (I can't remember when – some time in the 1960s), and on that occasion, I think it would generally be agreed, Lucas succeeded in sustaining Lewis' side of the argument. If one were to think in terms of winners or losers, I think maybe that Lucas was the winner on points, but there wasn't on *that* occasion any kind of tension.

AW: What was Lewis' argument against naturalism?

BM: Well, the point in Lewis' book on *Miracles*[3] that Elizabeth Anscombe particularly fastened upon was his claim that a naturalistic philosophy is logically incoherent. By which he meant that if you try to explain everything that happens in the world, including human decisions and human beliefs, in terms of scientific laws (*e.g.*, that at such and such a point, such and such an individual would be persuaded by certain arguments) – it follows that that person's acceptance of that argument cannot be the result of his being influenced by rational considerations, but is simply the result of whatever the antecedent scientific conditions were.

However the thesis is worked out in detail, the essence of the claim is that, if on the basis of scientific laws, whether physical or biological, someone's beliefs can be predicted, then it follows that those same beliefs cannot be arrived at by a process of reason.

Elizabeth attacked this argument of Lewis', maintaining that he had failed to distinguish between various senses of causation, and that, if you made the required distinctions, you could see that it is quite possible for a belief to be caused by some scientifically explicable process and yet at the same time to be a rational belief.

Now in the debate – I mean the re-run debate – Elizabeth and John agreed as to what the original Lewis–Anscombe dispute had been about, and Lucas simply maintained that on the substantial issue Lewis was right and that, for the sort of reasons Lewis had put forward, a thoroughly naturalistic philosophy was logically incoherent. And the outcome of that debate was to make it perfectly clear that, at the very least, Lewis' original thesis was an entirely arguable philosophical thesis and as defensible as most philosophical theses are.

So there was no warrant for supposing that in the original debate Lewis had been shown to be just hopelessly wrong. It was rather that he was not equipped with the kind of philosophical techniques which were needed at that stage to cope with a highly professional performer like Elizabeth Anscombe. And so Lewis probably drew the correct inference and decided that he couldn't take on the professional philosophers at their own game.

AW: I think we've established something very important here, because what you have suggested is not that Lewis had no inkling of how to do philosophy, but that his methodology was deficient, and particularly, I suppose, in terms of the post-Russellian, Moore and Wittgensteinian revolution in philosophy just after the First World War.

Lewis never, so far as we know, really read modern philosophers, did he? And in that sense one doesn't see him as being able to wield the techniques necessary in order to confront the philosophers of his day. Do you think this was really just a deficiency of method?

BM: I think it was a lack of familiarity with the way that philosophy was done at that particular time. Lewis and most of the educated people of his generation had been brought up on an essentially Platonist philosophy, whose methods were literary rather than scientifically analytical. When they were confronted with the so-called 'revolution in philosophy' pioneered by Russell and later, of course, sharpened by Logical Positivism as represented by Sir A. J. Ayer and others, they were simply baffled.

They were not only baffled, they were convinced that it couldn't be true: they knew in their heart of hearts that this was too narrow and arid a conception of what philosophy ought to be. On the other hand, they saw no particular point in spending a great deal of time in trying to master this sort of philosophy in order to come to grips with its exponents. Not being professional philosophers themselves, they had other things to do.

And I suppose that Lewis, after the encounter at the Socratic Club, realised that if he was going to take on people like Elizabeth Anscombe, he would have to do a lot of homework. He had no particular aptitude for – and no particular interest in – the dominant philosophy of his day, and he could better spend his time doing the other things that he was supremely good at.

AW: Which, of course, he went on to do in the 1950s.

BM: Yes.

AW: I think there are one or two things we could pick up here. Let me start, if I may, with an analogy.

In the 1970s, when I was doing my doctoral studies on the philosophy of science, one of the big disputes in those days was between Sir Karl Popper's conception of what philosophy should be about and what he felt a certain kind of Oxford philosopher thought philosophy should be about.

I wonder if that isn't really very far removed from what you've just said about Lewis. The issue is not just a question of method, but also a question of purpose: What is philosophy *for*? As you said earlier, there was a certain aridity about the new philosophical climate that Lewis noticed. It was almost as if he said, 'If this is what the new philosophy is, do we need to bother?' I'm not saying that he just dismissed it out of hand, but that, to use your phrase, 'in his heart of hearts' he felt it wasn't right.

We, however, have come a long way since the 1940s and the 1950s, when Logical Positivism and conceptual analysis held sway. Are we now in an atmosphere in which a more traditional metaphysics is likely to make a comeback? Because, although Logical Positivism is dead, conceptual analysis isn't quite, is it?

BM: Going back beyond that question a bit – if I ask myself why it never occurred to me to go into this sort of question with Lewis, I think the answer is that at the time I met Lewis I was a young philosophy don, and I realised, firstly, that I was going to have to spend my professional career in an intellectual atmosphere where philosophical analysis was dominant and, secondly, that if I intended to continue to take religion seriously, I was going to have to meet this challenge head-on. Now, for the reasons that we've already discussed, Lewis wasn't the man to help in that endeavour, so it was clear to me that although I'd been very greatly influenced by Lewis, and was enormously indebted to him, so far as this particular matter was concerned my vocation was different from his.

As a result of that realisation I found myself getting together with a number of people like Austin Farrer, Eric Mascall, Ian Crombie, Michael Foster – and at an earlier stage Iris Murdoch and Richard Hare, and at a later stage John Lucas – all of whom were more or less uncomfortable with what seemed to us to be the unduly circumscribed nature of the task of philosophy as understood by the analytical school at the time. And we tried to master the techniques of logical analysis in such a way as to open up once again the possibility of genuine metaphysical discussion.

In fact this particular group went on meeting for virtually forty years. It ended only three or four years ago. What its influence may have been I simply don't know, but it is true to say that in the last fifteen years or so the narrow philosophical orthodoxy which prevailed, in this country at any rate, since the War has loosened up quite remarkably, and the need to vindicate metaphysics as a respectable enterprise has been widely recognised, with the result that, for example, philosophy of religion is now quite widely practised and accepted as an entirely respectable discipline.

Interestingly, this development has been even more marked in the United States than in this country. The Society of Christian Philosophers in the States numbers, I'm told, something like nine hundred teachers of philosophy, and it is the largest single section in the American Philosophical Association. It is a quite remarkably flourishing institution.

AW: I think it's worth pointing out, I'm sure you'll agree, that this is really quite remarkable if we look back to the 1940s, and even the early 1950s, when metaphysical philosophy really was ruled out of court.

BM: Yes.

AW: I suppose we could specifically relate your intention to continue this sort of work to the fact that you took over the presidency of the Socratic Club.

How long were you involved with the Socratic Club – to its close in the 1960s?

BM: Well, as you know, I became President of the Socratic in 1954, when Lewis went to Cambridge. I remained as President until the Socratic finally came to an end round about 1970. So that was quite a long period.

And when the Socratic came to an end it wasn't, I think, anything specifically to do with a general lack of interest in the philosophy of religion, but rather to do with a lack of interest in University societies of that kind. The effect of the late 1960s was to cause a massive reduction in the number of undergraduate societies at Oxford. People just didn't any longer want to meet and discuss in this rather formal way.

AW: I'd like to turn to something else now, if I may.

We've seen how Lewis had an influence on you in your early professional life, and how to a certain extent you continued the sort of work he was doing, specifically of course with professional philosophers. I'd like to pursue two topics with you now.

Firstly, I'd like to ask you about Lewis' weaknesses as a philosopher – if you can think of anything specific. Can you, for example, identify any particular kind of argument that he used that you yourself would not use?

And, secondly, when we've considered those weaknesses, I'd like to turn the whole thing on its head – because I think it would be really rather misleading to suggest that Lewis couldn't do any philosophy at all – and I would like then to consider his strengths. After all, what was it about Lewis' work that influenced you? Which particular books that he wrote did you find the most profound?

So those are two questions really. Let's start with the weak side of Lewis. As an apologist, speaking now in the philosophical sense, not just in the broader rhetorical sense, where do you think Lewis' weaknesses really showed? Particularly in those books such as *Miracles* and *The Problem of Pain*,[4] and perhaps even *Mere Christianity*.[5]

BM: I don't think that I want to think of it in those terms, because to think in those terms of Lewis' weaknesses as a philosopher would imply that one *regarded* him as a philosopher, whereas it is much more true to say that one didn't at that time regard him as a philosopher *at all*, because a philosopher, as one understood the term, was someone working within certain fairly precise limits, and arguing in certain fairly clearly delimited ways, and Lewis just didn't fit into this pattern. One regarded him as a lively independent thinker, but not specifically as a philosopher. He'd read Greats, he'd taught philosophy for a while, he was well acquainted with the philosophical classics, he had the sort of mind which, had he addressed himself to the questions that engrossed philsophers of the time, would have made him into a good philosopher by professional standards – but he simply wasn't 'one of the club', so to speak, and if you were asked to give a list of the leading philosophers in Oxford – or even of *the* philosophers in Oxford – Lewis wouldn't have been mentioned among them. So it wasn't a question of specific weaknesses; I mean, he produced some good searching arguments and clearly had a feeling for what was philosophically interesting and what wasn't, but he didn't go into questions with the kind of meticulous care for detail that was particularly characteristic of the philosophers of that period . . .

AW: Can I just take you up on that? I think this is a very good point you've made, because one of my criticisms of John

Beversluis' really rather devastating critique of Lewis' work, *C. S. Lewis and the Search for Rational Religion*,[6] is that he tends to treat him as if he were a professional philosopher who didn't do very well. But you're really suggesting that to treat Lewis by that criterion is unfair, that he never really claimed to be a philosopher, he was just a chap who felt he ought to take on, as it were, the fashionable theories of the day.

BM: Yes. You see, I think that with hindsight one can see that even the best philosophy of Lewis' day, done in this particular analytical tradition, was subject to a number of pretty severe limitations.

The whole idea of philosophical analysis assumed that it was possible to isolate certain questions and deal with them very, very rigorously, in such detail that almost inevitably you couldn't attempt large and subjectively important questions – they were simply unmanageable. So perhaps it wasn't entirely accidental that the philosophers of that period thought that you couldn't *in principle* handle philosophically very large questions.

Now I think that you can see in retrospect that if you're going to do that, and handle somewhat limited questions very minutely, you can only do it at the expense of making some very large assumptions which never enter into the argument at all, which are just not questioned.

AW: You mean the hidden presuppositions by which one allows oneself to continue to do this kind of micro-philosophical work?

BM: Yes. Quite. That's right. And I think that among Lewis' strengths as a thinker was his ability to see that there were very large assumptions being made, and to attack those assumptions.

A work that provides a very good example of this approach is *The Abolition of Man*.[7] A great deal of what passed for moral philosophy at that time did assume a subjectivist (or what in his book *After Virtue*[8] Alasdair MacIntyre calls an emotivist) position. In *The Abolition of Man* Lewis attacked this head-on – and I think in retrospect one can see that he was entirely right to do so.

It took people like MacIntyre, who'd gone through the mill of logical analysis, to show by precise philosophical reasoning what was wrong with the subjectivist approach to ethics. However, as we have seen, this was not the sort of task Lewis himself was equipped to undertake, but he had the larger vision to see intuitively that there was something profoundly wrong with it, and he marshalled arguments against it which are of considerable philosophical weight, although they are not technical philosophical arguments.

AW: I think that is an extremely helpful way of highlighting the value of *The Abolition of Man*. It demonstrates something you said earlier, that to a certain generation of Christians who thought that one couldn't any longer consider Christianity intellectually respectable, Lewis showed that you really could put up some quite reasonable arguments in its defence – that one didn't have to assume that the enemy has all the good arguments. So, regardless of whether judged by the philosophy of his day they were sufficiently philosophically technical, Lewis' arguments persuaded many people of good intelligence that Christian apologetics was still possible.

Furthermore, *The Abolition of Man* is important not simply because in it Lewis uncharacteristically (in comparison with his method in his other works) builds up very good critical arguments against certain kinds of fashions, particularly against 'subjectiveness' (as he calls it) and relativism, but also because he spells out almost disarmingly the position of classicism, or what he calls the *Tao*, which he doesn't so much defend philosophically as present as an accumulative argument.

Do you feel that *The Abolition of Man* is an apologetical book that has lasted?

BM: Oh yes. I think remarkably well. And I think it is very interesting, the convergence between Alasdair MacIntyre's argument – both in *After Virtue* and in his most recent book *Whose Justice? Which Rationality?*[9] – and the line that Lewis was taking in *The Abolition of Man*. You could say that in *The Abolition of Man* Lewis had a sort of intuitive vision of the kind of argument that in a more philosophically sophisticated way MacIntyre has marshalled in these books.

And of course another very interesting thing is the extremely circuitous route by which MacIntyre has arrived at his present position.

For a short period he tried to hold together the philosophy of Logical Positivism and the theology of Karl Barth. (And you can see how they would fit together, in that the Positivists assert that theological statements are nonsense and Barth says 'Yes, of course, you're absolutely right; looked at from the standpoint of human reason thcy're nonsense – that's why it has to be a matter of divine revelation!') Well, Alasdair was holding these two things together and arguing that, for this reason, there couldn't be a rational debate between theism and atheism. And I wrote an article entitled 'The Justification of Religious Belief' which was concerned with querying this and suggesting an alternative, which I later developed in the book entitled *The Justification of Religious Belief*.[10]

AW: I would have thought that the argument of *The Justification of Religious Belief* is something of a bridge between Lewis and the more recent MacIntyre – in fact it's MacIntyre before MacIntyre – in that it thinks through the presuppositions on which a great deal of modern thought has been based.

BM: Yes.

AW: I particularly remember the way in which you deal in that book with the idea that only the belief in theism has these intellectual problems. In fact all philosophies of life have these same sorts of problems. And in that respect, would it offend you to say that one can see you in the Lewis tradition?

BM: Oh no, not in the least. I'd be very pleased to be told that.

But the interesting thing I was suggesting about MacIntyre is that I had rather hoped that my article might, among other influences, persuade him into a more central tradition of rational Christianity. In the end, though, he gave up Christianity altogether and only came back to it comparatively late in his career, and came back to it by way of actually passing through the states of mind which he subsequently criticised – so he was criticising, so to speak, his past self. And it's particularly noteworthy that some of the criticisms that he eventually made of the positions that he used to occupy do very much reflect the general line that Lewis was taking in *The Abolition of Man*.

AW: I absolutely agree with you. *After Virtue* is a book which many people have recognised as a major work. And yet it constantly reminds me of Lewis' approach.

Perhaps, though, it has one or two advantages over Lewis. The first is that it has, I think, a sociological grasp Lewis simply didn't have. And secondly it is more professionally marshalled.

BM: The point of convergence between MacIntyre and Lewis is that, like Lewis, MacIntyre argues that there is a central moral tradition which one can't dispense with – which can be developed, but which can't be altogether rejected. And that this tradition is a shared tradition. It can't be thought up, as it were, by a single individual – it has to be something that is widely accepted in the society. And that is not far from saying what Lewis says in *The Abolition of Man*, that the acceptance of the *Tao* is a function of being human, and that those people who, post-Nietzsche (or maybe even post-Hume), have been trying to regard ethics as essentially the creation of individual preferences are eventually depriving themselves of what makes them human. Now I think that this is very much the central theme, both in MacIntyre's book and in Lewis' essay.

MacIntyre is – and always has been – someone who is extremely sensitive to the cultural currents of the age. He has had, as it were, to be carried along by all these currents before coming to a point at which he can make a true evaluation of them.

I'm intrigued that quite often people remark on the resemblance between the book I wrote about morality, *Morality:*

Religious and Secular,[11] and MacIntyre's book, and ask did I get it from MacIntyre or did MacIntyre get it from me? And the answer must be 'Neither,' because I certainly didn't get it from MacIntyre. When *After Virtue* appeared I was intrigued, because it was so different from the things I last heard MacIntyre saying. And I'm perfectly sure that MacIntyre wouldn't have read anything that I wrote – it's very unlikely, because he was moving in really rather different intellectual circles. But there is quite a considerable convergence there.

What has happened now – and not only in the case of Alasdair MacIntyre – is that there's a great sense of the wheel having come full circle, and the issues which were supposed to have been disposed of twenty or thirty years ago are now all being hotly debated again. And that means that some of the people who were writing then, and whose works have been neglected, have been revived and are being studied once more.

AW: Yes, I agree. John Macmurray's personalist philosophy, which is exemplified perhaps most clearly in his *Persons in Relation*,[12] and which went through a period of almost total neglect, is now being taken up – rediscovered – by various theologians concerned with theological anthropology.

What do you think has caused 'the wheel to come full circle'?

BM: I think that the chief influence was the development of the philosophy of science. If you remember, the Logical Positivist movement started as an attempt to make a clear demarcation between science and common sense on the one hand, and metaphysics and theology on the other. But work in the philosophy of science convinced people that what the Logical Positivists had said about science was not true, and, by the time the philosophers of science had developed and amplified their accounts of how rationality works in science, people discovered that similar accounts applied equally well to the areas which they had previously sought to exclude, namely theology and metaphysics.

I think the work of Thomas S. Kuhn was crucial here –

particularly the thesis developed in his book *The Structure of Scientific Revolutions*.[13] Although subsequent criticism has shown that Kuhn exaggerated the incommensurability of these 'paradigms', as he calls them, nevertheless the essential truth of his discoveries remains – namely, that when it comes to making a choice between large-scale scientific theories there isn't any system of rules that will enable you to do it. It's got to be done by a careful comparison of the two systems, each of which claims to provide a complete overall explanation of the phenomena. You either have to say that there's no way of choosing, or you have to say that there is a way of choosing, but that it's a matter of which explanation offers the best overall account – and this will eventually be a matter of judgement. But then, if that's true in comparing large-scale scientific theories, it's equally true in comparing metaphysical systems – whether theistic or materialistic – or indeed in comparing different moral theories. So you find yourself, simply as a result of taking seriously developments in the philosophy of science, embracing a concept of rationality which is broad enough to include all the things that Lewis and his contemporaries took for granted were worth arguing about. And that's why a lot of the stuff that Lewis wrote doesn't seem anything like as out of date as one would have expected.

AW: I have to agree with you about that. In 1988 I did a tour of American and British cities during which I gave lectures on Lewis to mixed audiences, ranging from a thousand people at Greenbelt to eighty people in the chapel at King's College London. The extraordinary thing was that not only were people obviously extremely well read in Lewis' works, but they were fascinated by his arguments and felt that people were still benefiting from them.

I'd like to change the subject now and, in drawing to a conclusion, raise something I'd like your views on. It's something I know you've been working on.

On the one hand it strikes me as almost a truism – not from a philosophical point of view but from a historical and cultural point of view – that if you have a daily face-to-face social interaction with people, of the kind that you get in a village (or that you used to get in any pre-industrialised society), where there is a certain amount of shared views about how the universe works (at least in ethical terms if not necessarily in physical terms), then to a certain extent it means that moral discourse can proceed – that at least we've got in common a basic idea of what's right and what's wrong.

But on the other hand I frequently find in modern industrial society, particularly with undergraduates – regardless of whether I'm doing theology or I'm doing sociology – that many of them share the view that everything is 'just a matter of opinion', and that to suggest that there may be some objectivity that exists almost irrespective of one's subjective opinion is a terrible cheek, or at the least a very strange idea.

Is this second feature, do you think, just a fashion that we're going through – one that Lewis almost prophetically saw forty years ago – or is it a result of features of our contemporary world such as vastly increased social mobility, mass immigration and emigration, and the mass media, where there are so many views on sale that people are very confused about what truth might look like? Do you think, for example, that we're witnessing a vast change in the way that our culture works, or do you see this as a philosophical problem?

BM: Well, first of all I meet you with an example from my own teaching experience.

I remember particularly – this was over ten years ago now – I was taking an undergraduate class of about fifteen students with someone else in the philosophy of religion at a 'prestigious liberal arts college' in the United States, and I became very rapidly aware that they reacted strongly against any attempt to provide a rational criticism of, or to look for a rational defence of, their religious views. And this is what I found – it was an interesting cross-cultural thing – that one would just get them to read essays, and I would start, habitually, in the way I would an Oxford tutorial, and I would say

'Yes, well that was an extremely interesting presentation. I'm not quite sure, however, that I understood what you were getting at in that first paragraph. I wonder whether you could explain it a bit more?' And then the chap would go on, usually saying a whole lot of further things. And I would say, 'No, I didn't want you to tell me some other things that you think. I just wanted you to explain to me what you actually meant by the things that you said in that particular paragraph.' And then with difficulty I'd get them to elucidate a bit, and then I'd say 'Yes, I think I see that . . . but in that case, is that really consistent with what I took you to be saying in your summing up? In your first paragraph you were saying such and such, in your final paragraph you were saying so and so. On the face of it these two aren't consistent.' And they *very* much disliked this. And I came to the conclusion that it wasn't just that they weren't used to this sort of Socratic method, but it was also that they were discussing the nature of their religious beliefs, and they thought that religion wasn't susceptible to this sort of treatment. What had been expressed were their opinions, and their attitude was 'If I contradict myself, then I contradict myself.'

So from my own experience I'm sure that you are right, and that it's very very difficult to get students today even to conceive of the possibility that there might be some truth of the matter, independently of what they happen to think about it.

And, of course, in argument one has to proceed by putting them into a situation where actually they're not prepared to leave it simply as a matter of opinion. For example, nowadays if you say 'Well, some people think that it is a good state of society in which all the arrangements are made for the convenience of men, but some people, on the other hand, think that such a patriarchal society unjustly exploits women', you'll find that they're not prepared to sit on the fence as far as *that* is concerned – they're against the patriarchal society, and they're against the exploitation of women, and you can then go on to say 'Well, in that case, what is it about the exploitation of women that is wrong? Because after all there are many societies – historically, probably more societies than not – which have grossly exploited women. It can't just be a matter of what is acceptable in society, and if it's a matter of individual opinion, well it wouldn't be a very difficult matter to go into the streets and find someone who would agree with the exploitation of women, though perhaps he wouldn't use that language.'

AW: I've had that experience. For ten years I taught social-workers social ethics – not because I was qualified to do so, but because no one else would do it. They were being taught sociology, psychology and 'social work practice'. But since nobody was sitting down and saying 'Well, considering you're making decisions every day, such as whether you're going to take an old lady into care, or are going to take a child away from its parents, let's consider the ethical implications of your job' – and being as they also had very strong views about such phrases as 'social justice' – I thought it would be a very good idea if we actually looked at those ethical ramifications and at phrases like 'social justice'.

And what I found time and time again was this scenario. We'd get a lot of people in a large room, all of whom claimed – or most of them anyway – that they didn't have any interest in morality in the traditional sense – certainly not in sexual morality – and then as time would go on we'd find that the room would be divided into people who felt very very strongly about one or two specific issues. Abortion would be one (they were against it because it was some kind of murder; or they were for it because it had nothing to do with killing, it had instead to do with the right of a woman to control her body; or whatever). So words like 'rights' would crop up. That was alright. But then, when I asked them to clarify why they held these views, they were lost, totally lost – and in fact most offended that I should ask them these questions. And that, it seems to me, is a demonstration of the fact we considered earlier, that we live in a culturally pluralistic world where there can't, as it were, be a common conversation.

BM: This of course is one of the points that MacIntyre makes very strongly, doesn't he?

AW: I think that is probably why his perspective has an enormous appeal for me.

But – given that we've agreed that the kinds of questions Lewis was talking about in the 1940s are now at least more respectable, and that we can once again ask the bigger questions – I suppose the question we must then ask is 'How do we get people to take traditional moral questions seriously if (a) they have no philosophical or moral training and (b) they tend to see morality very much as a matter of personal opinion?' I mean, what's the way forward?

Maybe we could end on that question, because we've gone a long way down a fairly drunken road, and because it seems to me a very practical and yet existential problem which people have to face: 'What do I believe in, and why?'

Given the fact that we've stated that there are these problems that we've both encountered, what do we do?

BM: Who is 'we'?

AW: I think, if you like, teachers, or anybody who confronts a group of people who are concerned about morality.

BM: I think that part of the answer is implicit in what you've been saying, namely that one does need education in ethical questions. And this is becoming increasingly apparent in various spheres.

I would have thought that what you were trying to do with your social workers was entirely the right way of proceeding, because in the intellectual situation which you have described, in which when you ask people if they have any moral principles they say 'No', it's no good just starting off with a discussion of moral principles which, *ex hypothesi*, they say they haven't got. But if you start off with the sort of situation in which they find themselves, and *then* you try to get them to take seriously how they would or should proceed in those situations, well the moral problems and the moral principles come out of it.

For example, we've got something called the *Ian Ramsey*

Centre in Oxford, and we've been having a seminar on the rights of elderly people. (Here too social workers are involved.) What are you to do if you have an elderly person who wants to go back home, but there are serious doubts about how competent she is (it's nearly always a she, because women last so much longer)? Well, usually the social workers feel that they ought to do what the patient or the client wants, so far as that is possible. But then what's going to happen if the old girl falls down the stairs? What about the responsibilities of the family and of the neighbours? Very often the family and the neighbours say 'Look, with the best will in the world, we can't be looking after her twenty-four hours of the day – and if we do less than that she's not going to be safe.' So, well, what matters? Take, for example, the autonomy of the individual. How much weight does one give to autonomy in the case of someone of doubtful competence? How does one measure competence? Should we ask what's best for the individual? But then 'best' in what terms? In purely physical terms? In social terms? And so forth.

One can't help feeling that your social workers, when presented with actual cases, would see that inherent in the situation is usually not one but a number of moral principles which they have to identify and then somehow or other weigh in order to resolve the question. What they certainly won't be prepared to say, when faced by the actual situation, is that they should do just what they feel like.

AW: No, they wouldn't.

It seems to me that an axiom of Lewis' approach to morality – probably following G. K. Chesterton – was that he tended to take it for granted that there was something called common sense.

Now I'm not sure that he ever articulated that in terms of a theory, but he felt that when he was appealing to people he could appeal to their sense – not only a logical sense, but a moral sense.

But I've found that when dealing with today's students it's no longer possible to make this assumption. I don't mean to say that I don't appeal to some 'innate sense of morality' – whatever that means – actually I do, but I have to make it conscious for them to believe that there are absolutes. Because, as you say, if you face them with a concrete, real-life situation all sorts of moral issues will emerge. To try and then relate those issues to general moral principles is, it seems to me, an enormous undertaking.

BM: I think it understandable that you should feel that way, because I think there are two things – maybe even three things – about Lewis' situation which would remove him quite a bit from the situation of your social workers.

The first is that he was aware of belonging to a common culture. I mean, the people that Lewis associated with at that period did represent, in this country, very largely a homogeneous group of people of a certain cultural background which could be taken for granted.

A second thing is that Lewis had a very strong sense of history. I mean, he was a good classical scholar, and a medievalist, and he was familiar with the whole sweep of English history and literature.

AW: But saw himself in a living tradition.

BM: And saw himself in a living tradition.

And the third thing is of course that, apart from the Great War, his experience was very much a one-class experience, wasn't it?

In these three respects his life-situation would be very different from your social workers'. And of course, as we see in his *De Descriptione Temporum*,[14] that splendid inaugural lecture at Cambridge, Lewis saw himself as really at the end of an age.

AW: 'A specimen', as he says. A dinosaur of the past.

BM: Yes, what I've just been saying about him he would have recognised.

AW: Yes. I think he would. He saw himself as one of the last of a dying species.

2

DID C. S. LEWIS LOSE HIS FAITH?

Richard L. Purtill

In 1986 a well-produced and well-acted television play based on the life of C. S. Lewis entitled *Shadowlands* was released.[1] The average television viewer, knowing little or nothing about Lewis and probably not a great deal about traditional Christianity, would, I think, get the following impression from that television play: A clever and somewhat arrogant Oxford professor thinks he can give an intellectual defence of Christianity. He meets and falls in love with a beautiful American woman who turns out to be dying of cancer. They marry, and she dies shortly after the marriage. His faith is shattered, his intellectual defences of Christianity now seem worthless. Gradually, he is brought to an acceptance of her death by the beauty of nature and the companionship of his stepson, his wife's child by a previous marriage. It is these natural consolations, rather than his religion, which heal the wound of his wife's death.[2]

Recently the American philosopher John Beversluis has examined Lewis' apologetics and his reaction to the death of his wife – in a book, *C. S. Lewis and the Search for Rational Religion*,[3] and in a short article (illustrated with pictures from *Shadowlands*), 'Beyond the Double Bolted Door'.[4] The book and article both give the same message as the television play :

C. S. Lewis' faith and his intellectual defence of the faith could not stand up to the death of his wife. The book also argues that Lewis' intellectual arguments for Christianity are philosophically naive and will not stand up to close scrutiny by a professional philosopher, and that those who defend or explain Lewis' arguments are uncritical partisans of Lewis.

In his book *The Inklings*,[5] which deals with 'C. S. Lewis, J. R. R. Tolkien, Charles Williams and their friends', Humphrey Carpenter tells the story of Lewis' debate with the then young English philosopher Elizabeth Anscombe in which Anscombe severely criticised one of Lewis' key arguments for belief in God. According to Carpenter, it was generally agreed, even by Lewis, that Anscombe won this debate, and Carpenter tells us that after this debate Lewis ceased to give intellectual defences of Christianity and moved closer to the position that 'all we can do is *choose* to believe'.[6]

Now the net effect of the television play, the books and the article has been to spread a certain general impression, even among people who have not seen the television play or read the books and the article, that C. S. Lewis at least to some extent lost his faith, or at least his faith in the possibility of a rational defence of Christianity. The two key events in this loss of faith were the debate with Anscombe and the death of Lewis' wife.

This general impression is deeply disturbing to many Christians, because for a good many contemporary Christians Lewis is seen as the outstanding – perhaps for some the only – contemporary defender of the position that Christianity can be shown not only to be intellectually defensible against unbelief, but even intellectually superior to unbelief.

If Lewis, the 'Defender of the Faith', as one author called him,[7] lost his own faith, or at least his own faith in reason in religion, how can we have any confidence in the rationality of religion? In fact, Beversluis explicitly draws this lesson from Lewis' life; since a rational religion would not stand up to argument and experience, even for Lewis himself, we must abandon the search for 'rational religion'.[8]

My purpose in this paper is to convince the reader, by evidence and argument, that the general impression given by the television play, the books and the article is not only false, but perniciously and perhaps deliberately and culpably false. It is in fact part of the counter-attack against Lewis' outstandingly successful defence of the rationality and probability of Christianity, and it is a particularly unfair and underhanded counter-attack, because it distorts Lewis' work and exploits his personal tragedy.

What, then, are the basic components of the counter-attack on Lewis? I have isolated five:

1 That Lewis' faith was unable to stand up to a very terrible but very common human tragedy: the loss of a dearly loved spouse.

2 That in crises such as this, the intellectual justification of religious belief is useless, and certainly proved useless to Lewis.

3 That Lewis' justification of Christianity will not stand up to careful and professional philosophical examination.

4 That Lewis was defeated in his argument with Elizabeth Anscombe and that this defeat convinced him that the rational justification of religious belief was hopeless.

5 That since Lewis was the major defender of rational religion, his failure to make out a rational case for religious belief shows that the project of the rational justification of religious belief should therefore be abandoned.

I will begin my rebuttal of the counter-attack on Lewis by considering Helen Joy Davidman Lewis' death and C. S. Lewis' reaction to it. Since we are speaking of his private life, I will make bold to speak of C. S. Lewis as 'Jack', the name his wife and his close friends used, and to speak of Mrs Lewis as 'Joy', the name which she preferred to her given first name, 'Helen'.

Let me first remonstrate gently with certain friends and supporters of Jack Lewis who have tried to counter the suggestion of some kind of emotional breakdown on Jack's part after Joy's death by citing incidents which seem to downplay his grief: incidents where he carried on academic or other commitments soon after Joy's death. Jack was a man of great personal courage, with a typically English dislike of showing his deepest emotions, but he did *feel* Joy's death very deeply, as plenty of evidence shows. To try to use his public behaviour to show otherwise can only defeat the purpose of those well-intentioned defenders by making Jack seem cold and unfeeling.

Jack did feel great grief at Joy's death and did love Joy very deeply. The real question is what effect this grief had on his faith. To understand this we must understand more about faith, and for this we can hardly do better than look at what Lewis himself wrote about faith. I will quote from one place in which Lewis examines the problems of faith directly and then from a fictional context in which he illustrates the points he makes in the longer extract.

In the first of two chapters on 'Faith' in *Mere Christianity*, Lewis raises the problem of how faith can be a virtue:

> I used to ask how on earth it can be a virtue – what is there moral or immoral about believing or not believing a set of statements? Obviously, I used to say, a sane man accepts or rejects any statement, not because he wants to or does not want to, but because the evidence seems to him good or bad. If he were mistaken about the goodness or badness of the evidence that would not mean he was a bad man, but only that he was not very clever. And if he thought the evidence bad but tried to force himself to believe in spite of it, that would be merely stupid.
>
> Well, I think I still take that view. But what I did not see then – and a good many people do not see still – was this. I was assuming that if the human mind once accepts a thing as true it will automatically go on regarding it as true, until some real reason for reconsidering it turns up. In fact, I was assuming that the human mind is completely ruled by reason. But that is not so. For example, my reason is perfectly convinced by good evidence that anaesthetics do not smother me and that properly trained surgeons do not start operating until I am unconscious. But that does not alter the fact that when they have me down on the table

and clap their horrible mask over my face, a mere childish panic begins inside me. I start thinking I am going to choke, and I am afraid they will start cutting me up before I am properly under. In other words, I lose my faith in anaesthetics. It is not reason that is taking away my faith: on the contrary, my faith is based on reason. It is my imagination and emotions. The battle is between faith and reason on one side and emotion and imagination on the other . . .

Now just the same thing happens about Christianity. I am not asking anyone to accept Christianity if his best reasoning tells him that the weight of the evidence is against it. That is not the point at which Faith comes in. But supposing a man's reason once decides that the weight of the evidence is for it. I can tell that man what is going to happen to him in the next few weeks. There will come a moment when there is bad news, or he is in trouble, or is living among a lot of other people who do not believe it, and all at once his emotions will rise up and carry out a sort of blitz on his belief. Or else there will come a moment when he wants a woman, or wants to tell a lie, or feels very pleased with himself, or sees a chance of making a little money in some way that is not perfectly fair: some moment, in fact, at which it would be very convenient if Christianity were not true. And once again his wishes and desires will carry out a blitz. I am not talking of moments at which any real new reasons against Christianity turn up. Those have to be faced and that is a different matter. I am talking about moments when a mere mood rises up against it.

Now Faith, in the sense in which I am here using the word, is the art of holding on to things your reason has once accepted, in spite of your changing moods. For moods will change, whatever view your reason takes. I know that by experience. Now that I am a Christian I do have moods in which the whole thing looks very improbable: but when I was an atheist I had moods in which Christianity looked terribly probable. This rebellion of your moods against your real self is going to come anyway. That is why Faith is such a necessary virtue: unless you teach your moods 'where they get off', you can never be either a sound Christian or even a sound atheist, but just a creature dithering to and fro, with its beliefs really dependent on the weather and the state of its digestion.[9]

The fictional context in which Lewis vividly illustrates what he says in *Mere Christianity* is the first chapter of *Perelandra* (*Voyage to Venus*), where a fictionalised version of Lewis himself is going down to a country cottage to visit his friend Elwin Ransom. The whole chapter is well worth reading, but it comes to a culmination in the following passage, where the fictional Lewis begins to have doubts about his friend Ransom:

> He was in league with them! How did I know he was even a dupe? He might be something worse . . . and again I came to a standstill.
> The reader, not knowing Ransom, will not understand how contrary to all reason this idea was. The rational part of my mind, even at that moment, knew perfectly well that even if the whole universe were crazy and hostile, Ransom was sane and wholesome and honest. And this part of my mind in the end sent me forward – but with a reluctance and a difficulty I can hardly put into words. What enabled me to go on was the knowledge (deep down inside me) that I was getting nearer at every stride to the one friend: but I *felt* that I was getting nearer to the one enemy – the traitor, the sorcerer, the man in league with 'them' . . . walking into a trap with my eyes open, like a fool. 'They call it a breakdown at first,' said my mind, 'and send you to a nursing home; later on they move you to an asylum.'[10]

So Lewis' idea of faith is this: it is an acceptance of certain beliefs which is not contrary to reason, but which is *supported* by reason. In most cases, what war against faith are not rational considerations, but imagination and emotion. So what we would expect to find in the situation in which Lewis lost his dear beloved wife and had to come to terms with his grief is that he would face a struggle in which imagination and emotion were at war with his reasoned conviction that Christianity is true. And that is precisely what we do find.

The major evidence usually cited for Jack's state of mind after Joy's death is the little book he wrote and published under a pseudonym, entitled *A Grief Observed*.[11] This is the *only* piece of evidence cited by those who claim that Lewis lost his faith after his wife's death, and if the book is carefully and objectively examined it is powerful evidence for exactly the opposite conclusion: that Jack's faith was in fact tested but in the long run *strengthened* by his grief at Joy's death.

First let us see what Lewis himself says about the book. In a letter to a Catholic nun with whom he had corresponded for years on literary and religious subjects, and whom he regarded as a good friend, Lewis writes: 'I will direct Fabers to send you a copy of the little book, but it may shock your pupils. It is *A Grief Observed* from day to day in all its rawness and sinful reactions and follies. It ends with faith but raises all the blackest doubts *en route*.'[12]

There has been some controversy over whether Lewis 'distanced' his experience by fictionalising it somewhat. Are the 'sinful reactions and follies' an accurate picture of Jack's *own* feelings, or are they fictional – or at least a fictionalised picture of what a person who had just lost a beloved wife *might* feel?

I think that it is possible to answer this question with some certainty because we have letters written by Lewis to close friends at about the time he was writing *A Grief Observed*, and we have another case where Lewis wrote a book on prayer, *Letters to Malcolm: Chiefly on Prayer*, which is closely related to real letters he wrote.[13]

In *Letters to Malcolm* the correspondent 'Malcolm' and his family are fictional. The incidents such as the illness of Malcolm's son are fictional incidents, carefully arranged by Lewis' literary artistry to bring out points about prayer. *However*, to someone familiar with Lewis' unpublished letters it is clear that the letters are exactly the *kind* of letters Lewis often wrote to real correspondents, and major parts of the *Letters to Malcolm* can be exactly paralleled in letters to real correspondents (even little touches like Lewis being able to go upstairs only with difficulty). So what Lewis did in *Letters to Malcolm* was to *organise* and *orchestrate* his real opinions and ideas about prayer, and real incidents involving a number of *different* correspondents, into a united whole which gives *literary form* to real ideas and incidents.

It seems quite clear that Lewis did exactly the same thing with *A Grief Observed*. He took his real grief in all its rawness, he took the doubts and fears which really came into his mind, and he organised them into a literary masterpiece. At times he certainly heightened the contrast by omitting balancing thoughts and feelings (for example in a real letter he remarks to a friend about the fact that work and sleep, and even food, can temporarily distract us from grief).

The literary form into which Lewis put his story is almost exactly that of his fictional masterpiece *Till We Have Faces*:[14] all the doubts, objections and anger are expressed in the earlier longer sections, and the reconciliation and understanding come as the 'joyous turn' in the final section. (Did those detractors of Lewis who cited *A Grief Observed* as evidence for a *loss* of faith never read the book all the way through?)

The great body of unpublished Lewis letters in the Marion E. Wade Center at Wheaton College shows that in the years after Joy's death Lewis went on arguing with unbelievers, counselling the doubtful and (despite his own grief) cheering the despondent – speaking of his own loss only to his close friends and long-time correspondents. Even the published correspondence bears this out for those who take the time and trouble to read it. Look, for example, at the last sixteen pages of Major W. H. Lewis' *Letters of C. S. Lewis*,[15] the last thirty pages of *Letters to an American Lady*,[16] and the last twenty-three pages of *They Stand Together*.[17]

So if we look at the *facts*, at the record, we get exactly the picture Lewis' discussion of faith would lead us to expect: emotion and imagination warred against Lewis' reasoned conviction. But Lewis went on believing and acting on his belief. To quote his vivid description of the war of emotion and imagination on his convictions as evidence of loss of faith is unfair and dishonest in exactly the same way that it would be unfair and dishonest to call a man who had just performed a heroic act 'cowardly' because he vividly described the fears he had overcome to do his act of heroism. Courage is *overcoming* fear to do what you ought to do. Faith is *overcoming* emotion and imagination to believe and act as you ought to believe and act. And in that battle there is no reasonable doubt that Jack Lewis was the victor.

I turn with some relief from the really despicable attempt to turn Lewis' personal tragedy into an argument against his faith by quoting him out of context, to the related question of whether Lewis found that intellectual justifications of Christianity were 'no use' in facing his wife's death. But again I am genuinely puzzled. What do Lewis' critics expect; that as a safeguard against grief he should rehearse his intellectual grounds for belief? But Lewis had no intellectual doubts about his faith, and no new data which might give him intellectual grounds for doubting his faith. He had lost both his parents and several close friends by painful deaths. He was also very well acquainted with the variety and scale of sin and suffering from the great flood of appeals for help which came in letters to him. There is in fact no evidence at all that Lewis was moved to any intellectual doubts at all by his personal loss, and thus there was no need to renew or rehearse his intellectual grounds for belief.

What he did suffer were torments of emotion and imagination. He was unable to *feel* that Joy still existed after death, he was tormented by *imaginings* of a cruel God. Against such feelings and imaginings you do not turn to intellectual arguments, you turn to prayer. And there is ample evidence that Lewis did just that.

On the night of Joy's death, he was driven to and from the hospital where she died by a man named Clifford Morris who had driven Jack for many years, first as a driver for a taxi company, then as the owner of his own car-hire business. Morris had become, as Jack says in a letter, 'almost a family friend'.[18] In a very moving interview Morris tells how after Joy's death Jack asked to be driven out into the country, where Jack and Morris prayed together for a good part of the night.[19] Jack's stepson Douglas Gresham recalls how Jack consoled and comforted him, telling him that grief always has an element of selfishness in it, and they should rejoice that Joy was free of her sufferings.[20]

In fact Jack Lewis did go through a period where all emotional and imaginative support for his faith was temporarily withdrawn. But of course many if not all of the great saints and heroes of the Christian faith have gone through such a 'dark night of the soul', and Jack himself had written often of the dangers of relying on imagination and emotion in religion. Far from giving rise to any intellectual difficulties, his own experience confirmed and gave him new insight into the experiences of many great Christians in the past.

What opponents of Christianity believe we Christians believe about pain and suffering in our own lives is often puzzling. If anything is made very clear in the gospels it is that Christians should expect pain and persecution in this life. But opponents of Christianity seem often to be under the impression that Christians expect to be exempt from suffering because of their faith, and that if they are not then this is an argument against that faith. This is very far from the truth. Really devoted Christians like Lewis not only expect suffering in this world but are a little worried if things go too easily; for example, Lewis once wrote to a friend: 'Pray for me . . . I am travelling through "a Plain called Ease"; things are almost too easy for me presently.'[21]

We now turn to the charge that a careful philosophical examination of Lewis' arguments for Christianity shows that they do not stand up. In my book *C. S. Lewis's Case for the Christian Faith*[22] I examine these arguments and conclude that they do stand up to criticism. In his book *C. S. Lewis and the Search for Rational Religion* John Beversluis concludes that they do not. Which of us is right? In a review of Beversluis' book in the *International Philosophical Quarterly*[23] I gave the following characterisation of it:

In his introduction Beversluis divides previous books on C. S. Lewis into two categories: (1) books critical of Lewis which offer 'not an assessment but a demolition' and (2) admiring studies of Lewis which are unduly uncritical and adulatory.

Beversluis offers his own book as belonging to neither of these classes, as an argument not a harangue, an assessment not a demolition, appreciative of Lewis but not adulatory, and above all as rationally and judiciously critical of Lewis. If the book lived up to these promises Lewis would have been the first to welcome it: he was a man 'hungry for rational opposition' and would have welcomed a rigorous debate of his arguments. I share Lewis's feelings, and as the author of one of the books Beversluis puts into his second category would be glad to be shown important criticisms of Lewis I had overlooked.

Unfortunately, Beversluis does not fulfill his promises and in the end what he says of previous critics of Lewis applies eminently to Beversluis himself: 'One begins to suspect that they have reached these negative conclusions a bit too easily' . . . His procedure in criticizing Lewis is typically as follows: he begins with a straight exposition of Lewis's views, often with extensive quotation. Then rhetorically negative characterizations of Lewis's views begin to creep into the description. Finally actual arguments against Lewis or criticism of his view are given. But these are extremely brief (ten percent of the total material at a generous estimate), quite cavalier, and more often than not are based on misinterpretations of Lewis's points.

Chapter Two, on Lewis's 'argument from desire' is typical. It begins with a rhetorical attack on Lewis's *The Pilgrim's Regress* ('this embarrassing work', 'this gratuitously censorious little book') based on misinterpreting satire as if it were straight assertion.

Finally, about a third of the way through the Chapter a version of Lewis's argument from desire is given; we have desires no finite object can satisfy, other desires do not exist without an object. It is likely, therefore, that this desire too has an object, and only God would be an adequate object.

Beversluis gives a flurry of objections many of which are beside the point, e.g., some things which *do* satisfy our desires only satisfy them for a time. He repeatedly begs the question by asserting that 'the desire in and of itself proves nothing, points to nothing'. Whether it does is the point at issue. The argument 'other natural desires have objects therefore probably this one does' is never squarely faced. It is typical of Beversluis that we are never quite sure if he is denying the existence of the desire, denying that God's existence is the best explanation of the desire, or claiming that the desire exists but is doomed to frustration.

The remainder of the chapter is a curious bit of theology in which it is claimed that *the* Biblical view of God is quite incompatible with the 'romantic view' that all men desire God, since all men desire true happiness and true happiness can be found in God alone, an alleged contradiction which would have surprised Aquinas, among others. There is also a strange muddle about Lewis's autobiographical report that when he found God there was a time when he was tempted to retreat from the commitment involved. Beversluis sees this as incompatible with the claim that God was what he desired. But surely any accepted lover has experienced the moment when the heart's desire has been attained and the attainment seems momentarily frightening.

The chapter on Lewis's argument from morality is distinguished from the chapters before and after it by an almost total lack of arguments. It is repeatedly asserted that Lewis has ignored important alternative explanations of morality, but it is never shown how these views meet the challenge he poses: how we are to explain our conviction that morality is objective without explaining it away. In general, as I argued in my book on Lewis, his strategy is to cite a fact about human experience (desire, morality, reason) and show that God is the best explanation of this fact, because other explanations explain *away* the experience. Beversluis never seems to understand, much less answer this strategy, often because he implausibly tries to interpret Lewis's arguments as deductive rather than inductive.

There is an unfortunate tendency in this book to take incidents from Lewis's life, interpret them tendentiously, and use them as against Lewis's arguments. Thus the famous debate with Anscombe is interpreted as a complete defeat for Lewis's argument from reason to God, on the alleged evidence of Lewis's psychological reactions, even though Anscombe herself is quoted in a footnote to the contrary.

More disturbingly, Lewis's honest exposition of his agonized feelings after the death of his wife is interpreted as a loss of his earlier faith in 'rational religion'. This ignores Lewis's own description of *A Grief Observed* (quoted in my book) '(it) ends with faith, but raises all the blackest doubts *en route*' as well as the body of serene and mature work, such as *Letters to Malcolm*, which Lewis did after Joy's death.

It would not be difficult, and may at some future time be useful, to answer Beversluis's criticisms of Lewis point by point. When misunderstandings, misinterpretations and irrelevancies are set aside, little of substance remains, however: answering Beversluis is not likely to advance our understanding either of Lewis or of the issues involved. This is, I think, because Beversluis never really enters into dialogue with Lewis, never asks himself how Lewis might reply to his facile and fragmentary criticisms. There is a notable lack of the principle of charity in the logician's sense, as well as of charity in the theological sense, despite much rather patronizing praise of Lewis. In the end, the faults Beversluis sees in Lewis are mainly faults which Beversluis himself possesses in an eminent degree: setting up straw men, producing false dilemmas, drawing fallacious inferences. And he has characterized his own work in describing that of earlier critics: 'not an argument but a harangue, not an assessment but a demolition'.

Here we have two professional philosophers disagreeing on the philosophical value of Lewis' arguments. Beversluis claims I am prejudiced in favour of Lewis and criticises my book: I criticise his book. The best way to settle the issue would be to read carefully both books and the parts of Lewis' writings to which they refer. But even if you were willing and able to do this you could not do it immediately. So perhaps we can call on a third party, the well-known philosopher of religion Thomas V. Morris of Notre Dame University. Morris is not a partisan of Lewis: in fact he tends to think his success is due to good writing rather than philosophical excellence. But his judgement of Beversluis is in many ways similar to mine, though more moderately expressed. I quote his review[24] in full so as not to falsify by selection.

Not many good philosophers are great writers. Not many good writers are great philosophers. But an exceptional writer who addresses philosophical and religious topics with verve and style, whose books are well marketed, and who succeeds in touching people's lives can on occasion be acclaimed a great philosopher by the appreciative reading public who have benefitted from his writing, a judgment which may sometimes be far out of line with the properly philosophical merits of this thought.

Some professional philosophers find themselves with an ambivalent attitude toward such an author's success. While grateful for whatever good he has managed to effect in the lives of his readers, they regret the confusion of rhetoric with philosophy pervading the public reception of his work. Other professional philosophers find themselves hardly ambivalent at all, but are just irked at the situation. Having worked hard at philosophy for years, having come to understand the difficulty of ever proving anything by pure reason alone, and having reconciled themselves to living with the uncertainties of this world, they are more than a little irritated to see their students and the general reading public idolizing some good writer as a great philosopher who has proved this, that, and everything else of real philosophical significance, when it is clear to a trained eye that no such results have been attained at all. The tone of his book indicates that this is precisely how John Beversluis perceives and reacts to the phenomenon of C. S. Lewis' extraordinary popularity as a Christian apologist and writer.

This book actually begins with a measured, judicious, even appreciative tone of presentation. But it soon changes into a somewhat shrill, harsh, strident assault which ends up portraying Lewis as something of a pathetic figure whose blustery posturing as a rational apologist for Christian truth finally gave way at the end of his life to a desperate faith-against-all-odds held onto only by means of blatant philosophical inconsistency. Beversluis is concerned to blow the whistle on the Lewis myth, and as a professional guardian of philosophical truth, to protect the general public from Lewis's egregious logical errors. He says this of the Lewis reading public:

> The people to whom he primarily addresses himself are not trained in philosophy; they are on the whole simply not in a position to recognize his distortions, omissions, and over-simplifications.

It is Beversluis's aim to put his readers into a position where they can see Lewis's failures. In representative passages, he characterizes Lewis's 'irresponsible writing' as exhibiting 'a persistent tendency toward carelessness, inaccuracy, and oversimplification whenever he discusses opposing views', and blasts Lewis's own positive positions and arguments with such epithets as 'confused', 'wrongheaded', 'shipwrecked', 'disgraced', 'considerably worse than fuzzy', 'tendentious', and 'desperate'. Colorful passages in Lewis are labelled as 'bellicose outbursts', and we find that Lewis doesn't just *state* his opinions on controversial matters, he 'gives vent' to them. The overall tone should be evident.

Beversluis's method is to isolate individual apologetic arguments in Lewis's writings and, taking his statements at face value, to employ the sorts of distinctions we introduce to first semester philosophy students to show those arguments to be unsound. Often we find the sort of barrage of questions leveled at one of Lewis's arguments which a tutor will sometimes direct at a careless student. The next assessment is that none of Lewis's reasons for believing there is a God is any good, and that in addition he has no good response to the most popular argument for believing there is no God, the problem of evil.

My main overall philosophical criticism of this book is that Beversluis seldom comes anywhere near to digging deep enough to really appreciate a line of thought suggested by Lewis. All too often he gives a facile, fairly superficial reconstruction of a line of argument, and after subjecting it to some critical questioning, declares it bankrupt and moves on. What is so disappointing to the reader who *is* trained in philosophy is that in most such instances a few minutes of reflective thought suffice to see that there are very interesting considerations to be marshalled in the direction Lewis was heading, considerations altogether neglected by [Beversluis]. There are far too many false alternatives posed for Lewis's arguments, and hasty judgments rendered about their soundness. In short, it seems that Beversluis is guilty of precisely those shortcomings in polemical discussion he attributes to Lewis.

Some of the main lines of thought Lewis produced as indicating the truth of a theistic worldview, Beversluis treats as deductive arguments meant to prove the proposition that there is a God. This in itself is, I think, a mistake. As is well known nowadays, a philosophical argument can have force without being a deductive proof. But even more damaging to the prospects of a fair assessment of Lewis are Beversluis's oversights concerning the ways in which the details of the arguments themselves could be defended. In some places, for example, Lewis seems to suggest that human beings have a deep longing or desire which can be determined to be a desire for the divine, or for God. It cannot be satisfied by any worldly object and is such that its very existence is a pointer to the reality of its proper object, an eternal divine being. Such arguments occur elsewhere in philosophy: We have an innate desire for everlasting life; innate desires are usually in principle satisfiable, and so their existence points to the existence of their proper object; so, probably, there is such a thing as everlasting life. Regardless of what we think of such arguments at first glance, sophisticated versions of them are possible which employ the basic apparatus of confirmation theory, and which deserve a careful hearing. Beversluis just states concerning any such desire, apparently, that 'The desire in and of itself proves nothing, points to nothing,' as if that were all that needs to be said.

Further, Beversluis argues that if C. S. Lewis's own deepest desire had been for God, he would not, according to his own testimony, have been a reluctant convert. Likewise, if we all had a deep desire for God we would recognize it as such. We don't, so there is no such desire. But of course, God could be the cause and the only proper, complete satisfaction of the deepest need in the human heart without its being the case at all that he must be immediately recognizable as such by any person in just any spiritual or moral condition whatsoever. It is hard to see how Beversluis could ignore this possibility. But then, in another context, Beversluis characterizes the claim that a person's whole condition (attitudes, emotions, etc.) is relevant to what he can see in religious matters as a claim that seems 'to imply that in the pursuit of truth it is not so much solid arguments as sunny dispositions that are decisive'. So perhaps his neglect of this possibility is not so surprising after all.

C. S. Lewis, of course, was not just a theist, he was a Christian. And one of his best known arguments was an argument for the divinity of Christ. Sometimes known as the Lewis Trilemma, Beversluis discusses it only as a dilemma. It goes something like

this: Even non-Christians recognize Jesus as a great moral
teacher. But he claimed to be God. So either he was a colossal
liar, which is inconsistent with the assessment of him as a great
moral force, or he really believed in his own deity, in which case
he was either a lunatic on the level of a man, Lewis says, who
believes he is a poached egg – a state also grossly incompatible
with his moral leadership – or he was and is God, the Lord of
Creation. Liar, Lunatic, or Lord – which was he? A positive
assessment of his other teachings forces one to a positive assessment of his apparent self-understanding. Such is the argument,
roughly put.

When disagreeing with assumptions Lewis makes here about
the general reliability of the New Testament text, assumptions
shared by many contemporary scholars of a traditional bent,
Beversluis gratuitously states that 'he is a textually careless
and theologically unreliable guide'. But textual issues aside,
Beversluis argues that even if Jesus *did* claim to be God, the only
alternative to his honest deity is not something like lunacy. We
are not forced to a Lunatic or Lord decision, Beversluis says.
Consider the reaction to Jesus in his own time, he suggests. How
did the unbelievers of his time react? Did they brand him a
lunatic? No, they branded him a blasphemer. It was perfectly
sane, given Judaic messianic expectations, for someone to be
believed the messiah, or even for someone to believe of himself
that he was the messiah, without questions of lunacy arising at all,
Beversluis suggests. So a false belief in his own deity would not,
in the original context, be good grounds for our judging Jesus
insane.

But the Jewish expectations for a messiah at the time in
question were not expectations for God himself, for a literally
divine person, to visit Jerusalem. They were expectations of a
special ambassador or political deliverer to be raised up by God.
To claim to be such a messiah would indeed not be decisive
grounds for an insanity judgment. But this was not Jesus's
self-assessment as portrayed on occasion in the New Testament
documents. It is clearly deity that is at issue. And Beversluis's
remarks fail altogether to undermine the reasoning Lewis based
on *this* assumption. The argument certainly requires more
scrutiny and comment; it cannot be so easily dismissed.

I can sympathize with the intent behind Beversluis's project. In one place he makes a remark about Lewis's BBC talks on which some of his written work is based, which could be extended to the written apologetic corpus as a whole:

> My complaint about the Broadcast Talks is not that Lewis fails to be as thorough as his subject matter demands, but that he gives the impression of being thorough. The philosophically unsophisticated reader cannot fail to get the impression that Lewis is covering the ground, that he *is* doing justice to the material, and that he *is* compressing everything that needs to be said into highly compact but basically accurate form, when in fact he is not doing so at all.

While not necessarily sharing Beversluis's assessment of Lewis here, I share his general concern about the way in which some apologetics is done, and received. Indeed, that is why I wrote my own first book, a critique of a very popular evangelical apologist. And, as someone who has attempted the same sort of task, I must say that much of Beversluis's book is well written from a purely stylistic point of view. He is clearly a good writer. Especially when writing about Lewis's views on the problem of evil, he is proving and provocative, although there again, I believe, in error. In a purely literary way, the book is a fairly good read, but I am afraid that it is academically one I cannot highly recommend, either in its tone or in the depth of its philosophical argumentation.

I have quoted from Morris at such length not only because he does an excellent job of analysing Beversluis' book but also because he cannot be called a partisan of Lewis – his own feelings are possibly nearer to those of the philosophers who 'Having worked hard at philosophy for years . . . are more than a little irritated to see their students and the general reading public idolizing some good writer as a great philosopher . . .' But Morris' very 'irritation' insulates him from Beversluis' charge that defenders of Lewis are always merely partisans of Lewis.

There are, however, two points in Morris' review to which I take exception. First, he seems to endorse Beversluis' claim that Lewis gives a false 'impression of being thorough', that

Lewis seems to think that he has settled certain philosophical issues when he has only begun to discuss them. In fact, if you look at Lewis' published work you will find that he is always modest about his own qualifications and his own success when he has time and space to express such modesty. (His book *Miracles*, for instance, is subtitled 'A Preliminary Study'.[25]) In *Mere Christianity*, which was originally a series of radio talks with strict time limitations, Lewis simply does not have room to qualify and modify his statements, but in the preface to the published book he says:

> I am a very ordinary layman of the Church of England . . . in this book I am not trying to convert anyone to my own position. Ever since I became a Christian I have thought that the best, perhaps the only, service I could do for my unbelieving neighbours was to explain and defend the belief that has been common to nearly all Christians at all times . . . far more . . . talented authors were already engaged in . . . controversial matters.[26]

In the face of such modesty the accusation that Lewis gives a false impression of settling philosophical controversies is patently silly.

I would also quarrel with Morris' implied claim that Lewis is a good writer but without much philosophical ability. Actually Lewis made strictly philosophical contributions (such as his critique of Hume's arguments against miracles[27] or his analysis of punishment[28]) which receive respectful attention from professional philosophers. Increasingly, selections from Lewis are appearing in books of readings for philosophy classes, along with such authors as Plato, Aquinas and Hume. Incidentally, in using such books, I have never encountered a student simply relying on Lewis *as an authority*; students who have read Lewis seem to get from him a good appreciation of the value of argument and of giving one's own arguments.

Lewis' most direct confrontation with a well-known contemporary philosopher was the famous debate with Elizabeth Anscombe, to which we now turn.

First, a little background. The confrontation was at a meeting of the Socratic Club, an organisation founded by students with Lewis' help. In an essay about the founding of the club, Lewis says:

> Socrates had exhorted men to 'follow the argument wherever it led them': the Club came into existence to apply his principle to . . . the *pros* and *cons* of the Christian religion . . .
> . . . Those who founded it do not for one moment pretend to be neutral. It was the Christians who constructed the arena and issued the challenge . . . [W]ith . . . pains and toil the committee . . . scoured [the pages of] *Who's Who* to find intelligent atheists who had leisure or zeal to come and propagate their creed . . . We expose ourselves, and the weakest of our party, to your fire no less than you are exposed to ours. Worse still, we expose ourselves to the recoil from our own shots; for if I may trust my personal experience no doctrine is, for the moment, dimmer to the eye of faith than that which a man has just successfully defended.[29]

The argument under discussion and the debate itself are briefly described in my book on Lewis:

> One way of getting a preliminary insight into Lewis's argument is to ask whether nature is a product of mind, or mind is a product of nature. If God created nature, as Christians believe, then nature is understandable by reason because it is a product of reason. It sounds superficially plausible to say that if mind is the product of nature, nature would be understandable by mind as well. But in fact, there is no acceptable general rule that a product can understand what produces it.
>
> Furthermore, if nature is seen as nonrational, as without intelligence or purpose of its own, a special difficulty arises. One thing may produce another by design, by chance, or by some process that unfolds or develops what is already inherent in the producing agent. I produced the words on this page of my manuscript by design. In doing so, I produced a random pattern of letters in the left-hand margin. If you had the manuscript page before you and found any words spelled out by reading down the first letter in each line, those words would be there purely by chance. (Since this page will be set in type after I have written it, another random factor is introduced; I have no idea if the first

letters of the lines on the resulting book page will form any words.) As I was writing, my body was producing blood, digestive juices, and other secretions by a process determined by my biological makeup.

If nature is without intelligence or purpose, it cannot produce mind by design. If there is no intelligence or purpose in nature, then it cannot produce mind as the unfolding or development of something already there. So a mindless nature could produce mind only by chance. But if mind is only a chance product of nature, how can we trust our reasoning powers, how can we expect our minds to give us the truth about anything? To use a more contemporary analogy, would you trust the results of a computer that had been constructed or programmed by some random process?

In his original statement of this argument in *Miracles*, Lewis overstated his case slightly, saying that as soon as we find that a thought or belief results from chance we immediately discount or disregard that thought or belief. Lewis used the example of a belief, produced by a childhood trauma, that dogs are dangerous. As a matter of practical reasoning, it is certainly true that we discount a belief if we discover it originates in chance, but as a matter of logic it does not follow that the belief is false. It might happen that the belief is true, as a matter of chance, just as it might happen as a matter of chance that the letters on the left-hand margin of this page spell out the correct answer to some question. One cannot rule out the possibility, though one ignores it for practical purposes.

It is sometimes alleged that Lewis's argument on this point was refuted in a famous debate with the Cambridge philosopher Elizabeth Anscombe. In fact, what happened was that Anscombe pointed out the overstatement we have discussed, and in typical philosopher's fashion challenged him to define some of his key terms. Lewis may indeed have been nonplussed at the vigor of her attack and its source, since as a Catholic she might have been expected to be an ally. The result of her challenge was that Lewis rewrote the chapter of *Miracles* in which the argument occurs, clarifying and strengthening the argument.[30]

When Elizabeth Anscombe spoke to the Socratic Club in February 1948, she was therefore not an atheist, but a practising, if somewhat eccentric, Roman Catholic. She and her husband Peter Geach had become converts to Catholicism while they were students of the philosopher Ludwig Wittgenstein, and Anscombe combined a Wittgensteinian approach on some philosophical questions with a very theistic one on others. Later she and Geach were to publish a book, *Three Philosophers*, in which they defended Aquinas' arguments for God.[31] So Anscombe was not an unbeliever attacking just any or all argumentation for God, but an honest rational believer attacking an argument she thought inadequate for a conclusion she thought true and justified on other grounds (as Aquinas criticised Anselm's ontological argument).

Anscombe undoubtedly pointed out weaknesses in Lewis' *formulation* of the argument. Lewis would have endorsed the remark in the club minutes, 'in general it appeared that Mr. Lewis would have to turn his argument into a rigorous analytic one, if his motion . . . were to stand the test of all the questions put to him'.[32]

Actually, Lewis began this task then and there. In the note of his reply to Anscombe in the Socratic Club minutes he is already making the distinction which went into his revised chapter of *Miracles*, the relation between CE (cause and effect) and GC (ground and consequent), and he says:

> If an argument is to be verific the conclusion must be related to the premises as consequent to ground . . . On the other hand, our thinking of the conclusion is an event and must be related to the previous events as effect to cause . . . It would seem therefore that we never think the conclusion *because* GC, it is the consequent of its grounds, but only *because* CE, certain previous events have happened. If so it does not seem that the GC sequence makes us more likely to think the true conclusion than not. And this is very much what I meant by the difficulty in Naturalism.[33]

So Lewis was already fighting back, and when a paperback version of *Miracles* was issued by Fontana Books Lewis took

DID C. S. LEWIS LOSE HIS FAITH?

the opportunity to revise and expand the chapter in question; a very powerful piece of evidence that far from abandoning the argument Lewis thought it was worth considerable effort to strengthen and restate.

Some of Lewis' younger friends seem to have thought that his argument had been defeated, even decisively defeated, and that Lewis was unwilling to venture into the philosophical arena again. His former pupil George Sayer describes the incident as follows:

His argument for the existence of God soon got him into trouble. At a meeting of the Socratic Club on February 2, 1948, Elizabeth Anscombe, who later became a professor of philosophy at Cambridge University, read a criticism of Jack's argument that naturalism is self-refuting. Jack replied, and an exciting debate followed. The audience disagreed about who had won the debate, but Jack thought that he had been defeated, and he was still unhappy about the evening when he spoke to me about it during Easter vacation. He told me that he had been proved wrong, that his argument for the existence of God had been demolished. This was a serious matter, he felt, because, in the minds of simple people, the disproof of an argument for the existence of God tended to be regarded as a disproof of the existence of God. He wanted to mount a counterattack, but he thought that it would be dangerous to do so unless he was quite sure of its validity.

The debate had been a humiliating experience, but perhaps it was ultimately good for him. In the past, he had been far too proud of his logical ability. Now he was humbled. He had been cheered on by the crowd of admirers at the Socratic Club, often young women who regarded him as the great defender of Christianity, almost like a knight of the Round Table. But he saw that he had underrated the difficulty of taking on the new school of Oxford philosophers, that the study of philosophy had changed very much since he had taken first-class honors. The Hegelians of his youth were now completely out of fashion. 'Logical positivism' was the current mode, and 'linguistic analysis' was gaining popularity. The former held that all statements about moral or religious values are scientifically unverifiable and therefore meaningless; the latter, that all philosophy should involve the criticism of language, and that the most important philosophical question to ask was why a particular word or expression was used. Jack could not cope with such developments and really had no desire to. They made what he regarded as philosophical thinking almost impossible. 'I can never write another book of that sort,' he said to me of *Miracles*. And he never did. He also never wrote another theological book. *Reflections on the Psalms* is really devotional and literary; *Letters to Malcolm*, published after his death, is also a devotional book, a series of reflections on prayer, without contentious arguments.[34]

But a reliable corrective to Sayer's account is contained in Elizabeth Anscombe's account of the event in the collected edition of her philosophical papers:

This volume contains the earliest purely philosophical writing on my part which was published: the criticism of C. S. Lewis's argument for 'the self-refutation of the Naturalist' in the first edition of his book, *Miracles*, chapter III. Those who want to see what the argument was, without relying on my criticism for it, should take care to get hold of the first edition (1947). The version of that chapter which is most easily available is the second edition, which came out as a Fontana paperback in 1960. The chapter, which in 1947 had the title 'The Self-Contradiction of the Naturalist', was rewritten and is now called 'The Cardinal Difficulty of the Naturalist'. The last five pages of the old chapter have been replaced by ten pages of the new, though a quotation from J. B. S. Haldane is common to both. Internal evidence shows that at least some of the rewriting was done after the first Sputnik and even after the hot dry summer of 1959. But I should judge that he thought rather hard about the matter in the interval. The rewritten version is much less slick and avoids some of the mistakes of the earlier one; it is much more of a serious investigation. He distinguishes between 'the Cause-Effect *because*' and 'the Ground-Consequent *because*', where before he had simply spoken of 'irrational causes'. If what we think at the end of our reasoning is to be true, the correct answer to 'Why do you think that?' must use the latter *because*. On the other hand, every event in Nature must be connected with previous events in the Cause-and-Effect relation . . . 'Unfortunately the two systems are wholly distinct' . . . And 'even if grounds do exist, what exactly have they got to do with the actual occurrence of the belief as a psychological event?'

These thoughts lead him to suggest that being a cause and being a proof must coincide – but he finds strong objections to this. (He obviously had imbibed some sort of universal-law determinism about causes.) After some consideration he reverts to the (unexamined) idea he used in the first edition, of 'full explanation': 'Anything which professes to explain our reasoning fully without introducing an act of knowing, thus solely determined by what is known, is really a theory that there is no reasoning. But this, as it seems to me, is what Naturalism is bound to do.' The remaining four and a half pages are devoted to an elaboration of this. Unluckily he doesn't explore this idea of 'an act of knowing solely determined by what is known', which is obviously crucial.

Rereading the argument of the first edition and my criticism of it, it seems to me that they are just. At the same time, I find them lacking in any recognition of the depth of the problem. I don't think Lewis's first version itself gave one much impression of that. The argument of the second edition has much to criticize in it, but it certainly does correspond more to the actual depth and difficulty of the questions being discussed. I think we haven't yet an answer to the question I have quoted from him: 'What is the connection between grounds and the actual occurrence of the belief?'

The fact that Lewis rewrote that chapter, and rewrote it so that it now has those qualities, shows his honesty and seriousness. The meeting of the Socratic Club at which I read my paper has been described by several of his friends as a horrible and shocking experience which upset him very much. Neither Dr Harvard (who had Lewis and me to dinner a few weeks later) nor Professor Jack Bennett remembered any such feelings on Lewis's part. The paper that I read is as printed here. My own recollection is that it was an occasion of sober discussion of certain quite definite criticisms, which Lewis's rethinking and rewriting showed he thought were accurate. I am inclined to construe the odd accounts of the matter by some of his friends – who seem not to have been interested in the actual arguments or the subject-matter – as an interesting example of the phenomenon called 'projection'.[35]

With all respect to Sayer, who has written a generally wise and insightful book about his old teacher, Sayer is no philosopher (he was a teacher of English at the English equivalent of a high school) and was quite young at the time of the incident. Anscombe's recollections are far more to be relied on; as she drily suggests concerning 'the odd accounts of the matter by some of his friends', Sayer may very well be attributing his own feelings of dismay to Lewis as he writes the account almost forty years after the event.

I wonder if Sayer was not himself influenced by the interpretation of this event given in Humphrey Carpenter's book *The Inklings*:

> *Miracles* was published in 1947. Early the following year, its third chapter, in which Lewis proved that human Reason is independent of the natural world, was publicly attacked at the Socratic Club, not by an atheist but by a fellow Christian, the Catholic philosopher Elizabeth Anscombe. Lewis was unprepared for the severely critical analysis to which she submitted his arguments, for she proved in her turn that his 'proof' of theism was severely faulty. It is true that Lewis's most fervent supporters felt that she had not demonstrated her point successfully, but many who were at the meeting thought that a conclusive blow had been struck against one of his most fundamental arguments. Certainly after it was all over Lewis himself was in very low spirits. He and Hugo Dyson had organised an informal dining club with four of their pupils, Philip Stibbe, Tom Stock, Peter Bayley and Derek Brewer, and the club happened to meet a couple of days after the Socratic duel. Brewer wrote in his diary: 'None of us at first very cheerful. Lewis was obviously deeply disturbed by his encounter last Monday with Miss Anscombe, who had disproved some of the central theory of his philosophy about Christianity. I felt quite painfully for him. Dyson said – very well – that now he had lost everything and was come to the foot of the Cross – spoken with great sympathy.' Brewer added that Lewis's imagery when talking about the debate 'was all of the fog of war, the retreat of infantry thrown back under heavy attack'.

> Lewis had learnt his lesson: for after this he wrote no further books of Christian apologetics for ten years, apart from a collection of sermons; and when he did publish another apologetic

work, *Reflections on the Psalms*, it was notably quieter in tone and did not attempt any further intellectual proofs of theism or Christianity. Though he continued to believe in the importance of Reason in relation to his Christian faith, he had perhaps realised the truth of Charles Williams's maxim, 'No-one can possibly do more than decide what to believe.'[36]

(It was probably this account that Anscombe was thinking of when she spoke of 'projection', for Carpenter's book was published before her account.)

If you actually look at Lewis' activities in the years after the debate you get quite a different impression than that conveyed naively by Sayer and somewhat disingenuously by Carpenter. (Note that in the above quotation Carpenter's second paragraph introduces a wholly unsupported *interpretation* of Lewis' reaction. The comments 'Lewis had learnt his lesson . . .' and 'Perhaps he had realised the *truth* [my emphasis] of Charles Williams's maxim . . .' are both examples of *editorialising* by Carpenter.)

As to the fact cited by Carpenter, that Lewis did not publish further apologetic books of the same type as *Miracles*, it is correct but misleading. Lewis wrote controversial books on religion such as *Miracles* reluctantly, and only when he received invitations to do so from publishers or organisations that he did not feel he could refuse. (*The Problem of Pain*,[37] for example, was written for a series published by Geoffrey Bles, Lewis' friend and long-time publisher, at Bles' pressing invitation, and *Miracles*, too, was written at Bles' invitation.) As Lewis' friend Austin Farrer wrote:

> Philosophy was not Lewis's trade and he had many other irons in the fire . . . He was never quite at home in our post-positivist era . . . his philosophical experience belonged to the time of his conversion. Philosophy is an ever-shifting never-ending public discussion, and a man who drops out of the game drops out of philosophy.[38]

So Lewis had little inclination to argue the whole positivist question. He was wise; our era is now post-post-positivist and the debates of that era are as dead as mutton.

Carpenter is far from impartial on the matter he discusses. Throughout his book *The Inklings* he shows a marked hostility to any attempt to give a rational basis for religion. He is on the side of Charles Williams in thinking that 'all we can possibly do is *choose* to believe'. Carpenter is entitled to take such a position, even to argue for it in a book about Lewis and others (Tolkien for example) who took the opposite view. What Carpenter is not entitled to do is to assume the truth of his position and *attribute* it to Lewis in the face of much evidence to the contrary.

One valuable piece of evidence is Lewis' essay 'On Obstinacy in Belief' published in 1955, seven years after the Anscombe debate.[39] In this essay, Lewis reiterates and reinforces his position in *Mere Christianity*: Faith *should* be arrived at by rational means.

> There is, of course, no question . . . of belief without evidence. We must beware of confusion between the way in which a Christian first assents to certain propositions and the way in which he afterwards adheres to them. These must be carefully distinguished. Of the second it is true, in a sense, to say that Christians do recommend a certain discounting of apparent contrary evidence . . . But so far as I know it is not expected that a man should assent to these propositions in the first place without evidence or in the teeth of the evidence. At any rate, if anyone expects that, I certainly do not. And in fact, the man who accepts Christianity always thinks he has good evidence; whether, like Dante, *fisici e metafisici argomenti*, or historical evidence, or the evidence of religious experience, or authority, or all these together. For of course authority, however we may value it in this or that particular instance, is a kind of evidence. All of our historical beliefs, most of our geographical beliefs, many of our beliefs about matters that concern us in daily life, are accepted on the authority of other human beings, whether we are Christians, Atheists, Scientists, or Men-in-the-Street.
>
> It is not the purpose of this essay to weigh the evidence, of whatever kind, on which Christians base their belief. To do that would be to write a full-dress *apologia*. All that I need do here is to point out that, at the very worst, this evidence cannot be so

weak as to warrant the view that all whom it convinces are indifferent to evidence. The history of thought seems to make this quite plain. We know, in fact, that believers are not cut off from unbelievers by any portentous inferiority of intelligence or any perverse refusal to think. Many of them have been people of powerful minds. Many of them have been scientists. We may suppose them to have been mistaken, but we must suppose that their error was at least plausible. We might, indeed, conclude that it was, merely from the multitude and diversity of the arguments against it. For there is not one case against religion, but many. Some say, like Capaneus in Statius, that is a projection of our primitive fears, *primus in orbe deos fecit timor*: others, with Euhemerus, that it is all a 'plant' put up by wicked kings, priests, or capitalists; others, with Tylor, that it comes from dreams about the dead; others, with Frazer, that it is a by-product of agriculture; others, like Freud, that it is a complex; the moderns that it is a category mistake. I will never believe that an error against which so many and various defensive weapons have been found necessary was, from the outset, wholly lacking in plausibility. All this 'post haste and rummage in the land' obviously implies a respectable enemy . . . [These possibilities] may be of some use in analysing a particular instance of belief or disbelief, where we know the case history, but as a general explanation of either they will not help us. I do not think they overthrow the view that there is evidence both for and against the Christian propositions which fully rational minds, working honestly, can assess differently.

I therefore ask you to substitute a different and less tidy picture for that with which we began. In it, you remember, two different kinds of men, scientists, who proportioned their belief to the evidence, and Christians, who did not, were left facing one another across a chasm. The picture I should prefer is like this. All men alike, on questions which interest them, escape from the region of belief into that of knowledge when they can, and if they succeed in knowing, they no longer say they believe. The questions in which mathematicians are interested admit of treatment by a particularly clear and strict technique. Those of the scientist have their own technique, which is not quite the same. Those of the historian and the judge are different again. The mathematician's proof (at least so we laymen suppose) is by reasoning, the scientist's by experiment, the historian's by documents, the judge's by concurring sworn testimony. But all these men, as men, on questions outside their own disciplines, have numerous beliefs to which they do not normally apply the methods of their own disciplines. It would indeed carry some suspicion of morbidity and even of insanity if they did. These beliefs vary in strength from weak opinion to complete subjective certitude . . . There are some who moderately opine that there is, or is not, a God. But there are others whose belief or disbelief is free from doubt. And all these beliefs, weak or strong, are based on what appears to the holders to be evidence; but the strong believers or disbelievers of course think they have very strong evidence. There is no need to suppose stark unreason on either side. We need only suppose error. One side has estimated the evidence wrongly. And even so, the mistake cannot be supposed to be of a flagrant nature; otherwise the debate would not continue.[40]

Incidentally, it makes for an interesting study of Beversluis' techniques to compare Lewis' clear, confident statement with Beversluis' account of it in his article in *Christian History*:

Lewis's worries about contrary evidence were already apparent in his 1955 essay 'On Obstinacy in Belief.' Although he had tackled this problem in *The Problem of Pain*, the arguments and assurances of that book are conspicuously absent. So is the earlier strategy of *Mere Christianity* in which religious doubts were traced to 'mere moods' and religious doubters banished to the ranks of those who 'dither to and fro' with their beliefs dependent 'on the weather and the state of [their] digestion.' Here Lewis is no longer amused but uncommonly sober, on the defensive, and willing to make unheard-of concessions. It is no longer atheism but his own previous position that is 'too simple.' The honest inquirer must now candidly acknowledge that the evidence for theism is, at best, 'mixed' and that considerable ingenuity is required if the believer's position is even to be 'rendered tolerable.' The 'philosophies for the nursery' have proved to be more troublesome and resilient than anyone would have ever guessed and, in waging his polemical warfare against them, the apologist must employ heavier artillery than in bygone years. Through the essay, it is noteworthy how far Lewis has retreated and how meagerly his apologetic arsenal is now stocked.[41]

Here in small compass is the characteristic Beversluis technique of selective quotation, distortion and unfounded assertion. To read the whole essay and then to read Beversluis' comments on it is to completely unmask Beversluis as an interpreter of Lewis.

In the same connection, contrast Beversluis' earlier-cited picture of a shattered, doubt-haunted Lewis after Joy's death with the serene confidence of his last book, *Letters to Malcolm: Chiefly on Prayer*, completed three years *after* Joy's death. Here is what Lewis' biographers tell us about that book:

> Lewis was lucky in his publishers but none of them, perhaps, knew how to shepherd Lewis's energies so well as did Jocelyn (Jock) Gibb who took over the management of Geoffrey Bles Ltd after Bles retired in 1954. Without his gentle and kindly perseverance Lewis might never have written his last book. What began in 1952 as a slightly dull and rather academic work on prayer suddenly caught the author's imagination and almost, as it were, wrote itself. *Letters to Malcolm: Chiefly on Prayer* was completed in May 1963 and a typescript sent to Gibb a few weeks later. 'Respect and admire you as I do', Gibb wrote on 13 June, 'this "Letters to Malcolm" . . . has knocked me flat. Not quite; I can just sit up and shout hurrah, and again, hurrah. It's the best you've done since *The Problem of Pain*. By Jove, this is something of a present to a publisher!'[42]

Now look at a passage from the book itself:

> I don't say the resurrection of this body will happen at once. It may well be that this part of us sleeps in death and the intellectual soul is sent to Lenten lands where she fasts in naked spirituality – a ghostlike and imperfectly human condition. I don't imply that an angel is a ghost. But naked spirituality is in accordance with his nature: not, I think, with ours. (A two-legged horse is maimed but not a two-legged man.) Yet from that fact my hope is that we shall return and re-assume the wealth we laid down.
>
> Then the new earth and sky, the same yet not the same as these, will rise in us as we have risen in Christ. And once again, after who knows what aeons of the silence and the dark, the birds

will sing out and the waters flow, and lights and shadows move across the hills and the faces of our friends laugh upon us with amazed recognition.

Guesses, of course, only guesses. If they are not true, something better will be. For we know that we shall be made like Him, for we shall see Him as He is.[43]

In the face of such evidence we can only look at Beversluis' picture in amazement. *This* is a grief-shattered man with no faith left? *This* is a man who now doubts all his former certainties?

I turn with some relief to our final question: how much the case for rational religion depends on how successful C. S. Lewis' defence of rational religion was. I say 'with some relief', because there is something almost indecent in the attempt to attack a man's plainly expressed views by selective misquotation and misinterpretation of his work and his life story. I have to try very hard indeed to entertain the charitable view that those who do this are sincere and blameless. It is at least clear that they could not do what they do without considerable self-deception.

As to whether the case for rational religion depends on C. S. Lewis' success in defending it, I can imagine very well Lewis' own reaction to the idea. He would laugh, laugh 'till the hills rang with . . . laughter'. Then he might say something like this: 'It's very kind of you to value my work so highly, but you've apparently admired it more than you've read it. Over and over again I've emphasised the richness of the Christian tradition; told my readers to read at least one old book for every new one they read. Among my contemporaries and near contemporaries, there are many great defenders of Christianity. It's come to a pretty pass if the whole weight of the case for rational religion is supposed to fall on poor Jack Lewis, a teacher of English literature who reluctantly wrote some popular books on religion in his spare time. Look to Aquinas, look to Chesterton, look to your own contemporaries. If this fellow Beversluis wants to make a case against rational religion, why does he attack me; why doesn't he take on some of his philosophical peers who can correct his misreadings and answer his attacks? I'm praying hard for him of course, but it really does seem a little like Falstaff pretending to triumph over the corpse of Percy, who in life would have made Falstaff run like a rabbit . . .'

Now Lewis, if he said that, would be as usual too modest. Lewis was for many ordinary Christians the prototypical 'defender of the faith' for our times. He had powerful philosophical abilities, but because he was not a professional philosopher he did not use the jargon of the professionals nor was he caught up in the transitory controversies of the academic philosophers. He was a fine writer; one of the foremost prose writers of our time, with an almost unequalled combination of clarity and energy. If you were allowed to read only one twentieth-century defender of rational Christianity, Lewis would be the best choice by far.

However, we are *not* confined to reading only Lewis, and if we read only Lewis we are ill-equipped even to appreciate Lewis himself, much less his message. It is certainly true that on all levels of the rational defence of religion there are several contemporary 'defenders of the faith' who command our respect: philosophers such as Richard Swinburne[44] and John Lucas[45] come to my mind, some preacher or teacher who has been of help to you in thinking and living your faith might come to yours. But Lewis does have a special position in the minds and hearts of many of us, and it would be a blow, though by no means a fatal blow, if he had really lost his faith, or even his faith in reason. That is why I have taken the trouble to show in perhaps excessive detail that he did no such thing.

Finally, let me conjecture, as charitably as I can, on the motives of those who spread these untruths about Lewis. First, I think that there is a considerable element of plain envy in the attack on Lewis. Why should Lewis be so successful at winning converts to Christianity when my efforts are so unsuccessful, why should his faith be so robust when mine is so feeble? Envy delights to see the object of envy falter or fail, and is prone to exaggerate the faltering or failure.

Second, Lewis' message is profoundly out of step with the 'conventional wisdom' of our times. Christians are supposed to be on the defensive, not on the offensive. Christians are allowed to have their faith if that faith is admittedly irrational and sufficiently tentative and agonised, but a rational and confident faith? No 'modern man' can be allowed to have *that*!

Finally there is a motive very well exposed by Lewis himself in his last book, *Letters to Malcolm*. He is speaking of those who object to the supernaturalism of his religion, his refusal to explain away the miraculous and the divine, but it is equally true of those who object to his rational approach:

> Don't, however, misjudge these 'liberal Christians'. They genuinely believe that writers of my sort are doing a great deal of harm.
>
> They themselves find it impossible to accept most of the articles of the 'faith once given to the saints'. They are nevertheless extremely anxious that some vestigial religion which they (not we) can describe as 'Christianity' should continue to exist and make numerous converts. They think these converts will come in only if this religion is sufficiently 'de-mythologised'. The ship must be lightened if she is to keep afloat.
>
> It follows that, to them, the most mischievous people in the world are those who, like myself, proclaim that Christianity essentially involves the supernatural. They are quite sure that belief in the supernatural never will, nor should, be revived, and that if we convince the world that it must choose between accepting the supernatural and abandoning all pretence of Christianity, the world will undoubtedly choose the second alternative. It will thus be we, not the liberals, who have really sold the pass. We shall have re-attached to the name *Christian* a deadly scandal from which, but for us, they might have succeeded in decontaminating it.
>
> If, then, some tone of resentment creeps into their comments on our work, can you blame them? But it would be unpardonable if we allowed ourselves any resentment against them. We do in some measure queer their pitch. But they make no similar

contribution to the forces of secularism. It has already a hundred champions who carry far more weight than they. Liberal Christianity can only supply an ineffectual echo to the massive chorus of agreed and admitted unbelief. Don't be deceived by the fact that this echo so often 'hits the headlines'. That is because attacks on Christian doctrine which would pass unnoticed if they were launched (as they are daily launched) by anyone else, become News when the attacker is a clergyman; just as a very commonplace protest against make-up would be News if it came from a film star.

By the way, did you ever meet, or hear of, anyone who was converted from scepticism to a 'liberal' or 'de-mythologised' Christianity? I think that when unbelievers come in at all, they come in a good deal further.[46]

Simply replace 'supernatural' with 'rational' in some of this:

They themselves find it impossible to accept [a rational religion] . . . It follows that . . . the most mischievous people in the world are those who, like myself, proclaim that Christianity [is essentially rational, and more rational than any alternative]. They are quite sure that [rational religion] never will, nor should, be revived, and that if we convince the world that it must choose between accepting [a rational Christianity] and abandoning all pretence of Christianity, the world will undoubtedly choose the second alternative . . . We shall have re-attached to the name *Christian* a deadly scandal from which, but for us, they might have succeeded in decontaminating it.

I think Lewis is quite right; this is why both in the case of the supernatural in religion and in the case of the rational element in religion, Lewis' most determined opponents are 'liberal' Christians. He is disliked by the atheists as a formidable opponent. But there is an element of distaste almost amounting to hatred in some of his opponents who call themselves Christians. Some of course fight with 'covered shields'; for example, it is difficult if not impossible to discover from Beversluis' book whether he is an anti-rationalist Christian from the liberal camp or a complete agnostic.

Attacks on Lewis from within Christianity please the opponents of Christianity: as Lewis said, an attack on religion from within is 'news'. However, we cannot dismiss such attacks merely because they give 'aid and comfort to the enemy'; if the charges they make were true, that would have to be honestly admitted. But as I have tried to show, the charges are not true.

What can we learn from all this? First, I think, not to pin too much of our faith on any one 'defender of the faith'. We should preach Christ crucified and resurrected, not Lewis – even though his agony and his recovery of both confidence and peace in the faith which he never lost together echo Christ's death and resurrection. Next we should make very sure that in thinking about the faith *we* are really thinking with the *aid* of great men like Lewis, not merely parotting their arguments without making them our own.

Finally, we should let our thoughts and our prayers work together, as they did for Lewis; and bring hope and charity to the aid of faith, until we can say with Lewis:

Our opponents, then, have a perfect right to dispute with us about the grounds of our original assent. But they must not accuse us of sheer insanity if, after the assent has been given, our adherence to it is no longer proportioned to every fluctuation of the apparent evidence. They cannot of course be expected to know on what our assurance feeds, and how it revives and is always rising from its ashes. They cannot be expected to see how the *quality* of the object which we think we are beginning to know by acquaintance drives us to the view that if this were a delusion then we should have to say that the universe had produced no real thing of comparable value and that all explanations of the delusion seemed somehow less important than the thing explained. That is knowledge we cannot communicate. But they can see how the assent, of necessity, moves us from the logic of speculative thought into what might perhaps be called the logic of personal relations. What would, up till then, have been variations simply of opinion become variations of conduct by a person to a Person. *Credere Deum esse* turns into *Credere in Deum*. And *Deum* here is this God, the increasingly knowable Lord.[47]

3

UNDER THE RUSSIAN CROSS: A RESEARCH NOTE ON C. S. LEWIS AND THE EASTERN ORTHODOX CHURCH

Andrew Walker

Lewis was a thoroughly Western man, steeped in the thought patterns of Augustine, Aquinas, and medievalism. If his philosophical idealism ultimately harked back to Plato, it was refracted not so much through the Fathers as through later Thomism and the comfortable Englishness of T. H. Green.

And yet it is surely one of the greatest accolades that we can bestow on Lewis that this 'Christian for all Christians' is avidly read and admired by thousands of people in the Eastern churches. In Great Britain, for example, in the bookshop of the Russian cathedral at Ennismore Gardens in London there are basically two types of books on sale: Orthodox books, and a huge array of the writings of C. S. Lewis. And Metropolitan Anthony is a great admirer of Lewis and of Lewis' friend Charles Williams (and is also, of course, the chairman of the trustees of the C. S. Lewis Centre).

My contact with the Orthodox in the United States, which ranges from the Antiochene Church, and the Greeks, to the more Russified flavour of the Orthodox Church of America, suggests that Lewis is probably the most widely read of all Protestant writers. And it is not only among the Orthodox diaspora in America and Europe that this is so. I remember being present at a dinner party in London some years ago at which a senior Greek bishop from Constantinople begged me to send him Lewis' *Out of the Silent Planet*, mentioning in passing that in his opinion Lewis was really an 'anonymous' Orthodox![1]

The evidence that Lewis himself was well acquainted with Eastern Orthodox theology and practice is, however, scanty. Certainly in his earlier writings he shows little acquaintance with the Greek Fathers, and his cast of mind, with its commitment to classicism and the moral law, was clearly of a more *cataphatic* mould than the *apophatic* die of the Eastern church.

Nevertheless, it is unfair to suggest that Lewis knew nothing at all of the Eastern Fathers. We have his own admiring comments concerning St Athanasius and his theology in 'On the Reading of Old Books'.[2] Furthermore, as I have argued elsewhere,[3] the 'deep magic' of Narnia invoked by the White Witch in *The Lion, the Witch, and the Wardrobe*,[4] is a clear echo of the ransom theory, much loved by the early Greek Fathers – especially by St Gregory of Nyssa – in which the devil is seen as holding rights over the human world because of the fall. These rights God respects, and because of his innate justice he is prepared to pay the devil his dues. But Christ, like Aslan, knows of a deeper and more hidden 'law' than the devil knows. In the event the devil is 'tricked' by the cross,[5] for Jesus is no mere mortal in thrall to Satan: he is the God-Man – pure, and without sin. In Gregory of Nyssa's words, Jesus 'was the bait on the fish-hook'.[6]

The fact that this theory of the atonement was abandoned by both East and West would not have worried Lewis, (though in the West, but never the East, Christ's death on the cross was later seen as a ransom necessary to appease the anger of a wrathful God). We know, anyhow, that Lewis was not attached to one particular theory of the atonement; but it is so typical of him to have used the primitive ransom doctrine in that most famous of all the Narnian chronicles, simply because it was good myth and worked well in the context of what I have called the 'divine drama' of salvation.[7]

All of this is in itself interesting – for Lewis 'buffs' at least – but it is hardly proof of Lewis' interest in Eastern Orthodoxy.

Lewis' apologetics and his imaginative stories are not liberally peppered with references or allusions to the Desert Fathers of the *Philokalia*,[8] nor to the later treasury of Russian spiritual theology. Nevertheless, he did encounter Eastern Orthodoxy, though not primarily in books, nor in Greece or the Baltic states, but in Oxford through the Russian diaspora. In particular he was a friend of Nicholas and Militza Zernov from the 1940s to his death in 1963. (He used to refer to Nicholas, who was one of the great characters of the diaspora, as 'an Oxford institution'.)

Militza Zernov told me[9] 'we have certainly talked with C. S. Lewis (we are calling him Jack) about the Orthodox church. He was deeply interested in it.' Nicholas Zernov, who had a reputation for being persistent and persuasive, managed to involve Lewis in a number of his activities. For example, Zernov helped to found the Fellowship of St Alban and St Sergius, which still exists today. Its purpose was to bring Eastern and Western Christians (especially Anglicans) closer together. Militza Zernov recalls that Lewis went to one of the early summer conferences at Abingdon, where he was involved in all the discussions of the differences between the Eastern and Western churches. She cannot recall the year. We know, however, that Lewis read at least one paper to the Fellowship, on 'Membership', for it was published in *Sobornost* 31 (June 1945) and is still available in various Lewis collections.[10]

Less well known is the fact that Lewis attended a meeting at St Gregory's House in Oxford (again Militza Zernov is not sure of the date) which was another one of Nicholas Zernov's ecumenical ventures to bring Christians of the East and West closer together. There Lewis read a paper entitled 'A Toy, an

Icon, and a Work of Art'. To my knowledge this paper has never been written up and published. (Perhaps someone somewhere can recall the content of this paper or maybe has even recorded it?)

For many years it has been a common practice in Oxford for the Greek Orthodox and the Russian Orthodox to share a common church, while maintaining their distinctiveness. Whether or not it was this Oxford church that Lewis attended I do not know, but Lewis certainly attended at least one Orthodox liturgy and was clearly moved by it:

> What pleased me most about a Greek Orthodox mass I once attended was that there seemed to be no prescribed behaviour for the congregation. Some stood, some knelt, some sat, some walked; one crawled about the floor like a caterpillar. And the beauty of it was that nobody took the slightest notice of what anyone else was doing. I wish we Anglicans would follow their example. One meets people who are perturbed because someone in the next pew does, or does not, cross himself. They oughtn't even to have seen, let alone censured. 'Who are thou that judgest Another's servant?'[11]

Curiously, but surely it is of some symbolic importance, the Orthodox faith was to play some (albeit small) part in Lewis' funeral. As Militza Zernov recalls: 'When Lewis died it was very little known in Oxford, and we knew about his death and we wanted to come to his funeral. It was in the church near where his home was, and I prepared a cross with white flowers for his grave. When we arrived the church warden said that C. S. Lewis' brother, Major Lewis, had made an arrangement that there were to be no flowers in church. (He was very severe in his opinions.) So my cross was put outside the church. But we were early, before the beginning of the service, and then the news came that C. S. Lewis' brother was very unwell.[12] So the warden said, "Well, let's bring your cross in."

'And so the coffin was very high up in the middle of the church, and the white cross was put at the foot of this arrangement. And when his coffin was put in the cemetery, which was around the church, my cross was put on his coffin. So in that I was very happy that I could say farewell to him. And I am sure he would be pleased with it, because he appreciated beauty very much.'

So there we have it. Who would have thought it? Jack Lewis was buried under a Russian cross of white flowers, beneath an English November sky. And in their distinctive ways all of Christendom's divided churches were represented there when it must have seemed that for a moment there was a synergy of heaven and earth – a suspension of time, an instance of 'big magic', when that 'other country' was fleetingly transported to our own.

4

THE CHRISTIAN INFLUENCE OF G. K. CHESTERTON ON C. S. LEWIS

Aidan Mackey

C. S. Lewis more than once testified to the fact that he was among the many people whose approach to Christianity was due, in part, to the influence of G. K. Chesterton. It would be wrong to lay too heavy an emphasis on this claim, for in the long run no one can convert or save the soul of another. If and when conversion comes, it does so through the working of the Holy Spirit and our own willingness to hear and submit to the Word. Other people frequently act as signposts along the route, and sometimes as a more positive impetus, but the steering wheel and the brake are ever in our own hands.

This essay therefore makes no attempt to treat of the larger question of Lewis' conversion to Christianity, or to re-hash the detailed and honest account that he has given us in *Surprised by Joy*.[1] I confine myself to following a thread of influence which has long interested me and which must be traced back to long before the day when Lewis, just starting on his spiritual journey, first encountered Chesterton's *Everlasting Man*[2] and at once came under his influence. By that time the older man had already completed his own long pilgrimage and had come firmly to anchor in Rome. It is a journey worthy of some consideration.

Many, probably most, people have two erroneous impressions about the circumstances of Chesterton's early life. The first is that he was born into a Christian home, and the second is that the norm of Victorian society and family life was orthodox and actively Christian. In fact the spiritual truths of Christianity were, in the years in which Chesterton grew up, very much under siege. It was the age of Herbert Spencer, Charles Darwin, and Thomas Huxley, and of industry and commercialism triumphant. Chesterton himself wrote that 'The real vice of the Victorians was that they regarded history as a story which ended well – because it ended with the Victorians',[3] and the prevalent feeling of being the full culmination of the march of Progress, of standing upon a summit of achievement, could only be materialistic in essence. As Thomas Carlyle, who coined the phrase 'Captains of Industry', put it, 'It is the age of machinery in every outward and inward sense of the word.'[4] For the majority of people, certainly for those in the middle and wealthier classes, religious observance was often largely formalistic, and a matter of support for the existing social order. To a considerable extent, the truly spiritual life had been replaced by a code of ethics.

The two dominant and mutually opposing influences of the age, then, were on the one hand the openly materialistic atheism of socialism and of the new schools of thought and, on the other, an almost equally (though not explicit, and very frequently unconscious) materialism of entrenched capitalism, which looked to the church for support for the existing social and economic system. It appeared as a brave and provocative challenge from the outside when, in 1891 (the very year in which Engels published his completion of Karl Marx's *Das Kapital*), Pope Leo XIII launched his great attack on the twin evils of monopolistic capitalism and socialism:

> By degrees it has come to pass that working men have been surrendered, isolated and helpless, to the hard-heartedness of employers and the greed of unchecked competition. The mischief

has been increased by rapacious usury which, although more than once condemned by the Church, is nevertheless, under a different guise, but with the like injustice, still practised by covetous and grasping men. To this must be added that the hiring of labour and the conduct of trade are concentrated in the hands of comparatively few, so that a small number of very rich men have been able to lay upon the teeming masses a yoke little better than slavery itself.

To remedy these wrongs, the Socialists, working on the poor man's envy of the rich, are striving to do away with private property, and contend that individual possessions should become the property of all, to be administered by the State or by Municipal bodies . . . the remedy they propose is manifestly against justice, for every man has the right to possess property as his own. This is one of the chief points of distinction between man and the animal creation, for the brute has no power of self-direction . . . Man's needs do not die out, but for ever recur . . . Nature accordingly must have given to man a source that is stable and always remaining with him, from which he might look to draw continual supplies . . . Man precedes the State, and possesses, prior to the formation of any State, the right of providing for the sustenance of his body.[5]

It was from this defence of man as a spiritual being and of the family as the natural unit of the State, that Chesterton, Hilaire Belloc and others were later to develop the social philosophy of Distributism.

The Chesterton family itself was never given to active worship, and in so far as it answered to any religious description it was vaguely, though passively, Unitarian. Years later Chesterton's school friend (afterwards to become his brother-in-law) Lucian Oldershaw recalled being given by his father a serious warning against the agnosticism and republicanism of the Chesterton household. It was therefore natural that when Chesterton consciously began his quest for truth he should start it not in the churches but in the ethical societies which then abounded.

The word 'consciously' is of some importance, for an earlier influence, unrecognised at the time but significant and endur-

ing, had already been at work on his mind. George Mac-
Donald, Christian minister, poet, literary critic and novelist,
was also writing fairy and fantasy stories for children in which
serious theological and philosophical concepts underlay the
tales themselves. As a child Chesterton came very strongly
under the spell of these, and in particular of *The Princess and
the Goblin*,[6] published two years before his birth in 1874. His
testimony to the effect of that book is of great interest:

[It is] a book that has made a difference to my whole existence,
which helped me to see things in a certain way from the start; a
vision of things which even so real a revolution as a change of
religious allegiance has substantially only crowned and confirmed. . . . When I read it as a child, I felt that the whole thing
was happening inside a real human house, not essentially unlike
the house I was living in, which also had staircases and rooms and
cellars. This is where the fairy-tale differed from many other
fairy-tales; above all, this is where the philosophy differed from
many other philosophies. I have always felt a certain insufficiency
about the ideal of Progress, even of the best sort which is a
Pilgrim's Progress. It hardly suggests how near both the best and
the worst things are to us from the first; even perhaps especially at
the first. And though, like every other sane person I value and
revere the ordinary fairy-tale of the miller's third son who set out
to seek his fortune . . . the very suggestion of travelling to a
far-off land, which is the soul of it, prevents it from achieving this
particular purpose of making all the ordinary staircases and doors
and windows into magical things . . . There is something not only
imaginative but intimately true about the idea of the goblins
being below the house and capable of besieging it from the
cellars. When the evil things besieging us do appear, they do not
appear outside but inside. Anyhow, that simple image of a house
that is our home, that is rightly loved as our home, but of which
we hardly know the best or the worst, and must always wait for
the one and watch against the other, has always remained on my
mind as something singularly solid and unanswerable; and was
more corroborated than corrected when I came to give a more
definite name to the lady watching over us from the turret . . .
Since I first read that story some five alternative philosophies of
the universe have come to our colleges out of Germany, blowing

through the world like the east wind. But for me that castle is still standing in the mountains, and the light in its tower is not put out.[7]

Elsewhere in the same introductory essay Chesterton commented that 'another recurrent image in [MacDonald's] romances was a great white horse; the father of the Princess had one, and there was another in *The Back of the North Wind*. To this day I can never see a big white horse in the street without a sudden sense of indescribable things.'

George MacDonald, then, formed and established one major aspect of Chesterton's view of creation and his response to the world about him. And it was from this base of an awareness of the wonder of existence that Chesterton grew, and it was the philosophy of being that he constructed from it that was later to save him from probable insanity and possible suicide during his dark and tormented adolescence.

In his *Autobiography* Chesterton records how, during his days at art school, he carried the scepticism of the age as far as it could be made to go:

The atheist told me so pompously that he did not believe there was any God; and there were moments when I did not even believe there was any atheist.

And as with mental, so with moral extremes. There is something truly menacing in the thought of how quickly I could imagine the maddest, when I had never committed the mildest crime . . . there was a time when I had reached that condition of moral anarchy within, in which a man says, in the words of Wilde, that 'Atys with the blood-stained knife were better than the thing I am.' I have never indeed felt the faintest temptation to the particular madness of Wilde; but I could at this time imagine the worst and wildest disproportions and distortions of more normal passion . . . overpowered and oppressed with a sort of congestion of imagination . . . I had never heard of Confession, in any serious sense, in those days; but that is what is really needed in such cases . . . Anyhow, the point is here that I dug quite low enough to discover the devil . . .

. . . When I had been for some time in these, the darkest depths of the contemporary pessimism, I had a strong inward impulse to revolt; to dislodge this incubus or throw off this nightmare. But as I was still thinking the thing out by myself, with little help from philosophy and no real help from religion, I invented a rudimentary and makeshift mystical theory of my own. It was substantially this: that even mere existence, reduced to its most primary limits, was extraordinary enough to be exciting. Anything was magnificent as compared with nothing. Even if the very daylight were a dream, it was a day-dream; it was not a nightmare . . . I hung on to the remains of religion by one thin thread of thanks.[8]

And this gratitude for the gift of existence he expressed in a famous early poem, 'By a Babe Unborn':

> If trees were tall and grasses short,
>   As in some crazy tale,
> If here and there a sea were blue
>   Beyond the breaking pale,
>
> If a fixed fire hung in the air
>   To warm me one day through,
> If deep green hair grew on great hills,
>   I know what I should do.
>
> In dark I lie: dreaming that there
>   Are great eyes cold or kind,
> And twisted streets and silent doors,
>   And living men behind.
>
> Let storm-clouds come: better an hour
>   And leave to weep and fight,
> Than all the ages I have ruled
>   The empires of the night.
>
> I think that if they gave me leave
>   Within that world to stand,
> I would be good through all the day
>   I spent in fairyland.
>
> They would not hear a word from me
>   Of selfishness or scorn,
> If only I could find the door,
>   If only I were born.[9]

And again and again this hymn of gratitude for the 'Great Minimum' of existence is sung throughout Chesterton's work. In his last radio broadcast, just a couple of months before he died in June 1936, he took issue with T. S. Eliot's description of desolation and defeat in 'The Hollow Men':

> This is the way the world ends,
> This is the way the world ends,
> This is the way the world ends,
> Not with a bang but a whimper.[10]

And he again reiterated and defended his joy in mere existence:

> I have been filled with life from within in a cold waiting-room in a deserted railway-junction . . . I have experienced the mere excitement of existence in places that would commonly be called as dull as ditch-water. And, by the way, is ditch-water dull? Naturalists with microscopes have told me that it teems with quiet fun . . . I do not think that I am unfair to the whole trend of the time if I say that it is . . . without that rich repose in the mind which I mean when I say that a man when he is alone can be happy because he is alive.[11]

Of the many qualities which Chesterton and C. S. Lewis had in common, one of the more striking is their capacity for so reaching the centre and essence of an issue that their comment and their judgements do not date, and we read them today with something approaching disbelief that their words are not newly uttered, but come to us across many decades, still with a freshness and pertinence which shames most contemporary commentators. Our own self-indulgent and effete attitude to life is in desperate need of the understanding that true happiness in life, as in fairy-tales, is always conditional. It is only within the rules, only under the law, that we can be free. The Victorians who in the name of individual liberty campaigned for easy divorce would be genuinely horrified if they could see the state of our family life today, and it surely cannot be long before the vociferous propagandists for the permissive society are faced with their responsibility for the ghastly physical and spiritual sicknesses which tear our society apart. The clamour has been for 'rights' without duties, for gratification without delay and without self-discipline or submission to lawful authority. They lack, in short, that concept of conditional happiness which runs throughout Chesterton's work, the seed of which was planted by George MacDonald.

On Lewis, MacDonald was at least as strong an influence. In that splendid tribute to MacDonald as a Christian mentor, his Preface to *George MacDonald: An Anthology*, Lewis wrote:

> I have never concealed the fact that I regarded him as my master; indeed I fancy that I have never written a book in which I did not quote from him. But it has not seemed to me that those who have received my books kindly take even now sufficient notice of the affiliation. Honesty drives me to emphasise it . . . It must be more than thirty years ago that I bought – almost unwillingly, for I had looked at the volume on that bookstall and rejected it on a dozen previous occasions – the Everyman edition of *Phantastes*. A few hours later I knew that I had crossed a great frontier. I had already been waist-deep in Romanticism; and likely enough, at any moment, to flounder into its darker and more evil forms, slithering down the steep descent that leads from the love of strangeness to that of eccentricity and thence to that of perversity. Now *Phantastes* was romantic enough in all conscience; but there was a difference. Nothing was at that time further from my thoughts than Christianity and I therefore had no notion what this difference really was. I was only aware that if this new world was strange, it was also homely and humble; that if this was a dream, it was a dream in which one at least felt strangely vigilant; that the whole book had about it a sort of cool, morning innocence, and also, quite unmistakably, a certain quality of Death, *good* Death. What it actually did to me was to convert, even to baptise, (that was where the Death came in) my imagination . . . The quality which has enchanted me in his imaginative works turned out to be the quality of the real universe, the divine, magical, terrifying and ecstatic reality in which we all live.[12]

This first discovery came early in 1916, before Lewis had begun to read Chesterton, but that passage shows how amazingly similar was the effect that MacDonald had on them both. It would have been entirely in place in the pages of Chesterton's *Autobiography*, which I quoted earlier.

The parallels between the philosophical and spiritual development of these two men are, then, clear and striking, though separated, of course, by a good number of years. (Although it was 1922 before Chesterton actually entered the Roman Catholic Church as the goal of his journey, his allegiance to it had long been apparent. *Orthodoxy*, the first of his great religious books, was published in 1908,[13] but nothing in it needed to be cancelled or modified by later events. In 1911, speaking to the Heretics Club at Cambridge, he commented that 'he was more than ever inclined to think, though he had not yet been admitted, that possibly the claims of the Greek and Anglican churches were less near the truth than the Roman Catholic church'.[14]) Each had grown up very far from Christianity, Chesterton remarking in his *Autobiography* that 'I then had no more notion of being a Catholic than of being a cannibal'.[15] Exactly as was later to be the case with Lewis, Chesterton was astonished to discover that those people around him with whom he found himself most in sympathy, and most able to respect, were Christian. Nurtured on the comic and ineffectual curate of farce and fiction,

> I was quite ready to believe that a dying superstition was represented by such feeble persons. As a fact, I found that they were very often by far the ablest and most forcible persons. In debate after debate I noticed the same thing happen . . . It was the farcical curate, it was the feeble-minded clergyman, who got up and applied to the wandering discussion at least some sort of test of some sort of truth; who showed all the advantages of having been tolerably trained in some sort of system of thinking . . . It seemed to me that the despised curates were rather more intelligent than anybody else; that they, alone in that world of intellectualism, were trying to use their intellects.[16]

Lewis' discovery of Chesterton came early in 1918 when as a Second Lieutenant in the Somerset Light Infantry he was recovering in a Field Hospital from a bout of trench fever:

It was here that I first read a volume of Chesterton's essays. I had never heard of him and had no idea of what he stood for; nor can I quite understand why he made such an immediate conquest of me. It might have been expected that my pessimism, my atheism, and my hatred of sentiment would have made him to me the least congenial of all authors. It would almost seem that Providence, or some 'second cause' of a very obscure kind, quite over-rules our previous tastes when It decides to bring two minds together. Liking an author may be as involuntary and improbable as falling in love. I was by now a sufficiently experienced reader to distinguish liking from agreement. I did not need to accept what Chesterton said in order to enjoy it. His humour was of the kind which I like best – not 'jokes' imbedded in the page like currants in a cake, still less (what I cannot endure), a general tone of flippancy and jocularity, but the humour which is not in any way separable from the argument but is rather (as Aristotle would say) the 'bloom' on dialectic itself. The sword glitters not because the swordsman set out to make it glitter but because he is fighting for his life and therefore moving it very quickly. For the critics who think Chesterton frivolous or 'paradoxical' I have to work hard to feel even pity; sympathy is out of the question. Moreover, strange as it may seem, I liked him for his goodness. I can attribute this taste to myself quite freely (even at that age) because it was a liking for goodness which had nothing to do with any attempt to be good myself . . .
    In reading Chesterton, as in reading MacDonald, I did not know what I was letting myself in for. A young man who wishes to remain a sound Atheist cannot be too careful of his reading. There are traps everywhere – 'Bibles laid open, millions of surprises,' as Herbert says, 'fine nets and stratagems.' God is, if I may say it, very unscrupulous.[17]

From that time Lewis read a good deal of Chesterton, a habit he retained to the end of his life, and the thread of influence remained unbroken, interwoven with all the other philosophical and spiritual experiences which he was meeting and absorbing into his own armoury.

It was not only upon religious and some literary issues that Lewis found himself fighting side by side with Chesterton. On social and political questions both men were deeply, instinctively, and genuinely on the side of the ordinary common people and the normal, poor families who were (and are) increasingly at the mercy of planners, sociologists and paternalists. It is impossible to read much of Chesterton without coming, time after time, upon this theme. Indeed, several of his books, *What's Wrong With the World* (1910), *Eugenics and Other Evils* (1922), *William Cobbett* (1925), *The Outline of Sanity* (1926) and the novel *The Napoleon of Notting Hill* (1904), are entirely devoted to it.[18] In a controversy with H. G. Wells and George Bernard Shaw, Chesterton wrote:

Now I happen to hold a view which is almost unknown among Socialists, Anarchists, Liberals and Conservatives. I believe very strongly in the mass of the common people. I do not mean in their 'potentialities', I mean in their faces, in their habits, and their admirable language. Caught in the trap of a terrible industrial machinery, harried by a shameful economic cruelty, surrounded with an ugliness and desolation never endured before among men, stunted by a stupid and provincial religion, or by a more stupid and more provincial irreligion, the poor are still by far the sanest, jolliest, and most reliable part of the community . . . No part of the community is so specially fixed in those forms and feelings which are opposite to the tone of most Socialists; the privacy of homes, the control of one's own children, the minding of one's own business. I look out of my back windows over the black stretch of Battersea, and I believe I could make up a sort of creed, a catalogue of maxims, which I am certain are believed, and believed strongly, by the overwhelming mass of men and women as far as the eye can reach. For instance, that an Englishman's home is his castle, and that awful proprieties ought to regulate admission to it; that marriage is a real bond, making jealousy and marital revenge at least highly pardonable; that Vegetarianism and all pitting of animal against human rights is a silly fad; that on the other hand to save money to give yourself a fine funeral is not a silly fad, but a symbol of ancestral self-respect; that when giving treats to friends or children, one should give them what they like, emphatically not what is good for them; that there is nothing illogical in being furious because Tommy had been coldly caned by a schoolmistress and then throwing saucepans at him yourself. All these things they believe. They are the only people who do believe them; and they are absolutely and eternally right. They are the ancient sanities of humanity; the ten commandments of men . . . They do not believe in the Socialist ideal any more than they believe in the Manchester ideal;[19] they are too healthy to believe in either. But while they are healthy, they are also vague, slow, bewildered, and unaccustomed, alas! to civil war. Individualism was imposed on them by a handful of merchants; Socialism will be imposed on them by a handful of decorative artists and Oxford dons, and journalists, and Countesses on the spree . . . The moral fact is that the Democracy definitely dislikes your favourite philosophy, but may accept it . . . rather than take the trouble to resist.[20]

With Lewis this theme is not nearly so pervasive, but it is strong and is unmistakably integral to his philosophy. Michael D. Aeschliman writes of it:

The sources on whom Lewis chiefly relied are Plato and Aristotle, St. John, and Augustine among the Ancients, and Aquinas, Richard Hooker, Samuel Johnson,[21] and G. K. Chesterton among the Moderns – all exemplars of what he calls 'the great central tradition' . . . With Hooker, Lewis believed that, '[t]he great and perpetual voice of man is as the sentence of God himself,' but he did not confuse this tradition with the idea that majorities are always right . . . What Lewis trusted was the fund of 'common sense' of men throughout history, . . . what Alexander Pope was referring to when he wrote that 'whatever is very good sense must have common sense in all times': the vast common sense of humanity, of which [Lewis] felt he was a trustee and which he articulated and defended in all of his writing, speaking, and living.

Part of the reason for Lewis's popularity is his assumption that almost all good men who have ever thought honestly share universal convictions which may differ in detail but not in substance. He felt that the amorality, agnosticism, and atheism of much of twentieth-century culture, and especially of the culture of modernism, amounted to an aberration within the historical tradition of common sense, and that its adherents were, in the terms of Augustine whom he quotes, 'divorced by some madness from the *communis sensus* of man.' His own idea of the perennial philosophy was that 'good is indeed something objective, and reason the organ whereby it is apprehended.' Like Dr. Johnson, he knew and tirelessly repeated the fact that most men, whatever they say or write, assume in practical conduct that they have free will and decision and that objective truth and value exist . . .

    . . . [Lewis's] great learning was always worn very lightly and always subordinated to common sense, which was for him, as for Chesterton, . . . something both luminously intelligible and joyously mystical . . .

    . . . This wisdom [common sense] consisted largely for Lewis in a trust in and loyalty to the traditional virtues as the outline of an encompassing reality. He resented and opposed the implicit claims of both scientists and 'humanists' to moral superiority over the common man.[22]

And in a newspaper article in which he expressed his opposition to the concept of the paternalistic Welfare State, Lewis wrote:

I believe a man is happier, and happy in a richer way, if he has the 'freeborn mind'. But I doubt whether he can have this without economic independence, which the new society is abolishing. For economic independence allows an education not controlled by Government; and in adult life it is the man who needs, and asks, nothing of Government who can criticise its acts and snap his fingers at its ideology. Read Montaigne; that's the voice of a man with his legs under his own table, eating the mutton and turnips raised on his own land. Who will talk like that when the State is everyone's schoolmaster and employer? . . . On just the same ground I dread government in the name of science. That is how tyrannies come in. In every age, the men who want us under their thumb, if they have any sense, will put forward the particular pretension which the hopes and fears of that age render most potent. They 'cash in'. It has been magic, it has been Christianity.

Now it will certainly be science. Perhaps the real scientists may not think much of the tyrants' 'science' – they didn't think much of Hitler's racial theories or Stalin's biology. But they can be muzzled . . . To live his life in his own way, to call his house his castle, to enjoy the fruits of his own labour, to educate his children as his conscience directs, to save for their prosperity after his death – these are wishes deeply ingrained . . . Their realisation is almost as necessary to our virtues as to our happiness. From their total frustration disastrous results, both moral and psychological, might follow.[23]

This seeming echo of what Chesterton had for so long been fighting is neither coincidence nor a case of Lewis copying the stance of the earlier writer. In each case, social and political attitudes sprang directly and inevitably from the Christian recognition of people as spiritual as well as material beings, with souls to save, and who must build a social order which offers the most fruitful soil for rounded growth.

Earlier (p. 77) I quoted Lewis' remark on first reading Chesterton: 'nor can I quite understand why he made such an immediate conquest of me'. To us now, I believe – and very possibly to Lewis himself later – the matter is less obscure. Most thoughtful readers have at some time or another experienced a seemingly inexplicable feeling of rapport on first dipping into some writer. A feeling so strong that 'rapport' may well be too pale and inadequate a word to describe it. It is almost as if, after meeting and conversing with a stranger for a very few minutes, one realises that this is no stranger at all, but an old, loved and trusted friend with whom one had for some time lost contact. This feeling frequently precedes any understanding of the reason for it. That it should arise from the meeting of these two minds seems to me to be entirely natural and to be expected. They had many qualities in common, even if in Lewis some of them had not then reached their fullness. Each had a fierce intellectual honesty and a taste for chivalrous and good-humoured – though entirely serious – battle for truth through controversy and debate. Both were, as Lewis was later to write to E. M. Tillyard, 'hungry for rational opposition'.[24] And the mental development of Lewis up to that time, and especially the influence of George MacDonald, must have made him ready to receive with joy the full impact of the mind and heart of Chesterton and to feel, as I and countless others have felt, the *rightness*, the almost inevitable-feeling rightness, of so many of Chesterton's utterances. Many years later, answering a criticism of Chesterton, Lewis expressed this feeling vividly:

> Does not the central theme of the Ballad [of the White Horse][25] – the highly paradoxical message which Alfred receives from the Virgin – embody the feeling, and the only possible feeling, with which in any age almost defeated men take up such arms as are left them and win? . . . Hence, in those quaking days just after the fall of France, a young friend of mine (just about to enter the R.A.F.) and I found ourselves quoting to one another stanza after stanza of the Ballad. There was nothing else to say.[26]

The years which separated the lives of these two Christian warriors are irrelevant. They stood, and stand, shoulder to shoulder, each generous to foe as well as to friend, each unmindful of self, and each bearing arms as volunteers in the service of the same Captain.

5

A PECULIAR DEBT: THE INFLUENCE OF CHARLES WILLIAMS ON C. S. LEWIS

Brian Horne

I

On 15 May 1945 Charles Williams died. Two years later C. S. Lewis recalled that it was a Tuesday morning, 'one of our times of meeting'. Williams had been admitted to the Radcliffe Infirmary in Oxford two days earlier, and Lewis, unaware of how seriously ill his friend was, had gone to the hospital expecting to see Williams, lend him a book, and carry a message from him back to the group of friends meeting, as was their custom, at the pub The Eagle and Child on the Tuesday morning. On arriving at the hospital he was told that Williams was dead. 'This experience of loss (the greatest I have ever known) was', he wrote, 'wholly unlike what I should have expected.'[1] He returned to the gathering friends with the news. 'The world seemed to us at that moment primarily a *strange* one . . . We now verified for ourselves what so many bereaved people have reported; the ubiquitous presence of a dead man, as if he had ceased to meet us in a particular place in order to meet us everywhere.' Whether Lewis was actually voicing the reactions of all the members of the circle we cannot be sure; there is no mistaking, however, the depth of Lewis' own feeling. The impact of Williams, both as a friend and as a thinker, upon Lewis can hardly be overestimated, and his death drew from Lewis a tribute possibly unsurpassed in its expression of love and admiration: 'No event has so corroborated my faith in the next world as Williams did simply by dying. When the idea of death and the idea of Williams thus met in my mind, it was the idea of death that changed.'[2]

The name of Charles Williams had been known to C. S. Lewis before the two men met and before Lewis had read anything by Williams. Nevill Coghill, an old friend and colleague of Lewis, described the way in which he introduced Lewis to the third of Williams' novels, *The Place of the Lion*.[3] The year was 1936, five years after its publication; 'Lewis read it, was captivated by the strange blend of Plato and Genesis, wrote to Williams, met him and introduced him to the Inklings (a group of us described in *Surprised by Joy*), to our great delight.'[4] Coghill's account is confirmed by Lewis himself, but there is something odd about Coghill's recollection of Williams' introduction to the Inklings. Williams might well have met Lewis' brother Warren, Hugo Dyson, J. R. R. Tolkien and the others soon after 1936, but it is unlikely that before 1939 he would have been able to be present at the regular gathering of friends who met in Lewis' rooms to read their work to each other and generally enjoy each other's company and conversation. Williams lived in London and worked for the Oxford University Press in the City; it was not until the outbreak of the Second World War that the Press evacuated Amen House, its London office, and moved its staff to Oxford. Lewis' welcome of Williams was warm and generous: not only was he introduced to the Inklings, he was invited, at the instigation of Lewis, to lecture in the university. Erik Routley was an undergraduate in Oxford during those years. 'I am profoundly thankful . . .', he wrote, 'they were the years when C. S. Lewis and Charles Williams were doing their astounding double act in Oxford. One can't think of one without the other (Lewis would have been the first to insist on that).'[5] Over and over again in the biographical studies of C. S. Lewis one encounters descriptions of the significance of Charles Williams for C. S. Lewis. As Routley says, 'Lewis always said he owed everything to Williams. In a sense he mediated Charles Williams to ordinary people.'[6] 'Not to name those who are still with us,' wrote Austin Farrer, 'his debts in personal wisdom and in literary inspiration to his wife and to Charles Williams were visible to all.'[7] Coghill observed: 'They seemed to live in the same spiritual world. I believe Williams was the only one of us, except perhaps Ronald Tolkien, from whom Lewis learnt any of his thinking.'[8]

In 1942 Lewis published his book on Milton, *A Preface to Paradise Lost.*[9] It had begun as a series of lectures at University College, Bangor, but it is dedicated, in the form of a letter written, with Lewis' customary generosity and candour, to Charles Williams. 'It gives me a sense of security to remember that, far from loving your work because you are my friend, I first sought your friendship because I loved your books.'[10] This love of Williams' work was demonstrated again when Williams died. He had left two substantial but unfinished pieces, one in verse, the other in prose. The poetry had already appeared in print in two volumes under the titles *Taliessin Through Logres*[11] and *The Region of the Summer Stars:*[12] it was idiosyncratic and difficult and had been received with a great deal of puzzlement in some quarters. But Lewis admired it, and to honour the memory of his dead friend, as well as to elucidate the poems for as large an audience as he could, he delivered a course of lectures on them in Oxford in the Michaelmas term of 1945. Williams' unpublished prose work addressed the same subject as his poems, the Arthurian legend. In 1948 Lewis' lectures and Williams' literary-historical study were published together under the title *Arthurian Torso.*[13] It is clear that Williams was loved and honoured by Lewis and that Lewis did all he could to 'mediate' his friend's vision of both Christianity and literature to the world. Because of this it is often assumed that the mediation was done by the incorporation of Williams' ideas into Lewis' own work after the impact of Williams was felt in the late 1930s, and that Lewis was speaking no less than the truth when he said (as Erik Routley recalled) he 'owed everything to Williams'. However, when one begins to scrutinise the texts of Lewis from 1940 onwards the difficulty of giving an accurate account of Williams' effect upon Lewis' thought soon becomes apparent. My concern is not biographical. I have no doubt that Williams illuminated and enriched Lewis' life to a degree and in a way that is incalculable. It was not until he met Joy Davidman that Lewis found another human being who could so move him to love and delight. But the question of influence in Lewis' work is problematic. If we look for evidence of Williams' ideas changing and shaping Lewis' own in any substantial way, we shall look in vain. Given the biographical facts, this strikes one, initially, as surprising and even disconcerting. But the influence is there, elusive and tantalising. When Lewis, years after Williams' death, was asked by Walter Hooper what he thought of 'the current vogue for tracing the "influence" of Williams in his work', he replied, 'I have never been *consciously* influenced by Williams, never believed that I was in any way imitating him. On the other hand, there may have been a great deal of *un*conscious influence going on.'[14] Bearing this in mind, we may make an attempt at tracing the relationship between Lewis' mind and imagination and those of Williams, noticing the contrasts as well as the similarities.

When the two men met, Williams was fifty years old and Lewis thirty-eight. Both were already intellectually formed. But although (as some have remarked) they seemed to inhabit the same spiritual world, they were formed in different moulds. Lewis was a scholar and a university teacher and had spent most of his life in the company of fellow students and fellow academics. Williams, through lack of funds, had not been able to complete his first degree at the university, yet his learning at times astonished even the most brilliant of the dons in Oxford. Whereas Lewis seems to have been genial and 'clubbable', Williams had an altogether more mercurial

personality and seems to have been charged with a kind of
'electricity' that either strongly attracted or strongly repelled
others. Apart from these differences of temperament, there
was also what might be called a difference of theological
sensibility. When it came to expounding the Christian faith,
Lewis, as Austin Farrer remarked, 'was an apologist from
temper, from conviction and from modesty'.[15] It was part of
Lewis' nature to be combative (not aggressive), to want to
argue and debate, and in the process of that debate to reach
conclusions. He had the capacity, which he shared with all
good apologists, for assuming the intellectual stance of his
opponents; and some of his most convincing theological
essays came from the need to answer what he saw as an
untenable intellectual proposition. One might say that he
never minded fighting on enemy territory and with any
weapons that were to hand.[16] The approach of Williams was
quite different. There were, of course, occasions when he felt
the need to answer specific questions, but usually when it
came to theology he was a 'theologian' pure and simple. The
delight lay in the art of speculation, not in argumentation. He
would take an orthodox formulary like the Trinity or the
hypostatic union or the bodily resurrection, and turn it this
way and that, place it in new contexts, trace hidden connec-
tions with other dogmas, find new possibilities of meaning.
The marvel of his theology lies in the audacity of the imaginative power. One comes away from Lewis' theological essays
either persuaded by the logic of his argument or clearly aware
of the flaws that prevent him from proving his case. (I am not
suggesting that Lewis believed either that Christianity was
merely a matter of the exercise of reason or that the existence
of God could be proved, I am indicating Lewis' *manner* of
theological discussion.) One comes away from Williams'
theological essays in a state of amazement: could the Christian religion be as strange, as beautiful, as frightening as this?

There is, perhaps, a yet more important difference between
the religious sensibilities of the two men. Both were Anglicans, but each offered a different aspect of the Anglican

character to the world. Lewis had been born into the austere tradition of Northern Irish religious practice and belief, had become an atheist, and had made a slow, sometimes painful, return to faith, convinced intellectually that Christianity alone could give the only possible answers to the questions posed by the problems of human existence. Williams had been nurtured in a 'high' Anglican tradition and had never left it. He was by nature ceremonial, and despite the strongly sceptical cast of his mind he saw no reason to move away from the sacramental religion into which he was born. It was a tradition which helped to cultivate the natural gift of his imagination, and, in its theological precision, it laid an intellectual foundation for his love of symbol and imagery. The talent of Lewis was analysis; the talent of Williams was synthesis. Lewis' mind worked naturally in polarities, and dialectically, arguing logically that 'if *this* is true then *that* cannot be true'. Williams' mind always tried, naturally, to overcome polarities and work with paradox. Where Lewis would exclude, Williams would include. Hence the aphorism which, perhaps, most people still associate with Williams: 'This also is Thou; neither is This Thou.' It is almost inconceivable to think of Lewis making any sense of this in his early life; it goes beyond what he could have stated as an acceptable paradox. Yet he accepted it in Williams and recognised that it was by such a paradox that Williams actually lived his life. And when he came to write *Letters to Malcolm*[17] he seemed to have incorporated it, though not without some awkwardness, into his own understanding of what the Christian life must include.[18] For Lewis the natural tendency was always 'EITHER this OR that'; for Williams the tendency was always towards 'BOTH this AND that'. I stress this matter because I think it goes a long way towards explaining how difficult it would have been for Lewis to ingest and reproduce Williams' ideas – even if he had wanted, consciously, to do so. I believe Nevill Coghill's assessment of Lewis' character (at least as it is reflected in his theological writings) to be accurate when he says:

Underneath all, I sense in his style an indefeasible core of Protestant certainties, the certainties of a simple, unchanging, entrenched ethic that knows how to distinguish, unarguably, between Right and Wrong, Natural and Unnatural, High and Low, Black and White, with a committed force on which his ramified and seemingly conciliatory structures of argument are invisibly based . . .[19]

Austin Farrer reinforces this estimate when he recalls of Lewis that 'when he considered man in relation to God he viewed him too narrowly as a moral will, and that relation as a moral relation'.[20] This is certainly true of the early apologetic work of Lewis, and when he met Williams he must have become conscious of both the strengths and weaknesses of his approach as he fell under the spell of a man who once commented angrily on contemporary preaching, 'The hungry sheep look up for the divine metaphysics of the Gospel, and what do we give them? Morals!' Something of this particular effect of Williams on Lewis is conveyed in the Preface Lewis wrote for the *Essays Presented to Charles Williams*:

> It is one of the many paradoxes in Williams that while no man's conversation was less gloomy in tone . . . no man at times said darker things . . . This scepticism and pessimism were the expression of his feelings. High above them, overarching them like the sky, were the things he believed, and they were wholly optimistic.[21]

The Preface tells the reader as much about Lewis as it does about Williams.

As I have already suggested, we shall look in vain for a complete exposition of the central themes of Williams' theology – or an imitation of Williams' style – in Lewis' work. (Nor should we be disappointed if we do not find them.) There were, of course, areas where Lewis' and Williams' preoccupations met and overlapped, but most of the distinctive features of Williams' thought and vocabulary – the theology of romantic love, the presentation of the Way of the Affirmation of Images, the concept of co-inherence together with the notions of exchange and substituted love, the unique blend of scepticism and belief, his abhorrence of all forms of Manicheeism – remained the property of Williams, and, except in a few and interesting cases, were not incorporated by Lewis into his own work. But we cannot leave the matter there: Lewis *was* changed by Williams, and any picture of his achievement would be incomplete if those instances when Williams' influence rises to the surface were ignored. It is to the most significant of those instances that we now turn.

II

Much of Charles Williams' time at the Oxford University Press was spent on editorial work, and in 1940 the Press published an edition of John Milton's poems in their World's Classics series. It had been prepared by Williams, and he wrote an Introduction to the volume which was an expansion of an essay he had written three years before for the *London Mercury*. What he said about the character of Satan in *Paradise Lost* so impressed Lewis that when he came to give his own interpretation of the Satanic rebellion in *A Preface to Paradise Lost* he followed Williams closely.

> I must frankly confess, however, that I have only lately come to appreciate the War in Heaven at its true worth. The only preparation for it, in our days, is to read Mr. Williams's *Preface*. When I turned back from that remarkable piece of criticism to a re-reading of Books v and vi, it was like seeing, at last properly cleaned, a picture we thought we had known all our lives.
>
> . . . . . .
>
> Mr. Williams has reminded us in unforgettable words that 'Hell is inaccurate', and has drawn attention to the fact that Satan lies about every subject he mentions in *Paradise Lost*.[22]

What caught and held Lewis' attention was not so much Williams' literary judgement, though he respected that, as his theological perspicacity. Williams saw deeply into the nature of evil: its self-deluding quality and its frequent silliness, as well as its profound malevolence. Some such perception of evil may already have been part of Lewis' understanding, because Williams' theology can be traced back to classical Christian sources – through Thomas Aquinas to Augustine of Hippo – but Williams' remarkable ability to throw new light on orthodox teaching delighted Lewis.

This insight into the real nature of evil was to be put to comic use in perhaps his most famous books, *The Screwtape Letters*[23] and *Screwtape Proposes a Toast*.[24] Here Lewis mocks the pretensions of the devil while taking evil seriously. This is very much the style of Williams. It is not Milton's Satan, but Williams' interpretation of Milton's Satan, that provides the theological substructure of both the high and the low comedy of *The Screwtape Letters*:

> In the heat of composition I find that I have inadvertently allowed myself to assume the form of a large centipede . . . Now that the transformation is complete I recognise it as a periodical phenomenon. Some rumour of it has reached the humans and a distorted account of it appears in the poet Milton, with the ridiculous addition that such changes of shape are a 'punishment' imposed on us by the Enemy.[25]

There is being portrayed here both the hatred of goodness and also, more importantly, the sheer inability to comprehend goodness; and so he makes Screwtape dismiss one of the humans tetchily as 'The sort of creature who'd find *ME* funny!'[26]

The notion that evil is both harmful and fatuous is a paradox to which Williams frequently averred in his writing on the subject. Lewis adopted the same position:

> Next to the curse of useless tempters like yourself the greatest curse upon us is the failure of our Intelligence Department. If only we could find out what He is really up to! Alas, alas, that knowledge, in itself so hateful and mawkish a thing, should yet be necessary for Power! . . . All that sustains me is the conviction that our Realism, our rejection . . . of all silly nonsense and claptrap, *must* win in the end.[27]

Evil is seen to arise not only out of perversion of the will (a moral act) but also out of a failure of intelligence (an intellectual act). To be evil is to be mistaken: to have read the facts of the universe wrongly.

In his book on the incarnation, *He Came Down From Heaven*,[28] Williams discussed this concept in the light of the story of the fall in Genesis. He called the chapter, significantly, 'The Myth of the Alteration of Knowledge', and interpreted the real sin of Adam and Eve as the wilful desire to know the facts of creation differently. They could be known either as good or as evil. The facts themselves did not change, and could not be changed, but they could be known in a different manner – as evil rather than good: 'They [the Adam] knew good; they wished to know good and evil. Since there was not – since there never has been and never will be – anything else than the good to know, they knew good as antagonism. All difference consists in the mode of knowledge.'[29] Lewis did not follow Williams in making this interpretation the centre of his own understanding of the fall, but that he was aware of it was shown in his brief discussion of the Genesis story in the fifth chapter of *The Problem of Pain*.[30] Characteristically, at this stage of his life he focused upon the disobedience of Adam and Eve, the moral content of the story.

In 1964 *Letters to Malcolm* was published posthumously. Lewis returned to the question of facts in the nineteenth letter:

> It is a permanent witness that the heavenly realm, certainly no less than the natural universe and perhaps very much more, is a realm of objective facts – hard, determinate facts, not to be constructed *a priori*, and not to be dissolved into maxims, ideals, values, and the like.[31]

Was he remembering Williams' insistence upon facts in 'The Myth of the Alteration of Knowledge'? I do not think it fanciful to hear many echoes of *He Came Down From Heaven* in *Letters to Malcolm*. Williams described heaven as the 'place' of 'bright mathematics' and boldly produced the imagery of mathematical precision as a means for portraying the nature of God. ' "God always geometrizes" said Plato, and the Hebrew prophets thought no less . . . The prophets are sent out from the visible mathematics of the glory to proclaim the moral mathematics of the glory. Morality is either the mathematics of power or it is nothing.'[32] In *Letters to Malcolm* Williams' aphorism 'This also is Thou: neither is This Thou' is referred to three times and he is mentioned by name in the last sentence of the penultimate letter.[33] *He Came Down From Heaven* had opened with a discussion on the concept of heaven:

> It is not, of course, possible to deny that heaven . . . can exist in space; that would be to deny the Incarnation. But heaven, as such, only exists because of the nature of God, and to his existence alone all bliss is related. In a Jewish tradition God was called 'the Place' because all places were referred to him, but he not to any place. With this in mind it might well be that private meditation should sometimes vary the original clause by 'Our Father in whom is heaven'.[34]

Would it be unreasonable to suppose that Williams' words had lodged in Lewis' mind and rose to the surface when, in the last letter to Malcolm, he wrote: 'At present we tend to think of the soul as somehow "inside" the body. But the glorified body of the resurrection as I conceive it . . . will be inside the soul. As God is not in space but space is in God'?[35]

In their biography of C. S. Lewis, Roger Lancelyn Green and Walter Hooper address the question of Charles Williams' influence, and remark of the third volume of Lewis' 'science fiction' trilogy, *That Hideous Strength*,[36] that it 'has been described as a Charles Williams novel written by C. S. Lewis. This is, of course, a wild exaggeration: but it bears the seeds of critical truth.'[37] The first two volumes owe nothing to Williams, the last, undoubtedly, owes a great deal. There is, first, the elimination of much of the element of 'science fantasy' which characterised *Out of the Silent Planet*[38] and *Voyage to Venus*;[39] the location of all the action is in an identifiable milieu: the English Midlands. In this 'known' country supernatural forces erupt: the sudden dissolution of the barriers separating the natural world and the supernatural world involves ordinary human beings in profound moral and spiritual choices: 'It came over her with sickening clarity that the affair of her dreams, far from being ended, was only beginning. The bright, narrow little life which she had proposed to live was being irremediably broken into.'[40] This formula was not, of course, invented by Charles Williams, but it is one which he uses in all his novels, and it is probable, as many have suggested, that Lewis' admiration for Williams persuaded him to consider a similar device for bringing his own trilogy to a conclusion. We know that he first made contact with Williams' work in *The Place of the Lion*. One of the more extraordinary ideas to appear in that book is that of Platonic archetypes entering the world of matter when a breach occurs in the barrier which separates the realm of Ideas from the realm of Nature. The Forms enter (the Lion, the Eagle, the Butterfly) and gather all the material types to themselves. One of the characters in *The Place of the Lion* discusses the theory that the world is created by 'the entrance of certain great principles into aboriginal matter. We call them by cold names; wisdom and courage and beauty and strength and so on, but actually they are very great and mighty Powers.'[41] Lewis adapted this idea for the fifteenth chapter of *That Hideous Strength*, 'The Descent of the Gods'.[42] Here the 'great and mighty Powers' descend into the house at St Anne's. He gives these powers the names of the five planets known to the ancient astronomical system of Ptolemy – Mercury, Mars, Venus, Saturn and Jupiter – and their descent is the metaphysical centrepoint of the narrative.

Woven into the pattern of the book is another thread from Charles Williams: the Arthurian legend. Lewis, as we have seen, had already immersed himself in Williams' Arthurian poems, as well as his prose work, *The Figure of Arthur*,[43] and the spirit of Williams' understanding of the legend informs much of Lewis' writing in *That Hideous Strength*. Logres, the name for an ancient and ideal Britain, and Broceliande, the mysterious forest, occur frequently; and he introduces a quotation from the fourth poem of Williams' *Taliessin Through Logres*, Mount Badon, into his own text – without naming the author of the words.[44]

Opinions differ about the success of this book. My own feeling is that Williams' influence worked against Lewis' natural talent here – to the detriment of the novel. He moved away from his gifts as an allegorist and story-teller into a realm of metaphysical fantasy where he occasionally lost control over his material. Apart from the scene at the beginning of the fifteenth chapter, the attempt at persuading us of the interpenetration of the natural and supernatural is strained and lacks credibility. Whereas Williams, at his best, can convince us that the world is much more extraordinary than we had ever imagined and that the supernatural might at any moment be suddenly revealed, Lewis found this difficult until he transposed the fiction into another key altogether, as in the Narnia stories.

Ten years later he returned to his talent for allegorical narrative in the book which became *Till We Have Faces*,[45] and which, despite its unpopularity, remains one of his most impressive creations. In it he managed, subtly and successfully, to make use of one of Williams' major theological and practical ideas: the doctrine of 'exchange'. It occurs only once, but it flashes in the text with such brilliance that it transforms the story from the re-telling of an ancient myth into a portrayal of the deepest mystery of Christian love. At the very centre of Williams' theology was his belief in what he called Exchange. 'All life is vicarious', he wrote; we live in and for each other, actually bearing in our selves the pains and joys of others, experiencing their sorrows and sharing in their happinesses. It is not simply that this is a possible way to live, it is the only way to live: 'At the root of the physical nature of man . . . lie exchange of liking, substitution, inherence. The nature of man which is so expressed in the physical world is expressed after the same manner, only more fully, in the mental and spiritual.'[46]

And at the centre of all the exchanges is the Great Exchange made by God in Christ: the incarnation and the cross. Nevill Coghill has given a description of the effect of this teaching on Lewis' personal life:

> It was Charles Williams who expounded to him the doctrine of co-inherence and the idea that one had power to accept into one's own body the pain of someone else, through Christian love. This was a power which Lewis found himself later to possess, and which, he told me, he had been allowed to use to ease the suffering of his wife, a cancer victim, of whom the doctors had despaired.[47]

There is a direct link between this personal knowledge of 'substituted love' and the closing scene of *Till We Have Faces*. At the end of the trial Orual finds herself in the arms of her old tutor, the Fox. He leads her into a place where the walls are covered with pictures which tell the story of Psyche over again, but as it truly happened and not as Orual imagined it as having happened.

> 'But are these pictures true?'
> 'All here's true.'
> 'But how could she – did she really – do such things and go to such places – and not . . . ? Godfather, she was all but unscathed. She was almost happy.'
> 'Another bore nearly all the anguish.'
> 'I? Is it possible?'
> 'That was one of the true things I used to say to you . . .'
>
> . . . . . .
>
> 'And Psyche, in that old terrible time when I thought her cruel . . . she suffered more than I, perhaps?'
> 'She bore much for you then. You have borne something for her since.'
>
> . . . . . .
>
> 'You also are Psyche,' came a great voice.[48]

The mysterious words, 'You also are Psyche', hint again at Charles Williams and carry the whole burden of the book: the redemptive power of self-sacrificial love, a love which substitutes the lover in the suffering of the beloved. Lewis did not need Williams to teach him the truth of this doctrine, any more than he needed Williams to instruct him on any other aspect of the Christian faith, but he seemed to have recognised in Williams one whose own life and work articulated the great doctrines of Christianity more vividly and arrestingly than anyone else whom he had ever met. It was inevitable that the impress of Williams upon his own very different personality should have found its own peculiar way into his distinctive contribution to both literature and theology.

6

JOURNEYS INTO FANTASY: THE FICTION OF DAVID LINDSAY AND C. S. LEWIS

Bernard Sellin

Most of C. S. Lewis' fiction is set in other worlds. His children's fairy-tales describe adventures in a fairy-land called Narnia.[1] We are in hell with *The Screwtape Letters*[2] and in heaven for *The Great Divorce*.[3] Other books take us back into the past (*e.g., Till We Have Faces*[4]). But Lewis also wrote three fantasies, perhaps the most famous of his books now, which use the theme of space travel. They were written within a span of seven years, shortly before and during the Second World War. *Out of the Silent Planet*,[5] *Perelandra*[6] and *That Hideous Strength*[7] are often presented as a 'cosmic trilogy' since they depict the adventures of the Cambridge philologist Dr Ransom in his fight against the forces of evil. The first two are located on Malacandra (Mars) and Perelandra (Venus) whereas the last, *That Hideous Strength*, should be treated separately since in themes and setting it is so different from the rest. In *Out of the Silent Planet* and *Perelandra* we have two outstanding examples of the modern cosmic voyage in literature.

For centuries the theme has been a traditional element of science fiction. It has attracted writer after writer, and Lewis has explained that he had developed a taste for 'scientifiction' that was even stronger than the common boyish attraction of early Greek and Roman stories. 'The interest, when the fit was upon me, was ravenous, like a lust,' he wrote in his autobiography.[8]

Born in Belfast in 1898, Lewis lived at a time when Jules Verne's popularity had reached its climax. In England, Lewis' life overlapped that of H. G. Wells, who published his *The First Men in the Moon* in 1901.[9] Wells was to be an enduring influence on Lewis, who acknowledges his debt to him in the Foreword to *Out of the Silent Planet* and later in various references scattered in the text.

However, it may be more surprising to find that Lewis was also inspired by the work of a writer of lesser repute, David Lindsay, the author of *A Voyage to Arcturus*.[10] Lewis never tried to hide this debt either. The name of David Lindsay recurs in his letters, in interviews and in comments on his own work. In a discussion with Kingsley Amis and Brian Aldiss in Magdalene College, Cambridge, Lewis was asked to give the name of a writer who had used the theme of space travel in an interesting way, and he referred to Lindsay:

LEWIS: It's only the first journey to a new planet that is of any interest to imaginative people.
AMIS: In your reading of science fiction have you ever come across a writer who's done this properly?
LEWIS: Well, the one you probably disapprove of because he's so very unscientific is David Lindsay, in *Voyage to Arcturus*. It's a remarkable thing, because scientifically it's nonsense, the style is appalling, and yet this ghastly vision comes through.[11]

The debt is acknowledged again in his letters: 'The real father of my planet books is David Lindsay's *Voyage to Arcturus* . . . I had grown up on Wells's stories of that kind: It was Linday who first gave me the idea that the "scientifiction" appeal could be combined with the "supernatural" appeal . . .'[12]

Lewis develops the same theme in a letter to Ruth Pitter dated 4 January 1941:

A Voyage to Arcturus is not the parody of *Perelandra* but its father. It was published, a dead failure, about twenty-five years ago. Now that the author is dead it is suddenly leaping into fame: but I am one of the old guard who had a treasured second-hand copy before anyone had heard of it. From Lindsay I first learnt what other planets in fiction are really good for: for spiritual adventures. Only they can satisfy the craving which sends our imagination off the earth. Or putting it another way, in him I first saw the terrific results of fiction hitherto kept apart, the Novalis, G. Macdonald, James Stephens sort and the H. G. Wells, Jules Verne sort. My debt to him is very great. I'm a little ashamed to find it so obvious that the affinity came through to you even for a talk about Lindsay.[13]

This letter was written in 1941, when Lindsay was not dead, as Lewis thought (he still had four years to live), although at the time it seemed that from a literary point of view Lindsay would not avoid oblivion.

In 1941 Lindsay was still struggling, trying to write books which he knew would not be published in his lifetime, although it is interesting to note that as early as 1941 there seemed to be a Lindsay revival. Lewis' description of Lindsay 'suddenly leaping into fame' is certainly exaggerated, although it foretells the reissue of *A Voyage to Arcturus* in 1946. By that time it seemed that Lindsay's literary career had been a fiasco. Only his first four books had managed to attract the interest of a publisher without reluctance. After 1926 Lindsay published only a single book (*The Devil's Tor*, in 1932[14]), though he never gave up writing until his death in 1945.

Many would have regarded his career as a failure. Few would have thought that this man dying in oblivion could have influenced such a literary personality as C. S. Lewis. Lewis, by the way, must have been one of the very few that took Lindsay seriously and recognised some of his qualities. By doing so Lewis has also contributed to Lindsay's redemption, although he was not blind to the shortcomings of the author of *A Voyage to Arcturus*. He has expressed himself on the subject with a frankness that equals his praise of Lindsay. He described it as 'that shattering, intolerable, and irresistible work, David Lindsay's *Voyage to Arcturus*' in an essay on science fiction.[15] Elsewhere he described Lindsay's style as 'at times (to be frank) abominable'[16] or 'appalling',[17] adding that the paradox was that such glaring defects could carry conviction. The verdict has been shared by many other readers.

Readers of C. S. Lewis may, then, have come across the name of David Lindsay, although they may not be very familiar with him.[18] Lindsay was born in 1876 in the suburbs of London. His father was a Scot who had come to work in London. David Lindsay came late to literature after a successful business career as an underwriter in the City of London, an occupation which started when he was still in his teens, rising from the position of office boy to that of manager. Many people would have envied him this position, but Lindsay's interests had always been literature and philosophical speculation. A voracious reader of fantasy and German literature, a connoisseur of music (particularly of Beethoven and Mozart), Lindsay might have remained a model employee if he had not experienced two emotional shocks which were to upset his life for the next thirty years. The first was the trauma of the First World War. Although he did not have to fight on the front, Lindsay accepted conscription badly, mostly because he thought that, in his late thirties, he was too old to join the war; but possibly also because his interest in German literature, philosophy and music urged him to maintain some neutrality. The second event was a late marriage to an enthusiastic young girl, his junior by some twenty-odd years, who stimulated his intellectual capacities and encouraged him to give up his job – something he had often dreamt of – and become a writer.

It was in those circumstances that, after demobilisation in 1919, Lindsay left the London firm that employed him and settled in Cornwall in a small cottage near the sea. His first novel, *A Voyage to Arcturus*, was written there as if the author were under a spell. It was an amazing story of space travel and the discovery of a star called Arcturus. Readers must have drawn a parallel with Wells' *First Men in the Moon* and other similar science fiction books. Yet it was difficult to deny that the book was packed with meaning. Indeed Lindsay had put into the book some twenty years of reading and philosophical thinking. Anybody expecting another version of the popular space opera was bound to be disappointed. The book was immediately accepted for publication by Methuen. In the next few years Lindsay was to write and publish three additional novels, all imbued with the supernatural but set in southern England. These were more conventional. All enhanced the malaise felt by a handful of upper-middle-class English people when they suddenly became conscious of the existence of a supernatural world. The appeal and significance of the supernatural, combined with a criticism of conventional society, became the main themes of Lindsay's books. Although each of the three subsequent novels deserves consideration, they do not succeed as much as *Arcturus*. In them Lindsay's ponderous style and stilted characterisation are no longer toned down by the magic of fantasy. For many readers they remain interesting philosophical speculations but faulty artistic objects, with the exception, perhaps, of *The Haunted Woman*.[19]

Many critics have said it before: *A Voyage to Arcturus* almost defies summarisation. The book starts deceptively with a spiritualistic séance in a middle-class London apartment. Hardly have we had time to be introduced to the guest who is to become the main character, one Maskull, accompanied by his friend Nightspore, than we are asked to follow them out, first to a steep cliff on the east coast of Scotland, then up to an observatory, and finally into a space vessel which whisks the main character to a star called Arcturus in a fraction of a second. There is no attempt at scientific credibility. The opening of the book is a succession of unexplained mysteries which sometimes look like jokes. Whereas C. S. Lewis tried to impart to the reader the magic of the cosmic voyage, Lindsay devotes only seventeen lines to the trip. The scene that awaits the traveller is what matters.

The book really starts in chapter 6, when Maskull awakes on the star Arcturus.

From that moment we are in a world of pure imagination where anything can happen. Maskull wakes up and finds that a tentacle now comes out of his chest and that his face shows new organs having special properties such as reading other people's thoughts. The plot of the book consists of a succession of meetings with representatives of Tormance, the inhabited part of Arcturus. A majority of these are women (Joiwind, Oceaxe, Tydomin, Gleameil, Sullenbode). One is an androgynous being: Leehallfae. As Maskull wanders over the face of the new world it becomes gradually clearer to the reader – and to the hero – that the people met all embody spiritual or philosophical doctrines. In other words, Maskull is confronted by these doctrines in succession and is also invited to react to them, either to follow or reject them. The journey is not so much a cosmic voyage of science fiction as a peregrination through philosophical doctrines in which notions of pleasure, pain, love, duty, etc., are ruthlessly tested and finally rejected. The world of Tormance, we realise gradually, is deceptively fantastic, since it is a parody of our world: a succession of delusions which hide the grandeur of a supernatural world called Muspel, whose god is Surtur. Tormance is a trap laid by Crystalman, the devil. We learn that all the creatures we have met so far, even the nicest, are children of Crystalman. Some of them, indeed, have been Crystalman himself, disguised to waylay Maskull the pilgrim. In the end, having escaped from the clutches of Crystalman, Maskull dies physically but his spiritual self, Nightspore, is saved. The latter becomes the last survivor of Muspel in his attempt to check the invasion of evil. The book ends with a presentation of Lindsay's cosmogony and grim moral philosophy, a struggle for life in which the forces of evil seem to be overpowerful:

> The truth forced itself on him in all its cold, brutal reality. Muspel was no all-powerful Universe, tolerating from pure indifference

the existence side by side with it of another false world, which had no right to be. Muspel was fighting for its life – against all that is most shameful and frightful – against sin masquerading as eternal beauty, against baseness masquerading as Nature, against the Devil masquerading as God . . .

Now he understood everything. The moral combat was no mock one, no Valhalla, where warriors are cut to pieces by day and feast by night; but a grim death struggle in which what is worse than death – namely spiritual death – inevitably awaited the vanquished of Muspel.[20]

The book is, in fact, much more complex than this summary suggests. Characters appear and vanish without warning. Whole episodes are unexplained. The symbolism of the book is very intricate. And Lindsay's philosophy comes close to the sort of cosmogony which was popular in the Middle Ages and the Renaissance.

Readers familiar with C. S. Lewis may have already noted some similarity of themes between his novels and Lindsay's masterpiece, for example in the 'moral combat' just quoted. Although the aim is different, the opposition between Muspel and Crystalman finds an obvious parallel in the fight between Maleldil and Weston in *Perelandra*, with Maskull and Dr Ransom as emissaries of what is good.

Lewis has explained what he found attractive in *A Voyage to Arcturus*. 'I know the geography of Tormance better than that of Tellus,' he confessed in his essay 'On Stories'.[21] In that essay Lewis is trying to define the pleasure derived from the reading of romance, and he comes to the conclusion that excitement or suspense is not what matters most. We can experience fear or suspense in many circumstances, but the effect produced on the reader will be totally different if the enemy whom the hero has to face is an Indian, a giant or an extraterrestrial. The best authors, then, according to Lewis, are those who manage to impress readers through the creation of an atmosphere of their own. The best stories are those that stimulate the deeper imagination, and this is why space travels have a special appeal. Mr Bedford from H. G.

Wells' *First Men in the Moon*, alone on the Moon just as the long lunar night is going to engulf him, is one example given by Lewis of this expansion of danger by the surroundings.[22] One of the functions of art, according to Lewis, is 'to present what the narrow and desperately practical perspectives of real life exclude'.[23] Hence the justification of science fiction.

In the course of argumentation Lewis mentions David Lindsay's *A Voyage to Arcturus*, which he calls 'perhaps the most remarkable achievement in this kind'.[24] He even gives a detailed analysis of Lindsay's method. He notes that, contrary to what happens in most books, in *A Voyage to Arcturus* danger never seems to come to an end. The book is a succession of threats which are never dissipated.[25] Lewis' analysis runs as follows:

> Unaided by any special skill or even any sound taste in language, the author leads us up a stair of unpredictables. In each chapter we think we have found his final position; each time we are utterly mistaken. He builds whole worlds of imagery and passion, any one of which would have served another writer for a whole book, only to pull each of them to pieces and pour scorn on it. The physical dangers, which are plentiful, here count for nothing; it is we ourselves and the author who walk through a world of spiritual dangers which makes them seem trivial. There is no recipe for writing of this kind. But part of the secret is that the author (like Kafka) is recording a lived dialectic. His Tormance is a region of the spirit. He is the first writer to discover what 'other planets' are really good for in fiction. No merely physical strangeness or merely spatial distance will realise that idea of otherness which is what we are always trying to grasp in a story about voyaging through space: you must go into another dimension. To construct plausible and moving 'other worlds' you must draw on the only real 'other world' we know, that of the spirit.[26]

It seems to me that there are two main ideas in this passage. The first is Lindsay's skill at renewing interest through an accumulation of dangers. The plot is made up of a succession of meetings which all imply some sort of threat, so that the reader, at the end of each chapter, keeps repeating: 'Now, what next?'

The second idea is the equation between theme and plot, the creation of a fantastic world which is above all a world of spirit, or as Lewis put it 'a passionate spiritual journey',[27] not a mere story of a voyage through space.

'He is the first writer to discover what "other planets" are really good for in fiction.' Indeed, before David Lindsay, journeys into other worlds had been a favourite theme of literature. In his study *Into Other Worlds: Space-Flight in Fiction from Lucian to Lewis*[28] Roger Lancelyn Green mentions some fifty books published on the subject before the First World War. The seventeenth century, especially, under the impact of the progress of science and astronomy, witnessed the development of certain stereotyped conventions in books which up to now have remained masterpieces of the genre: Johann Kepler's *Somnium* (1634), Francis Godwin's *Man in the Moone* (1638) and Cyrano de Bergerac's *L'autre monde ou les états et empires de la Lune* (1657). Many other attempts followed, but with very few exceptions they have been forgotten until we reach the second half of the nineteenth century: Jules Verne's *De la Terre à la Lune* (1865) and H. G. Wells' *The War of the Worlds* (1898) and *The First Men in the Moon* (1901).

Leaving aside the most extravagant tales related to this genre, it seems to me that they took three different forms.

The first is embodied by Jules Verne: technical and scientific considerations are the main motivations, as if the author were trying to persuade the reader that such adventures could happen and that man could survive on a distant planet without the least preparation or even equipment. Plausibility is an ingredient which is never forgotten.

In a second group of stories the notion of conflict dominates and the plot is not so much the discovery of an alien world as the danger of a cosmic invasion from extraterrestrial people or robots. An example is Wells' *War of the Worlds*.

Finally, the best stories are often those which use the alien world as a pretext for moral or philosophical analysis. In this last category the planet may become a utopian experiment or the setting for a society endowed with different rules. It must be added that before the twentieth century few cosmic voyages reached that level of seriousness or speculation. Excitement seemed to be the only motivation for most of these authors. One exception is Cyrano de Bergerac, a writer whom Lewis does not seem to have read. He would have found the adventures of the narrator extremely stimulating, a combination of invention and seriousness such as he admired about *A Voyage to Arcturus*.

There is no hint that when he was writing *A Voyage to Arcturus* in 1919 Lindsay was aware that he was breaking new ground. There is no indication either that he had thought much about the constraints and rules of a cosmic voyage, and the plot of *A Voyage to Arcturus* remains an exception in his works. What is striking is that there is no attempt to justify it on scientific grounds: not only the voyage through space, but even Maskull's metamorphoses and the problem of language. These are all taken for granted, a fact which certainly appealed to Lewis, as can be inferred from his essay 'On Science Fiction'.[29] There he explains that it would be a waste of time to try to justify the plot. 'The more plausible, the worse,' he adds.[30] Interest lies elsewhere, in the invention of a new world, in the creation of atmosphere or in the writer's attempt to impart to his readers the experience of waking up on the Moon as the sun rises in the distance. In Lindsay's book there is no attempt to create a structured society either – at least as we imagine it on the Earth, with different social ranks and occupational activities. Lewis must have remembered it, and, in that respect, the shift from *Out of the Silent Planet* to *Perelandra* is revealing. Whereas in the first we find social groups (*sorns, pfifltriggi* and *hrossa*), each with clearly iden-tified activities and characteristics, in the second book society has shrunk to one single person, the Lady. This change is not accidental. It reveals Lewis' concentration on spiritual states. Compared to Lindsay, the difference is that the plot of *Perelandra* revolves around one single meeting (Ransom and the Lady, and the interference of Weston), whereas in *A*

Voyage to Arcturus we have a succession of meetings, too many perhaps if we remember Lewis' remark about Lindsay's building 'whole worlds of imagery and passion, any one of which would have served another writer for a whole book'.

In each example we have a journey which develops along unexpected lines. The space ship does not invite us to consider a rational explanation of what life may be on Venus or Arcturus, but to discover an invented world which is a construction of mind and spirit. The traditional theme of the quest, so common in fantasy, has become a confrontation of ideologies. In *Out of the Silent Planet* the Cambridge philologist Dr Ransom is captured by two men who are planning an expedition to Malacandra (Mars) in order to exploit mineral resources there, but they also bring evil, corruption and death to a planet which has remained in a state of primeval innocence. The inhabitants of Malacandra are morally and spiritually superior, not scientifically or technologically, as in Wells' *First Men in the Moon.* Through a technique of contrast Lewis' book is a severe criticism of our own civilisation, of war and strife, of slavery and domination, of prostitution, *etc.*

In *Perelandra,* where we meet Dr Ransom again, now personally involved in a redemptory mission, Lewis carried the technique one step further, stripping it of inessentials. There is no space ship to carry Ransom away: he is placed inside a sort of coffin and whisked away. The complex social structure which could be found in the first part of the trilogy has disappeared. As noted earlier, the book is limited to a confrontation between three people: the Lady; Weston, who embodies the devil; and Dr Ransom, who is acting as a redeemer to save the Lady's innocence.

Lewis' masterstroke was to make the 'other world' of the planet an unfallen world, thus finding a correlation between spatial and physical otherness and moral difference. As Ransom acknowledges at the beginning of the journey, this was a daring novelty, as human imagination had been used to conceiving of outer space as a place of darkness and death, an alien world which could only be the abode of monsters. Now we have a radically different conception of outer space: a place of beauty, colour and life which upsets traditional conceptions, although as Hélène Tuzet points out, locating the heavens in the sky was also a rather common reaction since the Middle Ages.[31] This is why *Perelandra* is a landmark in space-flight literature. It is in Tuzct's own words 'a resurrection of living space'.[32]

On the surface, Lindsay's Tormance is similar – a planet which is not inhabited by monsters and which has an abundance of life. Far from being a dead planet it shows an excess of life. New plants or beings appear all the time, as if they had just been created out of nothing. It is also revealing that Crystalman is also called Shaping, the creator of new shapes. Equally Tormance is a colourful world as bright as Perelandra. Lindsay invents two primary colours which he calls 'ulfire' and 'jale'. The water of Tormance produces an effect similar to some drugs: it heightens colours.

At first glance it seems that both Lindsay and Lewis depict their planets in a similar way: places where life is generous, where colours are plenty, where scenery is impressive. Yet they diverge in the response they expect of their readers. Whereas Lewis builds an attractive world which we are expected to admire, Lindsay is so treacherous that he adds shade after shade of colour, like a careful painter, only to decide at the end that colours are a travesty. Colours are Crystalman's traps. His own body is depicted as a 'painted shadow'. In *A Voyage to Arcturus* what is attractive is meant to be rejected whereas in *Perelandra* beauty is positive, something to be remembered with nostalgia by the traveller when he is back on Earth.

The similarities between Lindsay and Lewis may now appear more clearly. Essentially, both combined the plot of a voyage through space with an exploration of moral, religious and philosophical issues centred on the conflict of good and evil. Whereas we are led to expect a science fiction adventure, what we get is, in the already quoted words of Lewis, 'a passionate spiritual journey'. Although the adventure and the excitement of discovering a new planet are not neglected, the exploration of ideas through discussions, confrontations, debates is an essential part of the books, in a manner reminiscent of George MacDonald's *Phantastes*.[33] In each case we find a hero who becomes involved in the adventure unexpectedly, who has to understand what is happening before having to commit himself to a mission. Both Dr Ransom and Maskull realise that they have been asked to play the parts of redeemers and that, to a large extent, the future of the human race depends on them. As in a lot of fantasy, characterisation is very sketchy and characters and actions take on a symbolical-mythic value. Whereas Lewis' fiction draws heavily from Christian mythology (the silent planet myth, the story of Paradise, the temptation of Eve, the integration of angels in the books), Lindsay resorts to Greek mythology (Maskull is compared to Prometheus, the robber of the sacred fire) and also to Scandinavian myths. For example, in *A Voyage to Arcturus* Muspell and Surtur (the ideal world and God) are names which come from Icelandic sagas, although Lindsay uses them with totally different meanings. Originally Surtur was a fire giant from the realm of fire or Muspell. According to mythology, at the end of the world (Ragnarok) the sons of Muspell ride out against the gods.

So far I have considered only the main contours of Lewis' and Lindsay's fictions. If we turn to specific passages, we are likely to find a lot of similarities between the two writers without being able to say whether these are mere coincidences. For example, both Dr Ransom and Maskull are naked when they awake on the new planet. The meeting between Ransom and the Lady bears some similarity to Maskull's encounter with Joiwind, as does their discussion of the Deity. The mystery that surrounds the god of Malacandra finds a parallel at the beginning of *A Voyage to Arcturus*. Fantastic animals, floating islands, and fish used as a means of transport to move about are common to both works. Compare, for example, the effect of food on the traveller:

It is to be noted all through this story that while Ransom was on Perelandra his sense of taste had become something more than it was on Earth: it gave knowledge as well as pleasure, though not a knowledge that can be reduced to words. As soon as he had eaten a few mouthfuls of the seaweed he felt his mind oddly changed. He felt the surface of the sea to be the top of the world . . .[34]

He found the water heavy, but bubbling with gas. He drank copiously. It affected his palate in a new way . . . but somehow the intoxication brought out his better nature, and not his lower . . .

Maskull now began to realize his environment, as it were for the first time. All his sense organs started to show him beauties and wonders that he had not hitherto suspected. The uniform glaring scarlet of the sands became separated into a score of clearly distinguished shades of red . . .[35]

Descriptions of scenery and new beings are important parts of the books also. Other parallels can be found: the bubble-trees, the stream of sparkling water, the jagged mountains, etc. There is little doubt that Lewis was attracted as much by Lindsay's ability to invent a totally new world as by his 'spiritual journey'. From that point of view Arcturus is a masterpiece of imagination which has not been equalled. Examples are too numerous to be listed, from Lindsay's double sun to the new sense-organs and a third sex. But what is most remarkable about this invention is that it is not gratuitous. A close reading of the text will show that most extraordinary episodes, and features within them, can be interpreted with reference to the author's symbolical intentions.

Lewis' *hrossa* and *sorns* are his own invention. They do not bear much resemblance to Lindsay's beings. However, as several critics have already pointed out, the Stinginman from an unfinished piece now called 'The Dark Tower' – which was being written at the time when *Out of the Silent Planet* came out – is reminiscent of Lindsay's Arcturian creatures, as the following quotations will show:

The Man had a sting.
It was in his forehead, like a unicorn's horn. The flesh was humped and puckered in the middle, just below the hair, and out of it stuck the sting. It was not very big. It was broad at the base and narrowed quickly to its point . . .[36]

When he lands on Tormance, Maskull finds that he has been physically transformed:

He felt something hard on his forehead. Putting his hand up, he discovered there a fleshy protuberance the size of a small plum, having a cavity in the middle, of which he could not feel the bottom. Then he also became aware of a large knob on each side of his neck, an inch below the ear.[37]

This resemblance does not mean that Lewis' planet books are mere copies of *A Voyage to Arcturus*. They have an artistic value of their own which nobody will deny. Although we have insisted on similarities, it is also fair to underline the contrasts between Lindsay and Lewis.

The first is a different approach to the new world. Although both writers reveal unbridled imaginative capacities and vie with each other in their invention of new creatures and modes of perception, *Perelandra* comes close to the picture of a utopian Paradise, something which is absent from *A Voyage to Arcturus*. The landscape, for example, is the expression of innocence. We find an extraordinary richness and profusion of colours and realise that the writer is trying to impart this sense of plentitude, 'an exuberance or prodigality of sweetness about the mere act of living'.[38] Tormance, on the contrary, is an essentially hostile world, or rather it is a treacherous world which looks bright and attractive but which, in the end, means death and degradation. For Lewis Mars and Venus are two projections of Paradise, unfallen worlds; the books are investigations of the meaning of goodness. Lindsay's Tormance, on the other hand, is deceptively alien since it turns out to be a parody of our world on Earth. *A Voyage to Arcturus* is an investigation of evil. Lewis and Lindsay meet only in their conclusion: in the necessity of a reaction to curb the progress of evil. Some may even find Lewis more successful in his method, since he found a correlation between moral singularity (the description of innocence) and physical strangeness (the unknown planet).

Both writers join in a similar denunciation of moral corruption, but their philosophies are poles apart. In *Out of the Silent Planet* and *Perelandra*, Lewis' belief is often presented negatively as an opposition to Weston's own creed, which is a kind of life-force philosophy and technical imperialism. Against that Dr Ransom embodies moral commitment and more especially the commitment of religious belief. Their opposition is conveyed through one short sentence: 'I'm a Christian,' says Ransom.[39] And we can rely on this definition of Lewis' work by Gunnar Urang:

> These books – *Out of the Silent Planet*, *Perelandra* and *That Hideous Strength* (the so-called space trilogy), along with *The Screwtape Letters* and *The Great Divorce* – function in part as implicit apologetic, as a defense of the Christian faith, which takes particular account of the skepticism or hostility of the nonbeliever.[40]

Lindsay's religious and philosophical thought, on the other hand, does not adhere so closely to Christianity. It is very much his own, a mixture of Schopenhauer, Plato and the Gnostics. This is not the place for a detailed presentation of Lindsay's ideology, an ideology which is far from clear, as his readers already know. However, to give only a sketchy account of it, it could be said that for Lindsay the phenomenal world is a deceptive veil which hides the glory of a transcendental world which he called the Sublime or Muspel in *A Voyage to Arcturus*. This is the original world of which ours is a distorted copy. The distortion seems to be the work of an evil god, Crystalman in *A Voyage to Arcturus*; and consequently, in all his books, Lindsay invites us to go beyond the world of appearances to ultimate reality. Contrary to that world which Lewis depicts, the 'other world' for Lindsay is not a place of delight and plenitude, since pain is an essential part of redemption, combined with loneliness, as Lindsay's posthumous book *The Witch*[41] shows.

In spite of the differences in their religious and moral beliefs, Lindsay and Lewis had a lot in common. Both belonged to that generation of the early twentieth century who had to come to terms with technology, science and the upheaval of moral codes. Both resented the evolution of the modern world and turned for shelter towards a mythical past, towards spirituality and literature. Both became writers of fantasy and found it hard to accept the rules of realistic fiction in both their own reading and their writing. It is also striking that they shared an interest in the same authors: H. G. Wells, Novalis, Spenser, Rider Haggard, and the authors of Norse sagas. But perhaps the greatest link between them was George MacDonald (1824–1905), the Scottish author of *Phantastes* and *Lilith*[42] whose debt Lewis acknowledges in *Surprised by Joy*.[43] The adventures of Anodos in *Phantastes* offered another example of 'spiritual journey' in literature, combining the allegorical and the mythopoeic. In his Preface to *George MacDonald: An Anthology*, Lewis calls MacDonald a genius of the mythic tradition in literature.[44]

David Lindsay also told his friend E. H. Visiak that 'the author who had most influenced him . . . was George MacDonald'.[45] From MacDonald Lindsay learnt how to use the theme of the spiritual journey into another world, the mythic tendency, the intellectual debate and the accumulation of symbols.

David Lindsay and C. S. Lewis are two writers who are not often associated. They remain two of the best representatives of fantasy in the modern novel. Although they have much in common it would be misleading to interpret Lewis' work as mere plagiarism of Lindsay. In his academic career and in his entire work Lewis proved the extent of his intellectual and artistic capacities. A comparison between these authors should not be detrimental to either of them but should be useful in pointing out how they have both contributed in an original way to the development of modern fantasy. What is more, they have shown that fantasy does not necessarily mean third-rate literature. In their books Lindsay and Lewis have developed themes of the utmost importance while, in Lewis' own words, enlarging 'our conception of the range of possible experience'.[46]

7

ELUSIVE BIRDS AND NARRATIVE NETS: THE APPEAL OF STORY IN C. S. LEWIS' CHRONICLES OF NARNIA

Peter J. Schakel

My students, coming mostly from Christian homes and often being long-time readers of C. S. Lewis, tend to attribute their love of the Narnia stories to Christian motifs and meanings. Some Lewis scholars do the same. One cites details echoing Christianity: 'The Narnia Chronicles contain powerful and deep Christian allegory woven into their very fiber. It is this allegorical thread, more than any other factor, which makes of the Chronicles "an integrated single conception". The theme is that basic of all themes, Redemption through Christ.'[1] Another points to general structures which imitate the pattern of the Christian life: 'The seven books, taken in order of publication, develop a unified theme which might be described as the emotional climate of Christian commitment at various age levels, from very young childhood to old age and death.'[2]

I think they're mistaken. True, such Christian elements are there, and they form an important dimension of the total effect of the books. But they do not explain the initial appeal.

My students usually admit they loved the Narnia books before
they became aware of the Christian themes and parallels; and
children from non-Christian homes, many of them reading
the stories in state-supported schools where Christianity is not
to be mentioned, love them as much as my students with their
Christian backgrounds do. The popularity of the Narnia
books is extensive: sales continue to be impressive, board-
games and now video games based on the series appear
regularly, and recently a syndicated newspaper comic strip in
the United States alluded to them in a way that assumed wide,
general recognition. Such popularity of 'Christian' stories in a
widely secular age must be explained by elements beyond
their Christianity.

Lewis himself, I think, provides an analysis which accounts
well for their appeal. It comes not in the several interesting
and insightful essays on children's books and fairy-tales
written after the Narnia stories and explaining how he came to
write them[3] – it appears in an essay delivered to an undergraduate literary society in 1940 and published as 'On Stories'
a few years before the publication of *The Lion, the Witch and
the Wardrobe*.[4] In it Lewis explores the nature and appeal of
'story' – not of the novel, with its emphasis on realism,
characterisation, and symbol, but of narrative, adventure,
'romance'. Most nineteenth- and twentieth-century literary
scholars are more interested in the novel, with its greater
'seriousness' and 'relevance', than in romance or fantasy
writing, typically dismissing them as casual reading and
'escapist' literature. Through his concern with and attention
to 'story', Lewis makes a unique and important contribution
to literary theory, and one which greatly helps us to understand his own literary works. The ideas about the appeal of
narrative put forward in 'On Stories' help clarify, and are
confirmed by, Lewis' own romance-like fairy-tales, the
Chronicles of Narnia.

Lewis offers in his essay a caution about fairy-tales that
applies equally to his fantasies: not all readers will like them.
It's not that children like fairy-tales, then outgrow that taste

as they become adults. Rather, some children and some adults like fairy-tales (and romances), while some children and some adults do not.[5] I have certainly found that true in teaching the Chronicles of Narnia. Whether the class be made up of children or adults, some in it respond enthusiastically to the fantasy world and unrealistic happenings, but some resist them, preferring realistic settings, characters, and events in their fiction, or preferring expository writing over fiction.

Within the Chronicles Lewis depicts such a reader. Eustace Clarence Scrubb in *The Voyage of the Dawn Treader* does not like fairy-tales or romances – or imaginative literature generally. His parents and his education have made him prefer expository writing ('He liked books if they were books of information and had pictures of grain elevators or of fat foreign children doing exercises in model schools'[6]) over fantasy ('as he was quite incapable of making anything up himself, he did not approve of that'[7]). He had avoided romances and fairy-tales: 'Most of us know what we should expect to find in a dragon's lair, but . . . Eustace had read only the wrong books. They had a lot to say about exports and imports and governments and drains, but they were weak on dragons.'[8] Eustace overcomes his dislike of fantasy by living literally what he refused to experience imaginatively: he becomes a dragon and is enabled to go beyond himself and the limited, materialistic, rationalistic world in which he had grown up. Lewis does not expect everyone to change the way Eustace did. It is not his purpose in 'On Stories' to convince people they should appreciate romance and fantasy – only to make clear what he and others who like them do enjoy. Similarly, in this essay my intention is not to convince people that the Chronicles of Narnia should appeal to them; it is simply to clarify – for readers who enjoy the Chronicles as well as those who do not – the basis of their appeal.

Lewis grants that the initial appeal of story is suspense and excitement. Almost all romances and fairy-tales include them, and for some readers they are the main appeal. They are present throughout the Chronicles of Narnia. Each story involves danger to the children, or Narnia, or both, and uncertainty and anxiety over whether, and how, disaster will be averted. Will Peter, Susan, Lucy, and the Beavers escape from the White Witch as she pursues them, and will the Pevensie children and the good creatures be able to defeat the Witch in battle? Will the four children reach Prince Caspian in time, and can Peter win a hand-to-hand combat against the older, stronger King Miraz? Can Jill and Eustace escape from the House of Harfang, and can they, Puddleglum, and Rilian overcome the enchantments of the Green Witch? Such adventures do seize one's attention, especially on the first reading.

For Lewis, however, the suspense and excitement are not the main appeal.[9] He believes that is true for most people who love reading romances and fairy-tales, especially for those who love to *re*read them. On a second or third reading, the suspense is gone – rereaders know what is going to happen: yet they still derive great pleasure from the account. 'It is the *quality* of unexpectedness, not the *fact* that delights us. It is even better the second time. Knowing that the "surprise" is coming we can now fully relish [it] . . .'[10] So it is with children: 'children understand this well when they ask for the same story over and over again, and in the same words'.[11] And so it is with the Chronicles of Narnia. Children do enjoy hearing again and again the suspenseful episodes of Aslan's death and rebirth in *The Lion, the Witch and the Wardrobe*, and the attack of the sea serpent in *The Voyage of the Dawn Treader*, and the escape from Tashbaan in *The Horse and His Boy*. Freed from the 'shock of actual surprise', they 'can attend better to the intrinsic surprisingness' of the outcomes.[12]

Suspensefulness, as opposed to simple suspense, is achieved when the appropriate 'feeling' of uncertainty or danger is conveyed by the story. Lewis gets at the difference by contrasting the original film version of *King Solomon's Mines* with the romance by Rider Haggard on which it is based. In the book, the heroes are 'entombed in a rock chamber and surrounded by the mummified kings of [the] land', awaiting death by starvation.[13] The film substitutes a subterranean volcanic eruption and an earthquake. The latter has more action and perhaps 'sheer excitement', but it ruins the story for Lewis:

> What I lose is the whole sense of the deathly (quite a different thing from simple danger of death) – the cold, the silence, and the surrounding faces of the ancient, the crowned and sceptred, dead . . . The one lays a hushing spell on the imagination; the other excites a rapid flutter of the nerves.[14]

Such a 'sense' of a particular suspense and danger characterises some of the most memorable scenes of the Chronicles of Narnia, and helps to account for their appeal, for children and adults. The visit of the *Dawn Treader* to the Dark Island is perhaps the best example. The danger and the fear the voyagers experience there is qualitatively different from the danger and fear of the storm, or of Lucy's venturing into the Magician's House. The Dark Island conveys not just physical danger (fear of being smashed and drowned, or caught and punished), but fear of darkness itself – inner darkness as well as external darkness, the darkness of the subconscious even more than the darkness of night or death:

> How long this voyage into the darkness lasted, nobody knew. Except for the creak of the rowlocks and the splash of the oars there was nothing to show that they were moving at all. Edmund, peering from the bows, could see nothing except the reflection of the lantern in the water before him. It looked a greasy sort of reflection, and the ripple made by their advancing prow appeared to be heavy, small, and lifeless. As time went on everyone except the rowers began to shiver with cold.
>
> Suddenly, from somewhere – no one's sense of direction was very clear by now – there came a cry, either of some inhuman voice or else a voice of one in such extremity of terror that he had almost lost his humanity.[15]

Here is not just suspense and surprise, which lose their impact after a first reading, but a sense of 'darkness' (quite a different thing, to paraphrase Lewis, from simple fear of the dark). It lays a spell on the imagination which is re-experienced upon each rereading. For Lewis, then, a central appeal in story is the invocation of a 'feel' or 'sense' that enables one to *experience* the danger and uncertainty. And one reason for the appeal of the Chronicles of Narnia is his ability to inject such feeling into them.

A distinctive 'feel' or 'sense' is important beyond the suspense level, however. Lewis, in 'On Stories', talks at length about a quality he calls 'atmosphere', a more inclusive 'feel' or 'sense' which gave him much of the pleasure he found in story. Its importance comes out as he explains what he did not enjoy about *The Three Musketeers*: 'The total lack of atmosphere repels me. There is no country in the book – save as a storehouse of inns and ambushes. There is no weather. When they cross to London there is no feeling that London differs from Paris.'[16] He dealt with the same quality when he discussed science fiction: one variety of it concentrates on atmosphere, on describing the 'feel' of a place, on showing what it might be like to walk among the mountains of the moon under a black crowded sky, to live in a place or condition no human being has ever experienced.[17] That is a central aim in Lewis' own science fiction books *Out of the Silent Planet*[18] and *Perelandra*.[19] And it is the aim in the Narnian Chronicles: the appeal of atmosphere in them probably exceeds the appeal of suspense.

For Narnia to have atmosphere, there must be a feeling, when the children cross over to it, that Narnia differs from England. When Lucy enters Narnia for the first time, the countryside looks like England (or perhaps the Carlingford Mountains of southern Ireland[20]), and she sees a familiar-looking London lamp-post. That this is not London or England is established by the first inhabitant she meets:

> . . . she heard a pitter patter of feet coming towards her. And soon after that a very strange person stepped out from among the trees into the light of the lamp-post.
> He was only a little taller than Lucy herself . . . From the waist upwards he was like a man, but his legs were shaped like a goat's

(the hair on them was glossy black) and instead of feet he had goat's hoofs. He also had a tail, but Lucy did not notice this at first . . . He had a strange, but pleasant little face, with a short pointed beard and curly hair, and out of the hair there stuck two horns, one on each side of his forehead . . . He was a Faun.[21]

He invites Lucy to his home for a thoroughly English tea, in an English-style drawing room (though in a cave), but the questions he asks ('Excuse me . . . but should I be right in thinking that you are a Daughter of Eve?' 'You are in fact Human?'), and the books on his shelves (*Men, Monks and Gamekeepers; a Study in Popular Legend* and *Is Man a Myth?*), and the stories he tells about the Nymphs who live in the wells and the Dryads who live in the trees, about the wild Red Dwarfs in deep mines and caverns, and about visits from old Silenus and even Bacchus himself, signal that Lucy has not found a previously undiscovered part of our world, but has moved entirely outside it.[22]

The distinctive atmosphere of Narnia is shaped by the blending of familiar things with unfamiliar, and by placing familiar things in an unfamiliar context. The technique is illustrated nicely as the four children together pass through the Wardrobe into Narnia for the first time: 'Behind them were coats hanging on pegs, in front of them were snow-covered trees.'[23] One should not find trees in a wardrobe, or coats hanging in a forest, but there they are. The mixture of the familiar (European types of plants and animals, the customs and codes of Edwardian England – and its foods and language, for example) with the unfamiliar (animals who think and talk, mythical characters actually existing, the lack of other humans, reports of a powerful but absent King) helps readers, especially young readers, adapt to and accept that world and engage with its atmosphere. That atmosphere, once established, is elaborated for its own sake. The abundant detail describing the Beavers' home and the supper the children help prepare, for example, has no role in furthering their adventure. It is there to help convey what ordinary existence in Narnia is like – what it would be like to live there.

That is one of the great appeals of the stories – the sort of thing that could induce a child to smash through the back of his parents' wardrobe and hack away at the wall behind it, in an effort to get into Narnia himself.[24]

The atmosphere of Narnia depends also on its depiction as a uniquely Lewisian pastoral paradise, blending the ordinary and the impossible. Narnia is rural, a land of grassy slopes, heathery mountains, plashy glens, mossy caverns, and deep forests. It is unspoilt by the side-effects of urbanisation and industrialisation: Lewis' ideal world has no cities, factories, pollution, or poverty. But it takes for granted the availability of many familiar, useful things which require labour, manufacture, and trade. Mrs Beaver owns a sewing machine: Where is the factory in which it was made? Where were the raw materials obtained? Where did she purchase it? Purchase it with what? One could ask the same questions regarding the 'gum boots and oilskins and hatchets and pairs of shears and spades and trowels' along the walls of the Beaver home.[25] Mr Beaver drinks beer with his supper: Who brewed it? If he brewed it himself, who grew the hops from which it was brewed? The story presupposes factories, shops, farms, labourers, shopkeepers, farmers: but they are invisible. It is as Lewis says of Kenneth Grahame's *The Wind in the Willows*: 'Meals turn up; one does not even ask who cooked them.'[26] It all helps shape the atmosphere and appeal of Narnia, a place of quiet natural beauty where simple wants are met without the messiness and unpleasantness which usually accompanies their fulfilment.

At the centre of the atmosphere of Narnia is the blending of childhood and adult experiences, established by the use of talking animals and of children. The effect is again similar to that of *The Wind in the Willows*: '. . . the life of all the characters is that of children for whom everything is provided and who take everything for granted. But in other ways it is the life of adults. They go where they like and do what they please, they arrange their own lives.'[27] Lewis' animal characters, like Grahame's, are supposed to be adults but seem in many respects like children. Humanised animals, even old ones, invariably do not seem to be as old as human equivalents would be – perhaps because the life-spans of animals in our world are so much shorter than those of humans: an old dog may have lived about as many years as some of the children in a family. Though Mr and Mrs Beaver in some respects have the feel of grandparents, they convey also the aura of children, who simply have potatoes and tea and hams and marmalade in a larder, without wondering how they get there.

Human adults, except for Professor Kirke, when they appear, are usually the enemy. Children and animals achieve victories over evil or misguided adults, achieve them notably without the help of parents: parents are absent, doing war work or visiting America, or invisible – referred to but not appearing in the action. In Narnia children and animals are independent and self-sufficient, adult-like without having passed into the distant and undesirable state of adulthood. All of this, then, is familiar but strange. Becoming absorbed in the atmosphere of the Narnian world – with its fascinating mixture of England and otherland, paradise and imperfection, animal and human, adult and childlike – being enabled to live imaginatively in that world for as long as the book lasts, is one of the powerful appeals of Lewis' stories.

The Chronicles appeal to readers, ultimately, because they satisfy an imaginative impulse as old as the human race, the urge to 'visit strange regions in search of such beauty, awe, or terror as the actual world does not supply'.[28] The appeal is that of the mythopoeic, the making of stories involving the marvellous or supernatural. Myths are imaginative stories – that is, they are nonrational, non-intellectual (not irrational or anti-intellectual); they are explorations of matters beyond and above everyday life, concerning origins, endings, aspirations, purpose, and meaning. They open huge vistas, plumb depths of the emotions and the spirit, in ways realistic fiction cannot; but they have a simplicity which enables children to enjoy and respond to them.

Myths deal with basic issues of existence, the kind children constantly ask questions about. Children ask: 'Where did I come from?' 'Why does the wind blow?' 'How do aeroplanes fly?' Though parents often respond with details about sperms and eggs, high and low pressure systems, velocity, vacuum, and lift – and by purchasing encyclopaedias – such responses may be missing the point, giving 'cause and effect' information where imaginative understanding was sought. We think children want answers science can give, when what they really crave is a perspective only story can supply. Here, perhaps, is the most important reason the Chronicles of Narnia appeal to children: the mythopoeic dimension. In the Chronicles, as myths, children find not answers to the questions they ask, but responses to the questions they did not know how to ask.

To read the Chronicles of Narnia is to add to life, feel sensations we never had before, be carried by myth to a new range of experience and to have our outlook dramatically enlarged.[29] It is to watch a world coming into existence:

In the darkness something was happening at last. A voice had begun to sing. It was very far away and Digory found it hard to decide from what direction it was coming. Sometimes it seemed to come from all directions at once. Sometimes he almost thought it was coming out of the earth beneath them. Its lower notes were deep enough to be the voice of the earth herself . . . [It] was, beyond comparison, the most beautiful noise he had ever heard . . .

. . . [The] voice was suddenly joined by other voices . . . They were in harmony with it, but far higher up the scale: cold, tingling, silvery voices . . . [Then] the blackness overhead, all at once, was blazing with stars . . . [A] thousand, thousand points of light leaped out – single stars, constellations, and planets, brighter and bigger than any in our world . . . The new stars and the new voices began at exactly the same time . . . Digory . . . felt quite certain that it was the stars themselves which were singing, and that it was the First Voice, the deep one, which had made them appear and made them sing.[30]

This may do nothing to clarify scientifically the origins of our world; it does, however, invite us to look at the world, not as a *thing* composed of analysable substances and organisms, but as a *being*, to which we are intimately, inextricably related. Myth shows that science does not have all the questions, let alone all the answers, and not the most important ones. In *The Voyage of the Dawn Treader*, when Eustace raises the kind of issue modern Western culture focuses on, he is given a reply which thrusts him into a larger, higher mode of conception:

> 'In our world,' said Eustace, 'a star is a huge ball of flaming gas.'
> 'Even in your world, my son, that is not what a star is but only what it is made of.'[31]

The creation story in *The Magician's Nephew* is not concerned with what the world is made of, or the physical processes by which it came into being, but with what kind of thing that world is and what (or Who) is behind it. It does not give answers, but 'an image of what reality may well be like at some more central region'.[32]

To read the Chronicles is also to watch a world coming to an end:

> Soon Tirian found that he was looking at a world of bare rock and earth. You could hardly believe that anything had ever lived there . . .
> . . . The sea was rising . . . You could see all the rivers getting wider and the lakes getting larger, and separate lakes joining into one, and valleys turning into new lakes, and hills turning into islands, and then those islands vanishing . . .
> . . . At last the sun came up . . . It was three times – twenty times – as big as it ought to be, and very dark red . . .
> . . . Then the Moon came up, quite in her wrong position, very close to the sun, and she also looked red. And at the sight of her the sun began shooting out great flames . . . [And] the two ran together and became one huge ball like a burning coal. Great lumps of fire came dropping out of it into the sea and clouds of steam rose up . . .

. . . The giant . . . stretched out one arm . . . took the Sun and squeezed it in his hand as you would squeeze an orange. And instantly there was total darkness.[33]

The Last Battle suggests nothing about how our world will end; the important thing is that it shows that worlds *do end* – myth forces cultural and physical existence into a wider perspective which exposes their temporality and fragility. But *The Last Battle* also offers a vision of a world beyond the end of the world:

> So all of them passed in through the golden gates, into the delicious smell that blew towards them out of that garden and into the cool mixture of sunlight and shadow under the trees, walking on springy turf that was all dotted with white flowers. The very first thing which struck everyone was that the place was far larger than it had seemed from outside . . .
>
> . . . it was not really a garden but a whole world, with its own river and woods and sea and mountains.[34]

Myth thus resists modern efforts to confine existence to the physical and the behavioural and asserts that such further existence is more significant and meaningful than the present one. Jewel the Unicorn conveys that for Lewis when he cries: 'I have come home at last! This is my real country! I belong here. This is the land I have been looking for all my life, though I never knew it till now.'[35]

The New Narnia, as the children go further up and further into it, should not spur speculation about what heaven will be like – this, like *The Great Divorce*, 'is a fantasy . . . The transmortal conditions are solely an imaginative supposal: they are not even a guess or a speculation at what may actually await us.'[36] In theology, as in science, myth supplies not answers but an experience, of a larger existence than we can know cognitively. Such an experience touches depths the intellect cannot reach and conveys, to children and adults alike, the certainty that this is not just true, but Truth.

To read the Chronicles is, finally, to encounter Someone immensely greater and higher than ordinary mortals. Myth regularly deals with heroes and supernatural beings: that, Lewis believes, is part of its powerful attraction to human beings, whose natures desire and need to have others above them to look up to and inspire them. 'There is no spiritual sustenance in flat equality,' Lewis asserts.[37] 'Under the necessary outer covering of legal equality, the whole hierarchical dance and harmony of our deep and joyously accepted spiritual inequalities should be alive.'[38] Lewis' inclusion of kings and queens in Narnia was deliberate and purposeful:

> . . . a man's reaction to Monarchy is a kind of test. Monarchy can easily be 'debunked'; but watch the faces, mark well the accents, of the debunkers. These are the men whose tap-root in Eden has been cut: whom no rumour of the polyphony, the dance, can reach – men to whom pebbles laid in a row are more beautiful than an arch. Yet even if they desire mere equality they cannot reach it. Where men are forbidden to honour a king they honour millionaires, athletes, or film-stars instead . . .[39]

To Lewis a hierarchical order is not confining and restrictive: to know one's place and to be aware of what stretches above is freeing and uplifting, drawing one's attitudes and goals upward, preventing them from sliding horizontally into mediocrity and sameness.

More important even than human kings and queens is Aslan, who, as the Narnian embodiment of Christ and the manifestation of God, shows the greatness and grandeur of the divine. An emphasis on the majesty and exaltedness of God was basic to all of Lewis' Christian writings. It was in part a response to a need: 'I have stressed the transcendence of God more than His immanence . . . [The] present situation demands this.'[40] Lewis saw a tendency, echoing the pervasive search for 'equality', to bring God to our level, to treat him with familiarity, as a 'big daddy in the sky'; he attempted, in his expository writings and his stories, to convey the sense of awe and mystery he thought was essential to a proper sense of self and relation to the Other.

That Aslan is a lion, therefore, is no coincidence. Lewis claimed that the assignment of animal figures in such books as *The Wind in the Willows* is never accidental: 'Does anyone believe that Kenneth Grahame made an arbitrary choice when he gave his principal character the form of a toad, or that a stag, a pigeon, a lion, would have done as well?'[41] So it is with Lewis' principal character: the situation required a lion.

> 'Is – is he a man?' asked Lucy.
> 'Aslan a man!' said Mr Beaver sternly. 'Certainly not. I tell you he is the King of the wood and the son of the great Emperor-beyond-the-Sea. Don't you know who is the King of Beasts? Aslan is a lion – *the* Lion, the great Lion.'
> 'Ooh!' said Susan, 'I'd thought he was a man. Is he – quite safe? I shall feel rather nervous about meeting a lion.'
> 'That you will, dearie, and no mistake,' said Mrs Beaver; 'if there's anyone who can appear before Aslan without their knees knocking, they're either braver than most or else just silly.'
> 'Then he isn't safe?' said Lucy.
> 'Safe?' said Mr Beaver; 'don't you hear what Mrs Beaver tells you? Who said anything about safe? 'Course he isn't safe. But he's good. He's the King, I tell you.'[42]

There would be biblical support for depicting Aslan as a lamb – and he does appear briefly in that form at the end of *The Voyage of the Dawn Treader*.[43] To make that his permanent form, however, would stress his meekness and vulnerability, while myth and Lewis' theology required the awesome.

Part of the appeal of the Chronicles to young readers is Aslan as lion and lord. As Lucy says, when Aslan tells her she will never come back to Narnia: 'It isn't Narnia, you know . . . It's *you*.'[44] In *Miracles*[45] and *Mere Christianity*[46] Lewis offers arguments to prove the existence of God. In Narnia there is no argument: through story and imagination one experiences God in a way that renders proof unnecessary.

Lewis quoted his friend and former pupil Roger Lancelyn Green as once saying that the reading of Rider Haggard romances was to many people 'a sort of religious experience'.

Lewis agreed, but qualified the statement: '. . . it would have been safer to say that such people had first met in Haggard's romances elements which they would meet again in religious experience if they ever came to have any'.[47] When allowed to work as story, the Chronicles can have just the effect Lewis granted to Haggard's stories: readers do encounter elements they have met, or may later meet, in religious experience. Some readers, when they encounter those elements, try to confine them to the Christian rather than the religious. They seek biblical equivalents to various characters and details in the stories.[48] To do so, however, limits and lowers Lewis' mythic achievement. To have captured – through myths about beginnings, endings, other worlds, and divine beings – impulses that lie behind all religion is more valuable than to have created biblical parallels: the latter are of value only to those who already know Christianity, while the former may arouse in someone who is not a Christian longings which may draw him or her to Christianity.

For children and adults who, unlike the predragonised Eustace, are open to romance and myth, the Chronicles of Narnia appeal in various ways, at various levels: there is the appeal of suspense and suspensefulness in the narratives, the appeal of the 'atmosphere' of the Narnian world, and the appeal of the mythic dimensions of the stories. They appeal also because children realise that, fantasy and 'other-worldly' though they may be, they are fundamentally like life. Lewis concludes 'On Stories' by suggesting that the tension in every story between the vertical movement of the narrative and the horizontal stasis of such qualities as atmosphere and mythopoeic resonance constitutes 'its chief resemblance to life': 'In real life, as in a story, something must happen. That is just the trouble. We grasp at a state and find only a succession of events in which the state is never quite embodied.'[49] Children – like adults – try to make friendship, happiness, or success permanent, something they can hold on to. But such states prove ephemeral and elude one's grasp: they are experienced momentarily in passing events, then slip into memory. So it is with Narnia: we want the story to last, the joy of being in Narnia to be permanent; but the book ends and we must, like the children in the books, return to our own world. The elusive 'bird' we tried to catch in our 'net' of passing moments escaped – as it always will in life. But in reading the Chronicles 'it was at least entangled in the net for several chapters. We saw it close and enjoyed the plumage.'[50] And until we pass to another world where all states are permanent, that is much, and must be enough.

8

C. S. LEWIS THE MYTH-MAKER

Paul S. Fiddes

'Whatever happened here would be of such a nature that earth-men would call it mythological.'[1] This reflection by Lewis' hero Ransom upon his adventures on Perelandra (Venus) has the same kind of general effect upon us as the verdict of Shakespeare's Theseus upon certain happenings in a wood on a Midsummer Night: 'I never may believe/These antique fables . . .'[2] As reader or audience we have actually witnessed the events that are being classified as myth, fable or dream and so we feel that the boundary between myth and reality cannot be as sharp as Theseus or 'earth-men' might suppose. We protest that life itself is something like a dream or tale that is told: 'It seems to me/That yet we sleep, we dream.'[3] For C. S. Lewis, however, the relationship between myth and fact is more precise than this vague impression, and underlying his fantasies for adults and children is an exact theory about myth that dates from at least the time of his conversion to Christianity.

Myth and Fact

As Lewis relates in a letter to his childhood friend, Arthur Greeves, he came to see that 'the story of Christ is simply a true myth: a myth working on us in the same way as the others, but with this tremendous difference that *it really happened*.[4] Where God had used the minds and words of poets to create the pagan myths, especially those about a dying and rising God (Balder, Adonis, Bacchus), in the life of Christ he had finally used actual events to express himself. As Lewis summarises the matter in a later essay, '. . . Incarnation transcends myth. The heart of Christianity is a myth which is also a fact . . . By becoming fact it does not cease to be myth . . .'[5] In both the earlier and later accounts we notice two intertwined aspects: the myth has become Fact, but the story of the Fact still retains the imaginative power and effect of a myth. The pagan myths are 'good dreams' sown by God in preparation for the gospel,[6] but when we awake from the dreams into the daylight of the Great Fact, we must receive it 'with the same imaginative embrace'[7] which we accord to the dream-myth.

It is of the greatest significance that Lewis was originally inhibited from moving onwards from theism to Christianity because he could not see *how* the sacrificial death of Christ opened salvation to people two thousand years later. He came to realise that a pagan myth about a god sacrificing himself moved and affected him even though he could not say exactly 'what it meant'; even more, then, could the historical event of Christ have a salvific power here and now 'without knowing how it works'.[8] The doctrines or explanations are 'less true' than 'what God has already expressed in a language more adequate, namely the actual incarnation, crucifixion, and resurrection'.[9] Of course, Lewis as a Christian apologist valued and defended the theories, since historical fact is open to being understood by the reason. But the story of the Fact cannot be confined within abstract theory; like a myth, it appeals to the imagination and gives 'a taste of reality' which goes beyond conceptual knowing. The two convictions that 'myth became fact' and that the Fact still remains a sort of myth are, I suggest, formative for all Lewis' fictional work, though it seems clear that the first receives more stress in his earlier writings.[10]

Here Lewis is making a most important contribution to a long-standing theological debate about myth and truth, as well as providing a guideline for the more recent interest in narrative theology, or 'theology as story'. We should be aware that the vexed and confusing word 'myth' tends to be used in at least three different ways by modern theologians and biblical interpreters. (The popular meaning of myth as an 'untruth' or 'lying invention' can be ruled out from the beginning, since all religious thinkers accept that myth expresses some kind of truth in a way that could not otherwise be portrayed.)

1. Some theologians refer to any talk about God's acting in the world as a myth, since the action of God cannot be described or analysed in scientific terms. It is then urged that we should 'de-mythologise', or separate out the kernel of truth about human life from the husk of the myth.[11]

2. Others reserve the term myth for only certain kinds of talk about God, namely fictional stories about the activity of God or divine beings, by which we project into the past the deepest experiences we have of life in the present.

3. Others insist that myth refers to an event which has actually happened, but that it interprets the event in a way that is completely disconnected from history. Talk about God's acting through Christ to atone for the sins of the world is then said to be a 'myth' because it operates on a totally different level from historical fact. In contrast to the first view this approach rightly stresses that we cannot dispense with the myth; but it urges that the historical story of the charismatic prophet from Galilee and the mythical story of the divine redeemer cannot be mixed into each other's space without confusion.[12]

Lewis' use of the term 'myth' for pre-Christian stories of divine sacrifice obviously has some similarity to the second definition, except that the pagan myths in his view are not simply created by human beings but are ultimately prompted by a mythopoeic God. When, however, he speaks of 'myth become fact' in the incarnation, he goes a certain distance with those who hold the third view; faith does interpret the event with a story that has the power of myth. But he refuses to accept any driving apart of faith and history, myth and fact. The Christian story of the becoming flesh of the divine Logos is both historical *and* imaginative. He would surely have agreed with the theologian Wolfhart Pannenberg that the meaning ('God was in Christ') is inherent within the event itself, so that history is revelatory, and yet that there is still a widening horizon of interpretation from age to age.[13] He would have had sympathy with the way that 'narrative theology' affirms the power of story to lay bare the truths of human existence, but he would have disagreed with those narrative theologians who see the story of Christ as opening up a 'secondary world of consciousness' quite separate from the life of history.[14]

Lewis' distinctive contribution to holding history and myth together is, however, made not in theorising but in the practical arena of his own making of myth. In writing his novels of fantasy, Lewis is becoming (in J. R. R. Tolkien's words) a 'sub-creator'. He is copying the creator in sowing the dreams which are open to becoming fact in the incarnation. This is the first sense in which 'myth becomes fact' through his stories; he is adding to the stock of myths which are to be factualised in the incarnation. But, second, he himself makes already existing myths become 'fact', in the sense of a factuality internal to the 'other world' of the myth itself. When Ransom, in *Perelandra*, catches sight of the shoulder of a mermaid beneath the waves, 'He remembered his old suspicion that what was myth in one world might always be fact in some other.'[15] This idea can form the basis for a self-contained story such as a meeting with the Gorgon's head on the moon;[16] but it is most effective when Lewis presents a myth within a myth, as Shakespeare often writes plays within a play (for instance, the 'most lamentable comedy' hilariously

played by the workmen in *A Midsummer Night's Dream*[17]).
Lewis is, as it were, experimenting with the way that myth
becomes fact, using other worlds as the laboratory. One result
is that we are the more ready to believe in a myth's becoming
fact in historical reality (the incarnation) when we have
experienced the same kind of thing happening within the
framework of the fiction.

Myth is always transcended by incarnation, the dream by
the awakening. When Lewis himself becomes a myth-maker,
there is thus a two-way traffic of imagination between the
myth and the fact. On the one hand, as we read his myths, our
minds are disposed to accept the Fact when it finally appears
to us; we are prepared to hear the Christian message or to
assimilate its doctrines. Although Lewis makes clear that his
stories began with a picture he wanted to portray (a faun
carrying an umbrella, a queen on a sledge, a magnificent lion,
the floating islands of Venus), rather than a theme he wanted
to promote,[18] his consequent shaping of the story was influenced by the conviction that 'any amount of theology can
be smuggled into people's minds under cover of romance
without their knowing it'.[19] On the other hand, since the Fact
of the incarnation retains the power of myth, Lewis' own
myths can open up our experience of the Fact, and even its
meaning, in ways that apologetic or doctrinal writing fail to
do. Here Lewis' experiments with the way that myth might
become fact in 'other worlds' can, as we shall see, play a
powerful part.

To make a myth which is a good dream, we must put
ourselves at least partly asleep; that is, we must live in some
way 'outside' or 'beyond' the Christian story. The rest of this
essay is concerned, then, with the various ways that Lewis
tries relating his own myths to the event of Christ. They
must not be muddled into the Fact of history, or there will
be no traffic between them; but the reader must also be
able to move from one to the other without strain. In his
development as a writer of fantasy, Lewis successively
tries placing the myth after, alongside and before the

incarnation; each method has, as we shall see, advantages and problems.

Myth after the incarnation: 'there is a time that turns a corner'

In his trilogy of novels written in the genre of science fiction, Lewis creates a myth which explicitly refers back to the incarnation. While Christ is spoken about under the name of Maleldil, the hero, Ransom, affirms that he is a 'Christian'. In the first book, *Out of the Silent Planet*,[20] the incarnation is given the coded description of 'Maleldil's strange wars with the Bent One' and 'what Maleldil has done in Thulcandra' (the earth). But in the sequel, *Perelandra*, there are direct references to the incarnation, the cry of forsakenness from the cross, the sacraments, the church, Bethlehem, St Peter, Pilate and the Trinity.[21] Nevertheless, in these first two novels the myth is located 'beyond' the incarnation in the sense that the action is set on other planets (Mars and Venus) where there has been no need for incarnation at all. It is consistent with keeping a space between this myth and the Fact in history, that when Ransom asks the unfallen Lady of Perelandra whether she knows why Maleldil became a man on earth, she replies that 'There was more than one reason, and there is one I know and cannot tell to you, and another that you know and cannot tell to me.'[22] This myth is not to be confused with the Fact which Ransom knows, though it presumes that the Fact has already happened. The third novel, *That Hideous Strength*,[23] is however set on earth, and this – as we shall see – presents special problems for Lewis' technique.

One advantage of locating the new myth after the incarnation is that, within the framework of the story, it can be made clear that myth *has* become Fact, rather than merely hinting that it will. Although the inhabitants of the other planets that Ransom visits are unfallen, the becoming *man* of Maleldil to redeem fallen earth has had a decisive impact upon the life of all worlds. When Ransom expresses regret that intelligent life takes only human form on Perelandra, rather than in the diverse shapes of rational creatures that had delighted him in the old world of Malacandra, the Lady explains:

> How could they come again? Since our Beloved became a man, how should Reason in any world take on another form? Do you not understand? That is all over. Among times there is a time that turns a corner and everything this side of it is new. Times do not go backward.[24]

The Fact of the incarnation, as the humanising of God and the divinising of man, is thus affirmed in terms of a myth that follows it. The objective change made in the status of human life by the 'turning of time's corner' is also expressed in mythical terms by the changing role of the Oyéresu. In these novels Lewis presents a universe in which the rule of each planet has been consigned by Maleldil to a tutelary spirit, or Oyarsa. This is an extension on to the cosmic scale of the biblical idea of 'the sons of God' who are assigned by Yahweh as guardian angels to the nations on earth.[25] It also takes us, of course, into the world of classical myths where the planets embody the deities of Saturn, Jupiter, Mars, Venus and Mercury. This idea lingers on into medieval Christian culture, where the planets reflect at least some characteristics of these deities, and Lewis professes to have obtained the name Oyarsa from Bernardus Silvestris, where Oyarses appears as a corruption of Ousiarches ('ruling essence').[26] The once-for-all fact of Christ's becoming man can thus be expressed in the mythical form that the rule of the Oyarsa of Perelandra is handed over to the Lady and the King:

> Today for the first time two creatures of the low worlds, two images of Maleldil that breathe and breed like the beasts, step up that step at which your parents fell, and sit in the throne of what they were meant to be . . . Because it did not happen in your world a greater thing happened, but not this. Because the greater thing happened in Thulcandra, this and not the greater thing happens here.[27]

We notice that this human pair have attained rule over their world not only because they have not fallen when exposed to temptation, but also because Christ has become man. Lewis here echoes the biblical idea that nature will only attain its intended harmony under the stewardship of man, and that human failure to fulfil this destiny has therefore blighted the whole cosmos, plunging it into futility. The New Testament presents Jesus as the New Man who does for the first time govern nature aright and control the unruly elements.[28] A part in this rule is promised to those who share in the life of the New Adam, Christ. As the apostle Paul puts it in an image quoted by Ransom, they are like children come of age and receiving their inheritance, released from the tutors and guardians they needed until they came to manhood.[29] Paul understands the 'tutor' to be the whole system of religious law that was needed to cope with the problem of sin until a new kind of life became possible, a life lived by faith in Christ. Since Paul had the Jewish belief that the law was mediated to human beings through angels, he naturally thought of human beings as now released from the control of cosmic 'principalities and powers'. Lewis' mythical story that the Oyarsa of Venus hands over her rule to the King and Queen and their future children has thus become fact already in the incarnation; indeed, it presumes the Fact.

Moreover, the very stuff of myth is the inhabiting of the natural world by spiritual beings of one form or another. Within the world-view of the science fiction stories there are lesser *eldila* below the Oyéresu, and at a yet lower level there remain on earth faint remnants of what in past ages were 'Neutrals' (as Dr Dimble calls them in *That Hideous Strength*) – neither ministering spirits nor enemies preying upon humankind, 'all the gods, elves, dwarfs, water-people, *fate*, *longaevi*' of the ancient myths.[30] Lewis had early on been convinced by Owen Barfield's theory (and Tolkien's similar belief) that in the societies of the ancient world this world-view was accepted as objectively real: to earlier peoples the stars, trees and rivers were alive with mythological beings, and the whole creation was 'elf-patterned'. We must not suppose, however, that Lewis himself believes in this mythical landscape, though he finds it has its own kind of truth. He does not confuse myth with the fact into which it wakes. Writing about the dragons, dwarfs and giants that fill fairy-tales, he remarks that 'Belief is at best irrelevant; it may even be a positive disadvantage,'[31] and that 'In a certain sense we spoil a mythology for imaginative purposes by believing in it.'[32] The point is that Lewis can use the historical phenomenon of the loss of belief in myths as a way of affirming the decisive fact of the incarnation; since God has become man, dreams have faded.

Thus, in *That Hideous Strength*, Merlin is forbidden to 'renew old acquaintance'[33] with the field, wood and water in order to suck up strength to heal Ransom's injured heel and defeat their enemies. Ransom replies not only that 'The soul has gone out of the wood and water,' but that such commerce 'is in this age utterly unlawful';[34] he adds that 'It never was *very* lawful, even in your day.'[35]

Myth became Fact when God became man. This decisive event is parodied by the enemies in the stories, exalting a new Son of Man who is the product of scientific progress, and whose rule must be extended through the universe at the cost of all other civilisations. In effect they are turning Fact back into myth, the myth of evolutionary materialism (or what Lewis dubbed Wellsianity), whose aesthetic claim as 'one of the finest myths which human imagination has yet produced' Lewis is prepared to acknowledge.[36] But the result of turning away from Fact back to myth is that they fall back under the rule of the elemental spirits of the universe, who in this case are the dark *eldila* of the Bent One.

In locating his myth after the incarnation, Lewis is thus able to make clear the difference *between* myth and Fact, though we notice that the 'mythical' quality of the Fact itself tends to be lost in this contrast. Closely associated with this is a second advantage, that the myth can exemplify one of Lewis' deepest convictions about the truly religious life, which appears constantly in both his fiction and apologetic: it is disastrous to try to make certain of joy by repeating an experience through which it once came. Hyoi, one of the *hrossa* of Mars, is shocked when Ransom explains human sexual behaviour by the general dictum that 'If a thing is a pleasure, a *hmān* wants it again'; as a poet, the *hross* replies that 'A pleasure is full grown only when it is remembered'.[37] In a very different world, the enchanted Turkish Delight offered to Edmund by the White Witch made the eater crave for more of the same.[38] In contrast, the Lady of Perelandra knows that she must throw herself into the new wave, or delight in the new fruit, that Maleldil sends. To walk in the will of Maleldil from one good to another is to 'turn from the good expected to the given good'.[39] If a heart clings to the good it has first thought of, then it turns 'the good which was given it into no good'.[40] This law of the spiritual life stems from the nature of Maleldil himself, of whom the *eldila* say: 'Never did He make two things the same; never did He utter one word twice.'[41]

Now, we can see this principle most clearly if we imagine a world in which a primeval pair face temptation as did Adam and Eve on earth, but *after* the moment when time has turned its corner:

> What had happened on Earth, when Maleldil was born a man at Bethlehem, had altered the universe for ever. The new world of Perelandra was not a mere repetition of the old world Tellus. Maleldil never repeated Himself. As the Lady had said, the same wave never came twice. When Eve fell, God was not Man. He had not yet made men members of His body: since then He had, and through them henceforward He would save and suffer.[42]

The immediate implication for Ransom is that, in a way quite unlike the original story of Adam and Eve, he must use force to prevent the tempting by the Un-man going any further. Through his body, as a limb of the body of Christ, the Redeemer can act. But the wider implication, within the framework of the myth, is that either Perelandra or Tellus could be the centre of the story; Perelandra could be looked upon as 'merely an indirect consequence of the Incarnation on earth'[43] or the Earth story might be a 'mere preparation for the new worlds of which Perelandra was the first'.[44] As readers of the story, knowing it to be a myth, we can nevertheless share the perception that 'nothing was a copy or model of anything else'.[45] In the image of the Great Dance, any participant – whether beast, man or grain of dust – can be at the centre of the movement, for 'Where Maleldil is, there is the centre.'[46] Only the Bent Will is out of the centre, by trying to grasp that place for itself. The temptation offered to the Lady thus takes the form of transgressing Maleldil's command not to sleep on the Fixed Land; this is to seize security for oneself, rather than welcoming the next wave that Maleldil sends. It is, in the language of a modern theologian, 'trying to make absolute a finite certainty' and turning away from what is really our ultimate concern.[47]

By placing his myth of the Venusian unfallen Paradise after the incarnation, Lewis can thus make clear that myth has become fact, and that we are to live with trust in the One who never repeats himself. There are, however, problems with adopting this sequence of myth and fact.

In the first place, since the incarnation is *explicitly* in view, we are bound to expect more consistency with Christian doctrine than the myth can possibly sustain. In particular, the lack of a trinitarian concept of God, fundamental to the Christian story, is jarring. Elsewhere, Lewis has written with insight on this doctrine, perceiving that what matters is 'actually being drawn into that three-personal life', rather than being able to *picture* the three-personal God. The doctrine is about 'being caught up into' the threefold communion of God.[48] It is all the more disconcerting, then, to read the *Hrossa*'s account that Maleldil the Young had made the world and lived 'with the Old One'.[49] Nor is it more enlightening to read at the end of *Perelandra* that the King had learned about 'Maleldil and about His Father and the Third One'.[50] During the course of these science fiction novels, the only dimension of divinity actually encountered is Maleldil, who is 'the one

God'; this is a virtual modalism, and hints at nothing of participation in the three-fold life of God. It may well be argued that we cannot expect more within the constraints of the myth, but we are led to expect more because the myth follows the incarnation.

In the second place, in *That Hideous Strength* Lewis faces the difficulty of presenting a myth which is both after the incarnation and located on earth. He cannot achieve the gap between myth and Fact by the device of travel to another world, and so attempts to solve the problem by using the distancing effect of the Arthurian myth. Ransom and his company are the remnant of Logres, or true Britain, which is present in every age to 'haunt' the degraded state of Britain as it actually is. Logres is set against Britain, as a microcosm of the cosmic struggle between the *eldila* and the Bent One. Ransom himself is the Pendragon, and his unhealed bleeding foot makes a symbolic link between the earlier myth and this one: he has sustained this wound fighting with the Un-man in the caves of Perelandra, but it also recalls the dolorous wound of the Fisher-King in the Arthurian legend, as well as being a sign of fallen humanity.[51] Merlin, awakened from the slumber of centuries, plays the key role in defeating the totalitarian regime of the materialistic scientists, but he does so by having the powers of the five Oyéresu poured into him. Lewis thus succeeds not only in linking the earth-myth with his former inter-planetary myth, but also in carrying through more thoroughly the factualising of myth *within* the framework of the story. Instead of sporadic bits of myth (giants, furry talking beasts, mermen and the dragon of the Hesperides), one coherent myth takes solid form.

However, while the Arthurian myth certainly achieves the necessary 'space' from the Fact of the incarnation, it tends to become disconnected from the earlier event. Setting the scene on earth and after the incarnation has the effect of replacing one interest by another. Though there are certainly references to Maleldil's coming to earth, the 'Head' of the spiritual body at St Anne's is Ransom himself as Pendragon, standing in contrast to the severed Head of the loathsome scientific experiments at Belbury; he has 'become a bridge' (mediator).[52] His bleeding foot does not here open up any depths of meaning into the death of Christ, whose feet were also pierced, though hints are given us in *Perelandra*.[53] The Arthurian theme is so powerful that it has taken over in its own right, even though Arthur/Ransom is a Christian prince. Obviously there are limits, as well as gains, in locating the myth after the incarnation, and in his series of children's tales Lewis takes a different way.

Myth alongside the incarnation: 'there I have another name'

The adventures of the children in the magical land of Narnia take place, formally speaking, after the time of the incarnation. The children belong to the nineteenth and twentieth centuries, and they come and go between Narnia and the modern world, which exist in parallel but differently elapsing time scales. The whole history of Narnia from creation to apocalypse takes place within the span of the human children's lives. However, there is no intention of giving any thematic importance to the fact that the incarnation has already happened in this world; the turning of 'time's corner' in Judaea has no effect upon other worlds, even though a 'son of Adam and daughter of Eve' from our era have been the first King and Queen of Narnia, and human beings must sit upon the thrones of Cair Paravel if the land of Narnia is to be restored to harmony after the ravages of evil. The stories, however, are not allegories; it is as if Christ in this world and the great Lion Aslan in Narnia are parallel incarnations of the Logos, resulting in events and patterns of experience which are naturally similar, but by no means identical. The reader living in the world of this myth will become sensitive to recognising similar patterns of love and courtesy when he meets them in the Fact. When Aslan, at the end of *The*

Voyage of the Dawn Treader promises to meet the children in their own world, he voices the intention of Lewis himself in writing the stories:

> 'Are – are you there too, Sir?' said Edmund.
> 'I am,' said Aslan. 'But there I have another name. You must learn to know me by that name. This was the very reason why you were brought to Narnia, that by knowing me here for a little, you may know me better there.'[54]

Though the name 'Christ' is not spoken, we notice that the enigmatic Christological title 'I am' has been, and often is. To achieve the impact of a breakthrough to recognition, of the reader making his *own* connection, Lewis scrupulously refuses to mix the myth and the Fact in any explicit way; though the story of Adam, Eve and Lilith is known to the inhabitants of Narnia, none of the human beings who visit it seem to have taken the story of Christ with them, and the children themselves are apparently (and healthily) pagan. It is a sign that Narnia is coming to an end when Lucy unexpectedly remarks that 'In our world too, a stable once had something inside it that was bigger than our whole world.'[55]

Lewis is thus making myth in quite a different way from the Silent Planet series. In his unfinished tale, 'The Dark Tower',[56] he had already experimented with parallel-time worlds, but as a continuation of the Ransom story, his hero was explicitly a Christian. His failure to finish the fragment perhaps shows that the two genres of a truly 'alongside' Other World and a post-incarnation Other World cannot mix. In one the Christian themes must be explicit, in the other implicit. As we have seen, Lewis finally continued *Out of the Silent Planet* with a story in the same genre (*Perelandra*), but with an even more direct location within the Christian story.

There are great gains in presenting an Other World, with a kind of incarnation of the divine personality, 'alongside' the one we know. In the first place, Lewis can portray the actual *happening* of events which mirror a large range of Christian themes. We live through events which are a kind of crucifixion, atonement and resurrection (in *The Lion, the Witch and the Wardrobe*), creation (*The Magician's Nephew*[57]), and end of the world (*The Last Battle*). In the tales between we experience the life of discipleship under forms of journeys over the sea, along the roads or under the ground, with plenty of battles. Once again there is no clear parallel to the doctrine of the Trinity, which, as we have observed, can hardly be portrayed in an invented myth, but this does not matter, as the Christian story is not explicitly in view; we can accept Aslan as 'King of the wood and the son of the great Emperor-beyond-the-Sea'[58] without further questions about this Emperor who plays no part in the stories.

Furthermore, the Christian themes – or rather the themes that have Christian parallels – can be handled with a playfulness that would not be possible if Christian doctrine were explicitly in view. While there are many echoes of the biblical text, they reflect from a landscape which is full of fauns, centaurs, mermaids, dryads and hamadryads. As in the previous science fiction trilogy, 'myth becomes fact' *within* the confines of a story which is itself awaiting factualisation. This is a world in which the myths of the Ancient World, the Arthurian legends and popular culture can all come alive. Silenus and Bacchus dance with the children and Aslan after his resurrection,[59] the mystic table of the Fisher-King stands in the castle of Ramandu,[60] and even Father Christmas makes a personal appearance to give the children the gifts that mark their royalty.[61] The becoming fact in Narnia of what is myth in our world certainly has the effect – as before – of inclining us to believe that the myth of this world can similarly become Fact in ours. But in these stories, the mythical elements also have the effect of opening up the Christian themes and images, not allowing them to be foreclosed as dogma. We feel that the meaning of such an event as the atoning work of Christ is not a fixed concept, but will go on expanding for us; new depths will open up so that, as Aslan promises Lucy, he will tell her the story for years and years.[62]

This is to underline the early remark of Lewis that in the

incarnation, myth becomes Fact 'without ceasing to be myth'.[63] When, for instance, Aslan is mocked and slain at the Stone Table in place of the traitor Edmund, we feel the demands of the moral law (written on stone tablets) as well as the sheer extravagance of love; but there is no attempt to confine the explanation of the sacrifice and the consequent triumph over death and the White Witch to a strictly penal theory of atonement. The words of Aslan about the deeper magic before the dawn of time leave room for an endless expansion of meaning, and catch the echoes of several images of atonement: 'when a willing victim who had committed no treachery was killed in a traitor's stead, the Table would crack and Death itself would start working backwards'.[64] In a later story, Aslan bids Eustace pluck a thorn from the thicket and drive it into his paw, so that a great drop of blood falls into the stream on whose bed lies the dead body of the old King Caspian; he leaps from the water as the young prince whom the children had known, to be with Aslan on his mountain for ever.[65] Many biblical echoes of salvation are awoken by this incident – among them the pierced hands of Christ, the ram caught 'in a thicket', the waters of death and the waters of baptism – but a new myth is being created which has a power of its own, and which opens up our perception of the old story. Similarly, the creation story can be told in terms of the command 'Be walking trees. Be talking beasts',[66] the last judgement can be pictured as passing through a door set up on a hill,[67] and the search for true joy as a journey to the edge of the world.[68]

A third advantage of placing the myth in a world parallel to this one is that it appears natural for Aslan to come and go from Narnia; the unspoken assumption is that he has work to do elsewhere. In each story there is an anticipation that Aslan will appear, and he does so in a way that both surprises and fulfils expectations. He is absent and yet present, veiled and yet unveiled. When he comes he can sometimes only be seen by those who love and trust him. He is, in short, 'not like a *tame* lion'[69] but one who is free to walk where he will. In the

Christian story we would be speaking about such themes as the 'hiddenness of God' within the world, the inability of the human mind to capture a transcendent God, and the need for faith as 'the evidence of things not seen'. The framework of the myth is, therefore, particularly apt to express that experience of faith in Another which is a particular kind of seeing:

> 'Will the others see you too?' asked Lucy.
> 'Certainly not at first,' said Aslan. 'Later on, it depends.'
> 'But they won't believe me!' said Lucy.
> 'It doesn't matter,' said Aslan.[70]

Lucy follows the path on which Aslan treads, as Shasta in another story also finds a fellow traveller beside him in the mist, announcing himself as 'One who has waited long for you to speak'.[71] By contrast, the dwarfs in *The Last Battle* are so determined 'not to be taken in' by anything they cannot see that they disable themselves from being 'taken out' from the squalid stable,and experience the summer fruits and flowers that Aslan provides as filthy litter.[72] Though Lewis may well have been influenced by Owen Barfield's belief that the perceiver largely creates the appearance of what is seen,[73] he is using the idea to say something about the life of faith; his mythical setting also makes cogent two key principles of faith which Aslan often enunciates: 'no one is ever told what would have happened',[74] and 'I tell no-one any story but his own.'[75]

As a final gain, the placing of a myth in parallel to the incarnation makes us wonder whether our *own* world contains regions where Christ is at work unknown to us. If the Lion of Judah is not a tame lion, then he cannot be trapped within the walls of the church. Lewis in fact prompts us to ask this kind of question by giving us the picture of one faithful servant of the god Tash who finally meets Aslan inside the door of the last judgement, and is welcomed by him as a son. Lewis, we notice, is careful to make Aslan insist that he and Tash are *not* the same, but to affirm that 'unless thy desire had been for me thou wouldst not have sought so long and so truly'.[76] We cannot help here recalling the search for joy that

Lewis pursued through the pagan myths before his own encounter with Christ.

There are, then, considerable gains in the strategy of making a myth 'alongside' the incarnation. But the ending of *The Last Battle* does perhaps show up a problem. Since the myth and the Fact are parallel, but the human characters inhabit *both* worlds, there is always the danger that we shall insist that the two worlds should be connected. This can no longer be avoided with the Day of Judgement for Narnia and the final unveiling of Aslan's land. When the children die in a train crash and are taken to be with Aslan for ever, the link with our world has to be made:

> 'The dream is ended: this is the morning.'
> And as He spoke He no longer looked to them like a lion . . .[77]

As soon as the worlds are connected, the myth tends to dissolve. According to the Christian story, the Son of God eternally keeps his identity as a man, but here Aslan no longer keeps his incarnate form as a lion. This can only mean that Aslan is really Someone Else. Lewis integrates the two worlds by depicting the mountains of Aslan as connected to all 'real countries' – to the inner reality of each country such as Logres in Britain.[78] Thus what is connected to the real England is not the Narnia the children have visited, but the 'real Narnia'. It is no detraction from Lewis' achievement, however, to remark that any attempt to relate a new myth to the Fact is bound to show strains somewhere, and here the discovery that Aslan 'no longer looked to them like a lion' does weaken a little the reality of Narnia as Another World; the dream, as Lewis himself says, is ended.

Myth before the incarnation: 'in that far distant day'

In *Till We Have Faces* Lewis finally adopts the method of myth-making which seems most obvious: to imitate the sequence of the dreams among the pagans, setting his myth in the period before the incarnation. This model must have been present to his mind from the beginning, as it is the approach of *Beowulf*. Why did he not try this earlier? An obvious disadvantage is that the reader of such a myth will not tolerate too close a resemblance to the Christian story: dreams are one thing, but crystal balls quite another. He cannot exploit too many echoes from the Bible and Christian history, as he could freely with the previous two methods. However, there are considerable gains with the indirect approach. The making fact of myth within the myth can be carried through much more thoroughly than, say, the appearance of Silenus or Father Christmas in Narnia, because the original myths belong to the atmosphere of a pre-Christian era.

The two levels on which myth becomes fact are beautifully integrated in this approach. The story is a new myth, awaiting incarnation in the Fact 'later on'. At the same time the story in itself is the 'becoming fact' of the old myth of Cupid and Psyche. For the readers it is 'a myth retold' – the old myth becomes fact in this new story. From the viewpoint of the characters of the tale it is myth after the fact, since Psyche is 'godded' near the end of the action, and Orual works back from this point to narrate their life together, commenting on the relationship between the new myth and the facts as she knows them to have been. The 'fact' as she understands it is that the gods hid the transformation of Psyche from her, setting her a riddle. When Psyche meets Orual again, after being offered to the 'Shadowbrute' on the mountain as a sacrifice to heal the nation, she explains that she is now married to the god of the mountain. Orual's failure to see Psyche's palace recalls a familiar theme in Lewis – the need for faith to be able to see what is real. When Orual discovers that the myth of Cupid and Psyche portrays the elder sister as jealous, she protests that this is absolutely wrong; the gods failed to give her a clear enough sign, and to add to her grievance they have now put the wrong dream into people's minds. But the sacred story is a dream of the reality – and in fact Orual was jealous, not of Psyche's good fortune, but of the loss of her love to the gods: 'The girl was mine. What right had you to steal her away into your dreadful heights?'[79]

For the reader the myth comes before the fact; for Orual it comes afterwards. But for both there is an illuminating dialogue between fact and myth. For Orual, the myth enables her to see the meaning of her fact, the terrible warping of her love into possessiveness and hatred. For the reader, this initial becoming fact sends the myth on to the later 'becoming Fact' of the incarnation in a form that makes the dream clearer and which also throws new light on the later Fact. There is, as it were, a stage between the dream and the waking, a half-waking.

This half-way stage is really not needed to make any clearer the most obvious motif in the myth – the dying and rising god. Psyche is an example of the theme of 'life through death' that is sown through all the pagan myths; it is fitting that the priest of her shrine should mix her story with the vegetation myth of the renewal of nature. In her dying to heal the nation, half-drugged, naked and desolate, Psyche is evidently a dream of Christ. As Lewis himself points out in commenting on the story, many good people who follow the pattern of sacrifice are like Christ: 'What else could they be like?'[80] Though in an unpromising form, the temple of Ungit represents that sacrifice which appears in a much more refined form in ancient Israel, and which defeats the intellect of the Greeks (represented by the Fox), who can only ask in their wise foolishness: 'How can the victim be both the Accursed and the best?'[81]

The retelling, or the making fact, of the myth *within* the story (a half-waking) does, however, expose some other patterns that are more hidden in the original myth and which are open to become Fact 'later'. First, there is the theme of the passion of the gods for mortal beings and the transformation of mortal beings into gods. It is not only Psyche who is a dream of Christ – much more so is Eros/Cupid, who in his tremendous final coming wears the lineaments of Someone greater than he: 'The earth and stars and sun, all that was or will be, existed for his sake. And he was coming . . . [The] only dread and beauty there is, was coming.'[82] The mythical dream of the love of the gods for human beings will come to an awakening in the self-giving love of God at the cross (*agape*), and metamorphosis becomes real in the raising of humanity to share in the fellowship of the divine life (*theosis*).[83] The sacrificial love which fosters personal relationships is not characteristic of the gods in Greek myths; but it does appear in this half-wakening from the Cupid-Psyche myth, in the making and distorting of relationships between Orual, Psyche and the gods. Central to the myth retold is Orual's jealousy of the gods who 'steal love'. At the same time, the myth opens up a dimension in the Christian view of *agape* which has often been unfortunately suppressed. It evokes the nature of divine *desire* for fellowship with humanity, the element of *eros* which Christian theology rejected in imitation of the Greek philosophical reaction against myths. In his book on the nature of love, Lewis himself subordinated Eros to Agape as 'the Pagan sacrament';[84] but in this story the desire of God cannot be transfused entirely into Christian charity. It has been a welcome move of much modern theology to return to the biblical image of a God who desires fellowship and who is humble enough to want to be fulfilled and glorified through his human partners.[85]

Associated with the theme of love is that of sight. We have already seen how the theme that faith is a special kind of seeing plays a prominent part in the Chronicles of Narnia. Here the old feature of the myth, that Psyche is not permitted to see her divine lover, is integrated with the new feature that Orual cannot see the god's house. Psyche is willing to trust and not to seek for security, where Orual is not. This theme of seeing and not-seeing is then extended through the image of the veiling of the face; the god's face is veiled, as is his presence more generally. Orual is full of complaints about the ambiguity of the gods' messages and signs,[86] but she comes to understand that this is because mortals have no face with which to gaze upon the gods and be seen by them: 'How can they meet us face to face till we have faces?'[87]

Orual's assuming of a permanent veil through her reign in Glome is an outward sign that she has already veiled herself to the gods and others. She has no face for them to see. The similar lack of a face on the image of the goddess Ungit is, however, ambiguous; in so far as she genuinely represents the mysteries of divinity and sacrifice ('the way to the true gods is more like the House of Ungit'[88]) she is veiled in the way that all the gods are. But in so far as she is a distorted image, projecting human greed for love and devouring others to get it, she has no face in the sense that Orual has none: so Orual comes to confess that 'I am Ungit.'[89] When Orual in her judgement before the gods at last realises her self-centredness and possessive love she is stripped naked. The veil is removed and she is bareface at last. As Lewis writes later in *Prayer: Letters to Malcolm*, 'By unveiling . . . we assume the high rank of persons before Him. And He, descending . . . reveals Himself as Person'.[90] To be unveiled is to be aware that God sees us, so that Orual echoes Job in confessing, 'Before your face questions die away.'[91]

Now, this theme of unveiling arouses in the reader a sense of anticipation and longing for the time when the veil will be removed; it is like reading the Old Testament prophecies that the day will come when there will be a new heart and a new covenant: 'In that far distant day when the gods become wholly beautiful, or we at last are shown how beautiful they always were . . .'[92] The half-awakening from the dream will reach full awakening with the incarnation, and so the final encounter of Orual with the god foreshadows the experience of the Spirit of Christ about which the apostle Paul writes: 'When a man turns to the Lord the veil is removed . . . And we all, with unveiled face, beholding the glory of the Lord, are being changed into his likeness from one degree of glory to another.'[93]

A third gain from the 'half-waking' from the myth is summarised in the god's pronouncement, both warning and promise, that 'You also shall be Psyche.'[94] The promise is fulfilled as Orual receives beauty of soul at the end, brought from the house of the dead as one of the labours of Psyche. The warning is fulfilled as Orual, in her own way, endures through the tasks set for Psyche. If Psyche bears the punishment for sin, wandering through the world and undertaking the tasks inflicted upon her by Venus/Ungit, Orual bears the sorrow of them in similar experiences in her kingdom.

In setting the myth before the incarnation, Lewis cannot work out parallel details of the passion and resurrection story as he does in the Narnia stories. It is not clear, for example, why Eros cannot simply forgive Psyche for her transgression, committed out of love; in the original myth it is the law of his mother, and here he speaks of 'those against whom I cannot fight',[95] but Lewis makes no attempt to elaborate on the theme of the demands of the law as in the Narnian 'deep magic from before the dawn of time'.[96] However, he *can* work out another theme of the cross – what Charles Williams called 'the way of exchange', or bearing one another's burdens in the substitution of love.[97] There is anticipated the mystery of the body of Christ, where we are all limbs and parts of the whole. Because the myth is about the love of the soul (*psyche*) for the divine nature, it makes sense on the intellectual level that Orual too should be Psyche. Nevertheless, to take a myth in which the expected climax is the restoration of Psyche to Eros, and to re-make its climax as the glorifying of the elder sister, is to startle us. It awakens us to the mysterious possibility of living each other's life and bearing each other's pains in the life of God. It looks forward to the incarnation.

In several ways then, Lewis has taken what has universal appeal as a myth, and has personalised and particularised it, shaping it for onward movement to the factual moment of incarnation. Moreover, the half-awakening, before the incarnation, enables him to integrate the appeal of the myth to the imagination with the appeal of fact to the reason. In the Fact of the incarnation the appeal to the imagination will continue; it does not cease to be myth, giving a 'taste' of reality rather than an abstract analysis of it. In his apologetic works, Lewis tends to subordinate the imagination to the reason. Here, as Peter Schakel suggests,[98] he can achieve a wholeness within himself, portrayed in the figure of Orual who brings together the dark mysteries of the House of Ungit and the intellectual light of the Fox.

In each of these three different ways of making myth, Lewis is working out the perception he had at the beginning of his Christian experience: there is historic fact at the heart of the Christian story, and yet the story is expansive enough to go on awakening new echoes and communicating truth in unexpected ways. Myth has become Fact, and yet 'remains myth'. In moving from the science fiction trilogy to his last novel Lewis shifts the stress on to the imaginative power of myth, but he never forgets that the incarnation is about the redeeming of history. Only because of this does the story never end.

9

C. S. LEWIS AND IDEALISM

James Patrick

From his return to Oxford in January 1919 (after war service) until the spring of 1925, when he at last won a fellowship at Magdalen, C. S. Lewis directed his efforts to the study of philosophy and ancient history in the honours school of *Literae Humaniores* and his ambitions to securing a position in which he would tutor and lecture in philosophy. He had of course always loved literature as well, and in 1919 had (under the name of Clive Hamilton) published a volume of his own poetry titled *Spirits in Bondage*.[1] In 1922 he had entered the English School, thereby providing himself with a 'second string' for his academic bow, but when he contemplated writing a D. Litt. thesis in 1924 he chose a philosophical subject, the seventeenth-century Cambridge Platonist Henry More.

That his appointment required Lewis to tutor principally in literature and to 'help out' in philosophy tells us little of his earlier expectations. During the period when he was looking for a fellowship, he had once considered taking the civil service examination and had contemplated a post in classics at Reading. In the 1920s in England men like Lewis and T. S. Eliot often did not think of themselves as committed to one narrow discipline. Lewis had assumed he would join the philosophy sub-faculty, but the man was more than the discipline. He left philosophy, he told his father, without

regret, because of the loneliness of philosophical study;[2] but
he had by then been formed by his philosophical interest, and
that interest had produced in him two distinct results. An
understanding of myth rooted in his study of literature had
played an important part, but it had made the form of his
conversion, which he allegorised in *The Pilgrim's Regress* and
carefully detailed in *Surprised by Joy*, essentially philosophical. Lewis, over a ten-year period, had been converted by
thinking, by making his way from realism to idealism, from
idealism to theism, and from theism to Christianity.[3] And this
love of reason permeated his apologetic works. Almost alone
among twentieth-century writers, Lewis successfully addressed the intellects of his unbelieving contemporaries. His
apology sometimes took a literary form, but its skeleton was
invariably a reasonable appeal.

The circumstances that surrounded Lewis' philosophical
passage from scepticism to faith set the tone for an Oxford
career which would be marked by loneliness as well as
success. He had been at Oxford briefly from March 1917 to
the following June, staying just long enough to pass the
entrance exam and receive an Officers' Training Corps commission as second lieutenant in the Somerset Light Infantry.
When he returned to the University, Lewis passed from the
ranks of the army which had just soundly defeated the Kaiser
into the trenches of another war, the superficially gentleman-
ly, deeply passionate, inevitable personal conflict of ideas that
marked Oxford philosophy in the 1920s and 1930s.

In 1919 the idealistic philosophy of the school of Thomas
Hill Green still possessed the field, but it was increasingly
embattled, under siege from the forces of the proto-
positivism of John Cook Wilson, H. W. B. Joseph, H. A.
Prichard and E. F. Carritt, the Oxford exponents of the
brittle, fashionable, Cambridge philosophy of G. E. Moore
and Bertrand Russell. Lewis enlisted on the side of the
revolutionaries, and for about three years, until about 1922,
was, if not zealous for the new realism, at least sympathetic to
some of its characteristic ideas.

Atheism was part of the 'new look' Lewis adopted when he returned to Oxford, as was a kind of radical dualism. Lewis informed Arthur Greeves in December 1918 that his *Dymer* reflected his new ideas, and that the poem was built around the theme of 'development by self-destruction'. 'The background', Lewis wrote, 'proceeds on the old assumption of good *outside & opposed to* the cosmic order.'[4] In September Lewis had described the poetry of his *Spirits in Bondage* to Arthur Greeves as 'mainly strung round the idea . . . that nature is wholly diabolical & malevolent and that God, if he exists, is outside of and in opposition to the cosmic arrangements'.[5] This sort of disappointed Hegelian outlook does not seem easy to relate to the new realism of Cook Wilson and E. F. Carritt, but it did represent for Lewis a move from the swamps of the magician (to use the language of *The Pilgrim's Regress*) into a philosophy at once realistic, manly, and devoid of self-pity.

Although the pessimistic Gnosticism of the new look was not likely to have been of much interest to his philosophy tutor, E. F. Carritt, Lewis' rebelliousness in the face of the older Oxford philosophy, his self-confessed tendency to be 'against Government', and his atheism were bound to make the realists see him as a promising disciple.[6]

Carritt actively helped Lewis in his search for a fellowship and duly introduced him to H. A. Prichard, the rising leader of the realist school at Oxford.[7] When Carritt visited the University of Michigan in 1924, he asked Lewis to lecture in his place at Trinity and gave him responsibility for his pupils.[8]

But as Lewis' reputation among the realists flourished, his commitment to realism began to weaken. As he later wrote in *Surprised by Joy*, he had begun to wonder how reason could exist apart from participation in some cosmic *Logos*.[9] And there had also been his studies in the English School in 1922 and 1923, studies which had introduced him to a fascinating body of literature written by immensely interesting, if (as he then thought) ultimately wrongheaded, Christians.[10]

By the time Lewis' studies in the English School ended in

November 1923, he had moved closer to the *retardataire* Oxford philosophy which had as its hero the reticent F. H. Bradley and as its acolytes Bernard Bosanquet, John Alexander Smith and Clement Webb. Lewis had in fact become part of a small but important Thermidorian reaction against the positivist revolution, a reaction which, if it could not deny the positivists victory, was still successful in challenging the realists' hegemony until the late 1930s.

In 1921 R. G. Collingwood, perhaps Carritt's most promising pupil, and an adult convert to the Church of England, rebelled against the new realism.[11] H. J. Paton, Collingwood's contemporary, remained a determined disciple of Kant and Hegel.[12] In 1919 John Cook Wilson, the father of the new realism at Oxford, died, and his demise made John Alexander Smith the senior and most influential philosopher in the University. Smith, originally sympathetic to the new realism, had moved back into the idealist camp under the influence of Benedetto Croce by the time of his election to the Waynflete Professorship in 1909, and from his powerful position in Magdalen College Smith encouraged Collingwood, Paton and finally C. S. Lewis in their interest in classical metaphysics and the idealism of the school of Green.[13]

Here it is important to note that Lewis' thought in the early 1920s, grounded in the Gnostic scepticism of *Spirits in Bondage*, was 'spiritual' in a sense which he later repudiated. Spiritualism was in the air in England. Not only were the Crocean idealism of Smith and the Kantianism of Paton 'spiritual', but late idealism opened out towards mysticism and theosophy. Lewis' friend Owen Barfield had become an anthroposophist, a disciple of Rudolph Steiner, in 1923. In the 1920s Charles Williams was an adherent of the mystical and mildly occultic Society of the Golden Dawn. T. S. Eliot was attracted to Eastern religious thought in the early 1920s. Nor should it be forgotten that Lewis' childhood faith had been lost not to adolescent atheism but to the spiritualism to which he was introduced by a matron at Cherbourg School.[14]

By 1915 or 1916 Lewis had read Wilde and Beardsley and had found himself attracted to Yeats and to the occult. Had an apt teacher appeared, he wrote, 'I might now be a Satanist or a maniac'.[15] Then George MacDonald had turned Lewis' mind from the dark spiritualism that belonged to 'a depraved romanticism' towards the glorious, monistic universalism of MacDonald's children's stories and novels. The 'new look' of 1919, the detached, almost cynical, commonsense philosophy of Lewis' brief alliance with realism, was adopted as a way of overcoming the imaginal miasma left by his flirtation with magic and spiritualism, as well as the fantasies provoked by MacDonald and the search for 'joy'. The 'spiritual' had become too real, too frightening – witness Lewis' recollection in *Surprised by Joy* of his attendance (during a 'nightmare fortnight') upon a friend who had 'flirted with Theosophy, Yoga, Spiritualism, Psychoanalysis, what not?' and who was going mad.[16]

Given his underlying interest in ways of thinking that comprehended spiritual philosophy in all its florid ambiguity, it is not surprising that Lewis made Henry More, a Cambridge Platonist whose thought extended the Renaissance revival of Platonism into the heart of the Anglican establishment and into the seventeenth century, the subject of his nascent doctoral research.[17]

What Lewis found in More was an anti-Cartesian rationalist, someone who understood reason not as an abstract, analytic faculty presiding over an indeterminate field of extension, but as the consubstantial light joining the intellect to reality. More's corpus (the *Antidotes* against atheism and enthusiasm, the *Manual of Ethic*, the commentary on the *kabbala*), his detestation of Hobbes and his friendly reservations regarding Descartes' philosophy, all reflected Lewis' interests and to some degree formed his mind. Like many Neoplatonists, More found intelligibility and the existence of God self-evident. Knowledge of truth lay innate in every man. And there was also in More an interest in spirits and spiritualism, a fascination with the quasi-magical and alchemical side of seventeenth-century thought. In his last year, 1963, Lewis was still quoting Barfield and Jacob Boehme with approbation.[18] More's thought, like the philosophies of Boehme and Barfield, pointed beyond the merely rational and merely material, and in him Lewis found an idealist who believed in God, in reason as a living principle, in nature as alive with *Logos*. More was also an admirer of Spenser, whom Lewis had first read in 1914 or thereabouts, and whose poetry would be the subject of *The Allegory of Love*, a work conceived in 1923.[19]

Lewis' study of More in the winter of 1924 was preceded by a period of intense labour during July and August on the philosophy lectures he had agreed to give at Trinity as Carritt's proxy. These lectures, the notes for which exist, began with a consideration of innate ideas, and went on to a consideration of Leibniz, Descartes, Hume and Berkeley. Hume was rejected and Berkeley applauded. Lewis was perhaps remembering his work on the Trinity lectures when he wrote in *Surprised by Joy* that the new idealism of his contemporaries seemed hardly different from and hardly an improvement on the philosophy of Berkeley.[20]

His studies in More and the great seventeenth- and eighteenth-century philosophers brought Lewis' philosophical development to a maturity that remained essentially unchanged. Lewis came away from his studies in philosophy and literature convinced that there existed a kind of Vincentian canon of the intellectual life, that if students would read old books they would come across the witnesses to that consensus and might then build for themselves an impregnable intellectual fortress which rested on that broad foundation.[21]

Lewis also came to the end of 1924 possessed of one fundamental argument which he would use perennially in defence of reason and traditional ethics. Very many of C. S. Lewis' arguments in favour of morality and God take the form of a *reductio ad absurdum* which requires the opponent either to concede the existence of fundamental truths or to forgo the rationality of criticism, including the critic's own. This intellectual form in things is the recollection that comes to Mark Studdock as he sits in the objectivity room at N.I.C.E. Reason appears as 'solid, massive, with a shape of its own, almost like something you could touch'.[22] Either truth or meaninglessness. This argument in its varieties was proof against naturalism, for one need only point out that the attempt to subsume thought under a psychological canon could not be undertaken as a half-measure. If *some* thought was the product of environment or heredity, *all* might be, even the thought of the naturalist or psychologist. Naturalism was, as Lewis would argue after 1926 or 1927, self-refuting, and when this argument was challenged by Elizabeth Anscombe in 1948 Lewis refurbished but did not abandon it.[23]

In the end we are given in all of Lewis' works a universe shot through with goodness and truth, with practical reason and *Logos*, a universe like but unlike the universe of Lewis' teachers. Philosophically, this representation of reality is eminently defensible. It is traditional, and within certain limits can claim as authorities Plato, Plotinus, Dionysius, and in part St Augustine and St Thomas, as well as Leibniz and Berkeley. It does explain experience, and it explains it because it is, unlike the niggling scepticism of the Oxford realists, and however flawed, still significantly true. In one sense C. S. Lewis, like his teachers Clement C. J. Webb and John Alexander Smith, had no systematic philosophy at all, but wrote out of his broad knowledge of a central philosophical tradition. All the great witnesses from Plato and Aristotle to Bradley and Bosanquet who believed that reflection might yield truth could be cited in favour of the Oxford idealism of the 1920s.

On the moral side, this kind of argument formed the structure of the various essays on the good which Lewis wrote beginning in 1922. It was first used in an essay entitled 'On the Hegemony of the Moral Good', which was submitted to Magdalen College as part of his unsuccessful application for a fellowship in that year.[24] Moral values, so the argument went, could not be invented. Although the original essay has either been lost or remains unpublished, its substance appears in *The Abolition of Man* (1943) and in the undated essay 'On Ethics' which was published in *Christian Reflections* in 1967.[25] Just as Lewis' defence of truth involved the proposition 'Either truth or meaninglessness,' his defence of moral values was developed from the axiom 'Either values as they are in the broad human tradition, and have been discovered by every generation, or amorality.'

The true and the good appear in Lewis as textures of great intellectual and moral principles to which mind and conscience have immediate access. Lewis' intellectual struggle had probably never really been a struggle against positivism. It had been a struggle first between the imaginally fetid spiritualism of Yeats and of the magicians, and the sceptical spiritualism of the early poems; then between this new look and the intellectually disciplined idealism, replete with references to the ancients, of the period after 1924. In the midst of this struggle Lewis was at last elected to his fellowship. Once inside Magdalen in the autum of 1925, his belief in reason was reinforced by great teachers who were to influence him for the rest of his scholarly life: John Alexander Smith, P. V. M. Beneke, Clement C. J. Webb, C. T. Onions. Smith, with whom Lewis habitually breakfasted from about 1927 to 1936, was especially influential. Living 'on the same college staircase with Professor J. A. Smith', Lewis wrote in the Preface of *The Allegory of Love*, was 'in itself a liberal education'.[26]

During the five years following his appointment to the Magdalen fellowship, Lewis became a theist and finally a Christian. His first Christian apology, *The Pilgrim's Regress*, was what the subtitle proclaimed: *An Allegorical Apology for Christianity, Reason and Romanticism*. His fiction convinces because it is led by philosophical insight. For Lewis, after he had passed through the narrows of scepticism in 1922 and 1923, philosophy was always idealism coloured by allusions to the classical philosophical tradition. At the point of his rejection of scepticism, Lewis had found himself 'driven back into something like Berkeleyanism'.[27] In 1932 he had made Kant and Leibniz philosophical tutors to Christ, and Berkeley's *esse* is *percipi* is the epistemological theme of *The Pilgrim's Regress*.[28]

Lewis' conversion had many roots. The argument from desire, the conviction that the longing of the human heart could be satisfied by no finite object, was important.[29] Equally important was his conviction that the *Logos*, the eternal, spiritual reality which had seemed so alien to the cosmic order, had indeed entered history. Myth had become fact. Goodness and reason, so alien to the historical order of the cosmos for the author of *Spirits in Bondage*, were real, accessible, and would finally be victorious.

Yet belief in the reasonableness and intelligibility of things, like scepticism, has its dangers. The relation between God and creatures is complex, and is further complicated by the problem of evil. Attempts to state the God–creature relation by thinkers committed to intelligibility have fallen broadly into two groups. On the one hand there have been those who see creatures as containing the divine being in some lesser degree than God himself. For these theologians creatureliness represents a paradoxical separation of the divine substance from the divine ground. Creation is in some ways a fall into being. These thinkers include perhaps Plato, certainly Origen, the Cambridge Platonists, idealists of the twentieth-century school of Bradley, and monists like Bergson. Creatures are paradoxically both God and not-God. Creation is an allegory, and allegory is, in Lewis' words, not a mode of thought but a mode of expression.[30] In contemplating creatures we both meet God substantially and not at all. Creation exists as degrees of incarnation of the divine substance.

According to the other broad pattern, God creates not by the alienation of his substance or its derogation but through his power and through the non-necessary gift of his vestiges and traces to all creatures and of his image to man. According to this theology only the divine Son is of one substance with the Father. Creation is not an act of self-alienation but the superabundant gift of the creator's will. The existence of each creature is willed precisely in its creation. God is known not by allegory, according to which there is no essential relation between creature and creator, but by analogy, through which we gain certain but limited and obscure knowledge of God.

Although C. S. Lewis' philosophy was never so systematic as to rule out one or other of these broad intellectual visions, he was more at home with allegory and with degrees of incarnation, with monism and idealism, than with analogy and the classical doctrine of creation. His rejection of neo-scholasticism was perhaps motivated in part by an abiding mistrust of its continental matrix, but also by a conscious rejection of the anti-idealist metaphysic neo-scholasticism presupposed.[31]

Christopher Derrick was right in his insistence that Lewis' *The Allegory of Love* contains a key text which illuminates the pattern of Lewis' thought.[32] In answering the charge that Spenser's allegory might seem to modern Protestants too Catholic, Lewis sees quite correctly that the element in Spenser which earns this judgement is its rich specificity. Lewis then suggests that the fundamental difference between Catholics and Protestants is the Catholic tendency to make religion too concrete, the Protestant tendency to refuse to push allegory too far: 'Catholics and Protestants disagree as to the kind and degree of incarnation or embodiment we can safely try to give to the spiritual.'[33] Lewis then goes on to say that this one difference explains all others.

The argument here is finally a literary one, Lewis is not making a point about religion, but is suggesting that Spenser ought not necessarily be read in a Catholic manner. But Lewis' analysis indicates the ease with which he construed allegory as the fundamental intellectual pattern. Lewis had discovered not the difference between Catholicism and Protestantism, but the difference between optimistic allegorising, according to which reality can be significantly represented by words and symbols, and pessimistic allegorising, according to which the ideal can enter history only with great difficulty or not at all. The difference Lewis had found is the difference between John Mason Neale, the Romantic poets, and the authors of *Lux Mundi* on one hand, and the Puritans and the Albigenses on the other. 'That sort of actuality which Catholics aim at and Protestants deliberately avoid' is something other than a difference about allegory.[34] In fact the medieval and patristic way of thinking about God and the world, as Lewis knew, is not allegorical at all, but theological and sacramental, and the key to it is an understanding of mystery.[35]

Lewis' thought often moves too easily in a world of abstractions becoming immanent. To theologians it is a familiar world, the world of Origen and the Gnostics and Clement of Alexandria, of that pattern of thinking which at its worst degenerates into Arianism and at best ascends to the beauties of Plotinus or of Bradley's *Appearance and Reality*. Derrick sensed this when he wrote that 'the natural bent of Lewis's mind was profoundly Gnostic and even Manichean'.[36] In *Letters to Malcolm: Chiefly about Prayer*, Lewis could contemplate the possibility that creation is a tragedy, an inevitable separation of creatures from their divine ground.[37] Students of the second century will of course hear in these words the voice of Valentinus, for whom creation was the result of some primal flaw.

When we ask why one with so great a mind as Lewis could occasionally write in this way, the answer is surely to be found in the tendency of allegorising theology, rooted in idealistic philosophy, to move between the poles of utter equivocity and complete univocity. Allegory in theology leads to paradox, to contradictions like those denounced in 1 Timothy and taught by Marcion. The monistic, allegorising pattern tends to the belief that every creature is simultaneously God and not God, and fails to do justice to the truth that every creature is itself, its own being, created good, willed by God as a creature, and fulfilled by God.

This kind of half-conscious philosophical bias was expressed fairly fully in Lewis' last work, *Letters to Malcolm:*

Chiefly about Prayer. The passage is one in which Lewis is dealing systematically with the theological relation between the creator and creation. 'Meanwhile', Lewis wrote,

> I stick to [Owen Barfield's] view. All creatures, from the angel to the atom, are other than God; with an otherness to which there is no parallel: incommensurable. The very word[s] 'to be' cannot be applied to *Him* and to them in exactly the same sense. But also, no creature is other than He in the same way in which it is other than all the rest. He is in it as they can never be in one another. In each of them as the ground and root and continual supply of its reality . . .
> Therefore of each creature we can say, 'This also is Thou: neither is this Thou.'[38]

This sounds in some ways like a straightforward exegesis of the golden tradition Lewis followed, especially the reflection that even existence does not belong to God and creatures in the same sense. But the rhetorical passion Lewis displays here is also, and perhaps more deeply, rooted in Boehme, Henry More and idealism. In this tradition the idea that God is 'in' creatures, while witnessing powerfully to God's creative act, tends to suggest that God is still the existence of creatures. But the paradoxical affirmation of something much like panentheism on the one hand and of the utter alienation of God from creatures on the other cannot easily be averaged into a Christian doctrine of creation. This paradoxical theology says nothing of the existence of a natural or created good which is perfected by a supernatural good. Indeed in this same letter Lewis proposes the paradox that 'The higher the creature, the more and also the less God is in it; the more present by grace, and the less present (by a sort of abdication) as mere power.'[39] There is more than a hint here of the reversal of the principle that grace does not destroy but perfects nature. Indeed grace does sometimes seem to destroy the natural or at least to render it irrelevant for Lewis. In one sense we are back in the world of *Spirits in Bondage*, in which God has nothing to do with the cosmic arrangement of things.

That Lewis frequently ignored the existence of a created order in which created goodness is perfected by grace occasionally caused strained conclusions. His strange argument that marriage might be of two kinds, Christian and non-Christian, since the indissolubility of marriage is not rooted in nature but in grace and the gospel, reflects this lingering doubt that every supernatural mystery reflects the perfection of a good commanded at creation and established within it. Thus Lewis suggests that the imposition of monogamy by English law upon Muslims was probably unjust.[40] Tolkien, in a letter he never sent, pointed out that monogamy was not primordially the creature of a revealed ethic and supernatural grace but the very pattern of natural goodness for every man and woman, not special behaviour belonging to any sect but God's will for mankind.[41]

So, too, Lewis' later exposition of the Eucharist in *Letters to Malcolm: Chiefly about Prayer* was one in which he unaccountably neglected his earlier conviction that the eating of bread and wine was the necessary natural act which the Eucharist transposed into a mystery.[42] In 1963 the bread and wine appeared arbitrary, and the best thought Lewis could produce was a reflection which was autobiographical, not theological. Nothing, or nothing reasonable, could be said. The eucharistic mystery was to be received with touching and beautiful piety as magic (Lewis' word), that is as allegory of the highest and most equivocal kind.[43]

A habit of mind which tends to the neglect of the original justice in creation explains in part as well why C. S. Lewis never entered into conversation regarding the place of the Blessed Virgin in the economy of salvation. True, these doctrines were highly controversial, and thus lay in a psychological space outside the perimeter of that 'mere Christianity' which Lewis defended, but it is also probable that he considered the Immaculate Conception and the Assumption theologically inconsequential, and it was probably this judgement, on which he surely knew he differed from the Fathers, that drove consideration of the place Our Lady holds in

Christian dogma and piety from his writings. Lewis' neglect of these questions was rooted not in fear of controversy or of the imputation of anti-Romanism but in his lack of interest in the source of the created humanity of our Lord through which and by participation in which the whole human race is saved.

Lewis was, of course, a forthright defender of the doctrine that Jesus was born of a virgin and begotten by the Holy Spirit. The virgin birth is the indispensable condition for the divine paternity, but it says nothing of the source or quality of the human nature of the Lord. It explains how God can enter history, but is silent on the source of that human nature which is joined to the Word. Of course, if humanity viewed as natural createdness is gradually swallowed up in the supernatural in a way that ignores created goodness, then the problem of the humanity of Christ and of his resurrected followers is not an important problem, and belief in the sinlessness of Jesus' human nature and hence the sinlessness of its source lack obvious significance.

Lewis was intent on proving that the Virgin's son was God, and not much interested in the whole panoply of concerns that form the traditional Christian insistence that he is human. The fifth-century denial that Mary is the Mother of God which sent monks into the streets and evoked a torrent of defence from the Greek Fathers did not involve the question of our Lord's divinity (which was uncontested), but the truths that the Blessed Virgin was both truly mother and truly human. These assertions did not seem very important to Lewis, since for him there was some lingering sense in which the humanity of Christ was an economic condition assumed for the salvation of mankind, a veil taken by the *Logos*.

The 'myth-became-fact' apology that had been helpful at the point of Lewis' conversion led too easily to a theology of transcendent ideas becoming concrete, with their concreteness understood as incarnation. In the essay 'Myth Became Fact' the incarnation is treated as the thickest of allegories, as an event in which a reality existing outside time occurs within it.[44] Certainly this is in some sense profoundly true. The

Lamb slain before the foundation of the world offers himself at Calvary; the eternal Son is present in time and place. But the Christian doctrine of the incarnation is not simply about the appearance of the eternal in time. The Divine Man does not appear on earth. Rather, the second person of the Trinity assumes not only a body but human nature, taking it from a woman.

Lewis tends to use the figure of Philippians 2, that Jesus is God in the form of man, as an *exemplum* and explanation too easily. This formulation is especially dangerous if by form we mean body, and if flesh is not a synecdoche for all of human nature. In explaining why he found theories about the Eucharist unsatisfying, Lewis wrote that he could find 'no connection between eating a man – and it is as Man that the Lord has flesh – and entering into any spiritual oneness . . . with him'.[45] This text poses difficulties. One reason was (apparently) Lewis' difficulty in understanding Jesus as the paschal Lamb. But there is also the implication that the flesh Jesus bore as man is somehow assumed temporarily or economically, not related to the Word in such a way as to require belief that eating the Lord's body is sharing his divine life.

Thus the incarnation might be understood as the allegory of allegories. In a letter of 6 May 1955 to the mother of a child who had found Aslan more real and lovable than Jesus, Lewis wrote:

> Of course there is one thing Aslan has that Jesus has not – I mean the body of a lion. (But remember, if there are other worlds and they need to be saved and Christ were to save them as he would – he may really have taken all sorts of bodies in there which we don't know about.)[46]

In fact, it would be nearer the mark to argue that since God became man, suffered, died, rose glorified and ascended, we know that there are no worlds with other, higher beings, for the personal union of the Word with human nature is the crown of all creation, not economic, not temporary, but summary and eternal. Christ is the centre of the new creation, and in him nature is joined to God the Word eternally and personally. There can be no other incarnation. But for Lewis the idealist the possibility seemed unremarkable, assuming as he sometimes did that the Word takes bodies as required for the salvation of creation. This murkiness need not imply a contradiction of passages in which Lewis speaks of the unique quality of the incarnation of the Word as man.[47] What it perhaps does imply is an incomplete understanding of the personal union of the Word with human nature.

A secondary clue to Lewis' meaning is his rejection of the idea that the glorified bodies of the saints are identical in some way with the bodies in which they lived and died. This was of course a problem over which the Fathers of the second century laboured, always arguing that, our senses and limited reason to the contrary, the very bodies of the saints are somehow restored and glorified.[48] Lewis doubted this in 1963, speculating that since the purpose of bodiliness was sensation, the resurrection might indeed consist of the reconstitution of the senses inside the soul. This idea is put forward because 'We are not, in this doctrine [the resurrection], concerned with matter as such at all'.[49] This kind of thinking is familiar in the American South, which is the intellectual child of Ulster. It involves formal affirmation of every anti-Gnostic platitude and the simultaneous nourishing of a habit of mind, inherited from the Puritan side of the seventeenth century, which is unreflectively committed to the repudiation of the created glory of matter. Beneath Lewis' treatment of the Christ and the saints there is always a fear of the incarnation. Lewis wrote that it is well to have holy places and holy days, but that these special 'incarnations' do harm if they cause us to forget that all times and places are holy could we but perceive it.[50] In fact it is impossible that there could be too many holy places if these places are really holy, and impossible that any place could be made holy by our perception.

Similarly, Lewis' doctrine of the church seems at times to rest upon the notion of a complete and ideally knowable idea refracting itself into a number of necessarily partial and incomplete incarnations. The famous figure of the ideal Christian hall off which specific denominational rooms open, each offering specific warmth and light,[51] is another version of the allegorical pattern, of imperfect incarnations of a true idea. What is of most interest is not the relation of the various rooms to one another or of any room to truth. The relevant assumption is Lewis' belief that the fundamental truths of Christianity are discarnate ideals that in some sense transcend or are typically prior to any historical mission or community. This model differs accidentally from the ecclesiology of modernism because the religion of the hall, the essential and converting truth as defined by Lewis, contains very clearly stated Christian beliefs, but it imitates the pattern of modern religious liberalism perfectly. Another human authority might restrict the necessary truths learnt in the hall to Deism or expand them to include the dogmas of Baroque Catholicism, but a merely historical argument remains a merely human argument, and we are left wondering if in fact men and women have ever been converted by abstract truth. Perhaps they have been piqued or even convinced through ideas found in books, but to be a Christian at all means, among other things, being baptised and making a specific profession. Christianity becomes real at the point at which it ceases to be an idea, and at that point the believer is part of what he professes to be the true church. The hall is not part of the house at all; it is at best a porch. Lewis often seemed to prefer the porch, not only because it made his apologetic task possible, but also because it avoided the specificity of church membership. Too great a degree of incarnation might be, as Lewis once wrote, unsafe.[52]

Lewis' greatest strength as an apologist was his appeal to reason. That appeal rested upon a metaphysic. It never seemed to fail Lewis. Indeed it was never seriously attacked until the late 1940s, when, in the famous Socratic Club debate, Elizabeth Anscombe seemed to put Lewis on the defensive. So successfully did she attack the most important salient, the argument that naturalism is always self-refuting, that Lewis, who was chagrined by the unexpected rout, rewrote parts of *Miracles*.[53] Anscombe did not of course cause C. S. Lewis to lose either his faith or his philosophy.

When Christopher Derrick asked Lewis in a Cambridge pub to name the philosophical school to which God might subscribe, 'Lewis's answer was immediate: God is a Berkeleyan Idealist.'[54] Idealism had given Lewis the vision of a world alive with reason and with God, and it is important to note that the systematic weaknesses of the idealist underpinnings of his thought usually have no obvious influence on Lewis' fiction. It is as though when Lewis moves on to poetic ground, imagination carries reason with it and the perplexities of his metaphysics move into the background.[55] (This is especially true of his fictive essays on the theme of Christian obedience. There is perhaps nothing in twentieth-century literature as powerful as the conversation between Ransom, Weston and the Green Lady in *Voyage to Venus*;[56] and *The Screwtape Letters* is the classic depiction of the warfare that rages around the human soul.[57]) But perplexities there are, and Lewis would be the last man to ask that his own thought be somehow exempt from critical reflection. Lewis was always careful to note that he was not a theologian, so we need not expect systematic completeness there. Blessings in the gift of idealism there were aplenty; difficulties some, and of some importance. To think these things through with patience and clarity, remembering that we need not decide at once, but that we must keep thinking, would be to vivify Lewis' work across the decades that separate us from his life.

10

'LOOK OUT! IT'S ALIVE!':
C. S. LEWIS ON DOCTRINE

Jacques Sys

'It is, of course, the essence of Christianity that God loves man and for his sake became man and died.'[1] This is 'mere' Christianity, the foundation of Christian belief, the 'very essentials of Christianity' as Richard Baxter expressed it. But this does not mean that religion implies blind belief in a few formulae. Doctrines and dogmas are not arbitrary norms to which our allegiance would merely be a matter of social conformity; they do not constitute a body of beliefs set up for convenience sake so as to strengthen the apparent cohesion of a community. Neither is 'mere Christianity' that form of 'reasonable' religion which amounts to no more than a simple moralism with a vaguely theistic or deistic outlook.

Doctrines (*i.e.*, positive statements about God in his relation to men) find their roots in the faith as it was first represented in Scripture, and as such are modes of appearance of the living God in this world, *this* God who is not interested in morality proper but in our becoming his sons. In this respect doctrines and dogmas are to be understood as helps towards our 'putting on Christ', and 'dogmatic Christianity' is wholly contained in this statement: 'Christ was killed for us, . . . His death has washed out our sins, and . . . by dying He disabled death itself. That is the formula. That is Christianity.'[2]

This 'formula' is essentially to be found in 'the faith preached by the Apostles, attested by the Martyrs, embodied in the Creeds, expounded by the Fathers',[3] and all the positive, historical statements made by Christianity are derived from the 'catastrophic historical event' which is to be found at the very centre of history.[4] C. S. Lewis, then, was not so much interested in speculative theology as in dogmatic theology, that is to say the study (to quote *Lux Mundi*) 'of those truths which the mind of Christ's Church upon earth has believed to be at once the most certain and the most important truths of man's history, nature and destiny, in this world and for ever'.[5]

It is a study which must on no account be evaded, even if at first it might seem to the student more 'obscure or repulsive'[6] than speculative theology. It is all the more necessary since for Lewis theology goes infinitely beyond mere speculation in that it is 'a practical science' the aim of which is to answer our most immediate necessities. Theology cannot be a *système de la nature*, but the echo or development of the central event which was produced in order 'to reveal our immediate practical necessities'.[7] Doctrine, then, is not a philosophical system answering our natural curiosity; in truth it is not a system at all, but the expression of a body of hard facts, the conspicuous and unmistakable facts in which Christianity finds its roots.

Everything, then, is contained in Scripture and in the definitions of the Apostles', the Nicene, and the Athanasian Creeds, and Lewis' whole work may be considered as a constant meditation on the central kerygma: 'I believe in God, the Father, the Son, and the Holy Ghost.' Beyond this we find only explanatory theories, particular theologies which may or may not help us in our understanding of the 'formula'; but all such illustrations and commentaries are never to be mistaken for the unalterable core of the Christian faith and of the Christian life. Lewis was indeed not so much interested in the 'how it works' as in the 'things themselves', things and facts which are infinitely more important than theories which will never 'be quite adequate to the reality'.[8]

All this is theoretically shared by all Christians, as it was shared by men like Keble, Newman, Chesterton, Gore, and Temple. Yet, in Lewis' works Christian dogma acquires a particular quality, I should say a particular flavour, which goes a long way towards explaining the enduring success of his teaching and of his apologetics.

Let us first consider Lewis' highly personal conception of 'facthood'. Facthood is the first ingredient of the formula, not merely in the historical sense of actual events, but in the more mysterious and so to speak 'magical' sense of the word. God is a 'thing', not an idea; God is also a person, he is 'this' God; and as an intensely personal thing, he is that 'resisting material', the 'untame' God whose nature and will cannot be reduced to reason, whose very 'facthood' cannot be forced into the corset of logical categories. It is indeed characteristic of Lewis' God that he is both intelligible and yet absolutely unknowable. He is the *Deus absconditus* yet also the 'Lord of terrible aspect', which does not mean that the gap between him and us, just as the gap between him and the higher angels, is of the nature of an unbridgeable chasm; there is an ontological continuity between God and man, a continuity which is implied in the very status of man as a rational animal. If God is this thing, then fallen man is to be remade, rebuilt, so as to take part in the 'great Game', the celestial dance of the very centre of facthood, that is to say the life of the Holy Trinity. It is in this sense that Lewis understands the nature of God as substance. This usually misunderstood word 'substance' is not to be taken as a philosophical concept but as an all-embracing presence. God is an all-encompassing being whose existence is not merely to be assented to intellectually, but who is also to be trusted and adhered to in the most existential way, which implies joy, fear, longing, awe, all emotions which arise from the first lesson taught by God's facthood: the sense of shame which results both from the infinite disproportion between creator and creature, and from the dolorous sense of our own unworthiness as persistent sinners. This is the basis of faith which, beyond assent (though that comes into it also), is that disposition of the will which 'involves a degree of subjective

certitude which goes beyond the logical certainty'; it is 'a gift
to be asked'[9] from a person 'known by acquaintance', that is
to say involving all the psychological and spiritual elements
pertaining to relationship: adherence to the self, struggle with
and surrender to 'otherness'.

It is in this way that one can say that Christian doctrines are
both illuminating and dark, intelligible and unknowable.
What is living through the veil of words has all the characteristics of otherness, of that thing which is not to be apprehended
as idea but as 'this' God whose will is to draw us *nella sua
voluntade*.[10] The substance of the Christian doctrines is,
then, to be fought with, in the manner of Jacob with the angel.
Within the very words of the Creeds there is also that thing
which must be appropriated and even eaten, just as John is
made to eat the book in Revelation. This is not to mean that
reason is to be rejected; on the contrary, the 'formula' is
addressed both to the intellect and to the senses, in other
words to the 'whole man', his mind, his heart, his feelings,
even his sensations. To quote *Lux Mundi* again: 'You can no
more shut up faith to the compartment of feeling than reason
to the compartment of the intellect. Religion claims the whole
man, and true religion is that which can make good its
claim.'[11]

It is, then, from within the Christian doctrines that is
produced what Lewis calls 'a new organization'[12] which is that
of 'the Christ-life' in the Christian.[13] This is possible because
the object of faith is not alien to man's nature but reveals itself
by claiming loudly every area in ourselves. If we are to 'put on
Christ', 'to dress up as Christ',[14] we must give up mere
ratiocination and the shallow rationalism of the positive kind
and surrender to the far manlier reason of the living God.
Yet, again, that reason – which according to Lewis belongs to
'*Zoe*' and not to '*Bios*'[15] – remains opaque to full intelligibility. 'This' God is not the Platonic world of ideas, not the
Hegelian adventure of the Spirit (although that also comes
into it), but the 'utterly concrete fact'[16] that keeps telling us
that 'I, the ultimate Fact, have *this* determinate character,

and not *that*.[17] Thus, the 'opaque centre of all existences' is both intelligible and unspeakable – 'unspeakable not by being indefinite but by being too definite for the unavoidable vagueness of language'.[18] Words, as Ransom says in *Perelandra*, are vague: 'The reason why the thing can't be expressed is that it's too *definite* for language.'[19]

If God is that opaque fountain of facthood, what then is the relationship between the ultimate object of belief and the very words of the Christian dogmas? The same fragrance rests on Lewis' treatment of this subject: it is one which suggests light and shade, illumination and darkness, distance and close proximity; opacity (yet of a radiating kind) seems to be the governing factor of the church's expression of her fundamental beliefs. In order to understand this, a detour by way of Lewis' literary criticism might be of some help.

C. S. Lewis was a literary convert, and his love of words and literature was of a kind that deserves attention. We all remember Ransom falling in love with the language of the *Hrossa* in *Out of the Silent Planet*, a language which he came to know so well as to understand it from the depths of its spiritual core on the occasion of Hyoi's funeral.[20] The same delight is experienced in *That Hideous Strength* when all the inmates of St Anne's are gathered in the kitchen, waiting for the 'descent of the gods'; when at last the tutelary angel of Mercury appears Ransom is said to be enjoying heavenly bliss while 'sitting within the very heart of language, in the white-hot furnace of essential speech'.[21] The same magic is at work in *The Lion, the Witch and the Wardrobe*, where the children, when told about Aslan by the Beavers, are so affected by the very name of the Lion that they experience a 'strange feeling – like the first signs of spring, like good news',[22] an expression which reminds us of the young Lewis' violent emotions when reading the words:

> Balder the beautiful
> Is dead, is dead.[23]

On this particular occasion what was conveyed to him was

not meaning or definition ('I knew nothing about Balder'[24]),
but a whole world of sensations, of which longing was
the most important. Some years later, when he discovered
Wagner's music, his attention was directed not towards the
music proper, but to the complex network of sensations and
emotions which it aroused in him: 'Pure "Northerness" en-
gulfed mc: a vision of huge, clear spaces hanging above the
Atlantic in the endless twilight of Northern summer . . .'[25]
Lewis was in fact confusing twilight in the temporal sense with
twilight in the spatial sense, and this last instance is characteristic of his treatment of words even in later life when, off his
guard, he forgets the rationale of apologetics and gives us the
substance of his vision, such as in the last chapters of *Miracles*
and *The Problem of Pain*, or in 'The Weight of Glory',[26] or
again in the concluding section of *Till We Have Faces*.[27] In
these pages words acquire a particular quality or flavour
which transcends deductive knowledge and reveals the wide
and mysterious worlds of love and desire, the romantic worlds
of 'fairy lands forlorn', with an intensity of vision which is
reminiscent of St Augustine's *torrens voluptatis* or Baxter's
visions of heavenly life.

Literary works were for Lewis windows opening on to a
deeper reality, instruments thanks to which one can perceive and even gain access to the only world that matters,
that world which extends its limitless shores 'beyond personality' in the Neoplatonic realms of 'heightened modes of
consciousness'.[28] This process implies what he elsewhere calls
'looking along' as opposed to 'looking at' objects:[29] a method
which demands a form of communion with the object under
scrutiny, a form of 'empathy' or imaginative fusion which
allows the reader or the critic to reach what might be called
the centre of gravity of the literary object, only to discover
that this centre is beyond both the poet and the poem. A
poem is a living object which must be wooed, courted and
loved so as to bring it to fruition; and one of the principles of
Lewis' criticism was (even by the long way round of contex-
tual studies) to understand the work from within, from the

mysterious but unmistakable core of its own independent integrity, and from this vantage point reach its archetypal foundations, 'further up, further in', beyond the 'personal heresy', 'beyond personality', in the world wherein all literary forms find their roots.

We might even say that Lewis' aim is not to respond to the text proper, but to respond to that to which the text itself is a response. A good example of this method is found in the concluding sentences of 'What Chaucer did to *Il Filostrato*': 'the love-lore of Andreas, though a narrow stream, is a stream tending to the universal sea. Its waters move.'[30] The value of any literary work is then assessed by reference to that 'universal sea' towards which the waters of literature are moving and which correlatively 'in-forms' any work of art worthy of the name.

This is what myth does at the frontier between nature and supernature: 'myth is the isthmus which connects the peninsular world of thought with that vast continent we really belong to'.[31] Two things can be derived from this statement. First, that the 'source' of stories is incomparably vaster than we imagine it to be, just as 'Narnia within Narnia' is infinitely greater than Old Narnia; and second, that the 'universal sea' is not something towards which one progresses but a source towards which one regresses, and this regress implies a reversal, even a subversion, of our everyday categories. What our own period thinks to be inessential (such as rites, ceremony, liturgy) may be, as it is said in 'Myth Became Fact', the most important aspect of life:

> Even assuming . . . that the doctrines of historic Christianity are merely mythical, it is the myth which is the vital and nourishing element in the whole concern. Corineus wants us to move with the times. Now, we know where times move. They move *away*. But in religion we find something that does not move away. It is what Corineus calls the myth that abides; it is what he calls the modern and living thought that moves away.[32]

It is interesting to note that the same point is made in Lewis' discussion of Chapman's *Hero and Leander*: 'We must realize

that what we should regard as the externals of civilization are,
for Chapman, essential and vital.'[33] In both cases, what might
otherwise be taken as unsubstantial proves to be an aspect of
something more important (a sea or a continent), which in
Perelandra is called 'the great Game' or 'the great Dance' of
which one can sometimes have a glimpse if one is willing to
'look along' the works of art.[34]

This approach to language and literature is governed by the
idea that both poet and reader enjoy 'higher modes of consciousness' which are themselves modes of appearance or
incarnations of the higher reality of what Chesterton calls 'the
larger pattern'. In this respect, as Lewis forcefully puts it in
The Personal Heresy, the poet is the 'game hunter' coming
back to his own folk with the much-coveted prize which is
going to enrich the common stock of humanity and make of us
readers 'better men', better equipped in our search for truth.
In the words of the good poem (sub-Christian or Christian) an
image, a somewhat adumbrated reflection of the living fountain of facthood, is fleetingly perceived: through language and
metaphors, through 'dreams and stories', tall tales and epic
narratives, the Word is progressively brought into focus, and
what was true of the progressive revelation of the Christian
truth is also true, as a variation on a minor mode, of all 'good'
literature.[35] Through stories and poems, but 'darkly, as in a
mirror', the reader 'sees life' just as Ransom had been seeing
life in his adventures on Perelandra.[36] Yet one should never
mistake words or images for the thing meant, just as one
should never mistake the poem for the poet. Words are
indeed the medium through which life is tasted or experienced, and this is precisely why they ought not to be over-
cherished but humbly made to take their part in what Lewis
defines in *The Pilgrim's Regress* as a 'lived dialectic'.[37] Or
again, as it is said at the end of *Surprised by Joy*, imaginative
experience is to be forgotten and to be considered as one of
these 'roadside objects' on the way to Jesus Christ, much
loved objects indeed, but whose purpose is to serve as a
'pointer to something other and outer'.[38]

Images, metaphors, even the very material substance of words, have thus to be forsaken so as to give place to what Christianity is about. This does not mean that the whole world of nature and of art is negated: conversion is both *metanoia* and *epistrophē*, a willed break with all dominant forms of representation, but also a return or regress to the genuine origin of these representations. If images and more generally imaginative experience must absolutely be surrendered, the best part of it is none the less going to be handed back, and so to speak baptised and assigned its legitimate place in the 'cosmic game' which Saint Augustine called the *Ordo Amoris*.

What is true of literature is also true of doctrines and dogmas. This does not mean that Lewis wants us to step beyond doctrine into a hazy nowhere of Neoplatonic ecstasies; one must on the contrary take it the other way round: we do not reach the absolute through words, it is the absolute which makes itself known through human modes of representation, which so to speak descends within its creation. In this way is the truth of doctrine *tasted* in all its modes of appearance, as something concrete and unmistakable, a living core which radiates from within Lewis' rather Wesleyan Christian library, the 'mixed bag' in which many churches and trends of thought are represented, such as in the works of Boethius, Saint Augustine, Dante, Saint Thomas, Richard Hooker, Jeremy Taylor, George Herbert, or George MacDonald. In all these works he experiences the core of Christianity, not as an 'insipid interdenominational transparency, but something positive, self-consistent, and inexhaustible'.[39] It is interesting to note that in his discussion of this 'almost invariable something' Lewis does not refer to language but to the senses, to the sensations produced by the text (enjoyed and not only contemplated), to the 'familiar smell' of Christian literature, its 'unmistakable flavour' which is received gladly and to which the whole man responds through all his senses after having divested himself of his contemporary self, his ideological or chronological presuppositions – stepping out of time so as to taste the eternal flavour of truth. The same attitude is advocated in *The Great Divorce*, where one of the characters is advised to forget ideas and follow one of the 'solid ones': 'I will bring you where you can taste [truth] like honey and be embraced by it as by a bridegroom.'[40] There is in this no idea of a Platonic ascesis towards the world of ideas, but on the contrary a total surrender to the power of the Word. This experience is, as we have seen, a baptism, the starting-point of a journey towards the very centre of Christianity, towards Christ.

Yet, this being said, what about the norm, the regulating principle of the words which are going to convey the doctrinal statements? Who is to judge the relevance or irrelevance of such or such a word, the conformity or heretical nature of this or that proposition? The flavour is certainly not enough, the ecstasies are not sufficient; thus we are left with the nagging question of the development of doctrine and that of the various modes of appearance of the central Fact of Christianity. The test, says Lewis in 'On the Reading of Old Books', is to step out of one's own times and steep oneself in these books which are not merely the product of individual fancy and imagination, but which have received the sanction of the church, that church of which Lewis says in *Mere Christianity* that in it (and in it only) one is to find 'fires and chairs and meals', and of which one must ask, while waiting in the hall of proto-Christian experiences, 'Are these doctrines true: Is holiness here? Does my conscience move me towards this?'[41] In other words, what about the validity of doctrinal propositions?

We have seen that for Lewis doctrine is not something towards which one gropes through the many levels of experience, something which would thus be indefinitely pushed beyond the limits of its intelligibility: on the contrary, if dogmas may be said to transcend immediate representations, it is because they are to some extent 'points of contact' between human powers of representation, human awareness of experience, and the vast continent of the supernatural. Dogmas, then, are landmarks, signposts on the way to the

'Landlord's Castle', and as such they are unmistakably and perfectly intelligible in despite of man's slow apprehension and fallen nature.

This is, for instance, what Aslan keeps telling Jill at the beginning of *The Silver Chair*: 'Here on the mountain, the air is clear and your mind is clear; as you drop down into Narnia, the air will thicken . . . That is why it is so important to know [the signs] by heart and pay no attention to appearances. Remember the signs and believe the signs.'[42] This is what Lewis calls elsewhere 'obstinacy in belief':[43] once assent has been given, then one must stick to one's original belief, 'donkey-fashion', even 'in the teeth of evidence'. Authority is not here the external authority of a church, it is not derived from obedience to a knowledge which would have 'percolated',[44] but to knowledge immediately revealed 'in the spirit'. There is in *The Silver Chair* a coincidence, a simultaneity between spiritual experience and revelation of doctrine: the signs are communicated directly by Aslan and not by the mediating authority of a church. In fact, Jill has so to speak 'lived' those signs, experienced them not as esoteric knowledge, but as 'knowledge by acquaintance'.

The same theme is developed in *That Hideous Strength* on the occasion of the rather formidable encounter between Merlin and Ransom.[45] In the chapter entitled 'They Have Pulled Down Deep Heaven on Their Heads', the questions put to Ransom by Merlin are as many tests of authority in the form of a whole series of questions and answers sounding like a catechism or a kind of esoteric knowledge of doctrine; but for Ransom this knowledge was not acquired by a disciple/master relationship, but immediately, as a result of his personal experiences on Perelandra.

This example leads us back to the 'lived dialect' of *The Pilgrim's Regress*. The process of trial and error implied in the dialectic of desire 'faithfully followed'[46] leads the subject, John, to a total surrender to the will of God through Christ and through the mediation of the rather ambiguous 'Mother Kirk', who is not, says Lewis, to be understood in the ecclesiastical sense, but as a perhaps unhappy synonym of Christianity.[47]

What Lewis obviously dreads is a body of doctrines violently imposed from without and adhered to blindly and fearfully, as John had once tried to obey 'the rules' of Puritania. Such a mechanical conception of doctrine is according to Lewis based on a false conception of authority, which, to quote Charles Gore's 1891 *Bampton Lectures*, is not in keeping with 'the method of our Lord' because 'this system leaves the individual churchman simply to accept what the Church teaches, and to practise what the Church enjoins';[48] what comes here under attack is that aspect of the Church of Rome which 'rejoices simply in clear and definite answers to all questions'.[49]

In *The Pilgrim's Regress* Lewis criticises this scholastic approach of revealed truth in his allegorical North; yet it is not Romanism which is the target in these passages, but the higher and drier forms of Anglo-Catholicism of the Neo-Scholastic type,[50] and Lewis is careful enough or subtle enough to warn the reader that 'The two extremes do not coincide with Romanism (to the North) and Protestantism (to the South).'[51] We may then infer from this that if Lewis undoubtedly shares the opinion of Charles Gore, he none the less emphasises the fact that this defect is not particular to any denomination, but that it is a universal tendency to be found (at least potentially) in all churches, so great is the temptation of over-rationalisation. If this extreme is to be avoided, so is the other, 'Southern', extreme.

Lewis' attack on over-formalised dogmas does not imply that he developed his conception of dogmatic Christianity on a private-judgement basis resulting from an immediate and unmediated understanding of revelation. He was no upholder of the simple faith of the fundamentalist: doctrine and Scripture do not derive their authority from what Burke called 'man's private stock of reason', but from the teaching of the church such as it first appeared in the New Testament epistles, and in the last analysis authority is ultimately derived from Christ himself.

The spirit, then, not the letter, is to be grasped and digested or incorporated; and here again Lewis' literary criticism is of some help. Just as a literary text ought to be understood from within, from the depths of its living heart, the Bible and tradition ought to be tasted by 'steeping ourselves in its tone or temper and so learning its overall message'.[52] It is there and there only that one is to perceive (with the help of prayer) the particular fragrance of Christianity, its own character and 'otherness'. In other words, an over-precise doctrine (such as that of Neo-Angular[53]) is as much faith-killing as the tepid Christianity of the latitudinarian modernists. This is also what Lewis meant when he defended the idea of the mythical dimension of Christianity: if theology is 'the systematic series of statements about God and about man's relation to Him',[54] it is also true that the core of these statements is received (or more exactly ought to be received) as myth, and there is no reason to be ashamed of 'the mythical radiance resting on our theology'.[55] The appeal is obviously to both reason *and* romanticism, in Lewis' own particular sense of the latter, which is largely reminiscent of seventeenth-century devotional poetry and theology. In the long run we are brought back to the origin of all authority: the birth, life, death and resurrection of Jesus Christ; he being the model, the archetype, the only source and object of all knowledge in the Pauline sense of the word. Christ is then the 'mere' on which the whole complex idea of Christianity revolves. Christianity is a living idea, and the measure of the validity of its doctrines is the individual's capacity (as a member of the body of Christ) to surrender to that life and become 'a little Christ'. This is the common assumption and revealed axiom shared by all Christendom. Let us repeat it: the incarnation of the Son of God is the model, the figure or the archetype of the whole living order – and what is now at stake is the growth of the body of Christ; to quote Charles Gore again, 'The Christian authority is simply Jesus Christ.'[56] It is from this standpoint that we are to understand Lewis' rather neutral ecclesiology.

Behind the words of the letter, in the spirit of the letter, what is discovered is not, as we have seen, a system but a 'fact' or 'thing' about which one is expected to exclaim: 'Look out! It's alive!' And it is from the living core of the Christian faith that Lewis addresses us in all his works, from *The Allegory of Love*[57] down to *Letters to Malcolm*:[58] 'Ever since I became a Christian I have thought that the best, perhaps the only, service I could do for my unbelieving neighbours was to explain and defend the belief that has been common to nearly all Christians at all times.'[59] This explains the Christocentric flavour of all his books, wherein the reader constantly discovers what Hopeful calls in Bunyan's *The Pilgrim's Progress* 'the beauty of Jesus Christ'.[60]

Beyond ambiguities – and there are theological ambiguities in Lewis' apologetics – the reader must be aware that Lewis was not a theologian *stricto sensu*, but a man of goodwill whose constant effort was to bring back his 'neighbour' to Jesus Christ. What he says is not addressed to theologians, and not primarily to the church, but to the 'modern Western man', puzzled or spellbound by the shallow rationalism of our age. Lewis' task, then, was that of the missionary among savages of a particular kind, which in *The Abolition of Man* are described as 'men without chests',[61] that is to say men of straw, merely modern men such as Mark Studdock in *That Hideous Strength*, wholly untrained in the 'severities both of abstraction and of high human tradition'.[62] In these circumstances, 'The task of the modern educator is not to cut down jungles but to irrigate deserts.'[63] In the same way the task of the Christian teacher or writer is 'to spread the immediately sub-Christian perceptions and virtues, the rich Platonic or Virgilian *penumbra* of the Faith . . .',[64] just as Ransom and Lewis at the end of *Out of the Silent Planet* emphasise that 'what we need for the moment is not so much a body of belief as a body of people familiarized with certain ideas'.[65]

Such are the very first steps in the 'lived dialectic', the preface to chapter one of the process of conversion being that cleansing of the beginner's reason and imagination, away from 'ideology' and back to a meaningful universe, to a universe packed full with light, music, and the enamoured acknowledgement of otherness. Little by little the taste and flavour of the solidity of otherness discloses to the reader the true origin of its charm, that is to say not sheer otherness but 'this' God, this super-personal or even 'trans-personal' God whose positive and concrete reality demands that our every-day modes of representation should be subverted: 'Gramma-tically the things we say of Him are "metaphorical": but in a deeper sense it is our physical and psychic energies that are mere "metaphors" of the real Life which is God.'[66] The discovery of consistent supernaturalism is the first step to-wards the Christian belief in the one God, it is the training of palates[67] in the recognition of the flavour of Christianity, a training of eyes and sensibility in the acknowledgement of the Christian Figure (together, of course, with the inescapable reality of sin).

Lewis addresses his reader from within 'the formula', yet his method is that of the long way round, that of a vast movement of regress towards the almost wholly forgotten roots of supernaturalism, a movement backwards to the dawn of times, within the *penumbra* or *chiaroscuro* of pre-Christian or immediately sub-Christian feelings. Lewis says somewhere 'Would that we were pagans!'; this is no paradox: the dangers which now threaten trinitarian Christianity are exactly the reverse of those which endangered the faith at the time, say, of the Arian controversy. In those days the danger was that of a retrogression to pantheism and idolatry, to the belief in the mediation of demi-gods between nature and supernature. That jungle had to be cut down, and it was cut down by Athanasius and the Councils; but in our own age the Christian faith such as it was defined by the early Councils has become a desert, a sterilised belief which is the fruit of the 'de-mythology' of our times, when so many theologians seem to be entertaining the thought that Christianity can do without miracles, without the 'mythical radiance' that rests upon it, that it can even do without dogmas.

Lewis' method, then, is that of a pilgrimage (in the form of a regress) towards the living heart of Christianity; and once reason and imagination have been baptised and purified of the dross of contemporary presuppositions by a conversion of both the *sentire* and the *intelligere*, a new picture appears, which is that of Christianity defined as the Christian life: the long way round has brought us back to Puritania, and just as John did in *The Pilgrim's Regress*, the reader discovers that 'The Island is the Mountains: or, if you will, the Island is the other side of the Mountains, and not, in truth, an Island at all,'[68] and that all the Christian life is still to begin.

Thus the voyage towards the core of the formula reveals itself as a voyage towards the glorious heart of the Christian life. The shadowlands, even the good dreams and good stories, can now be forgotten and the reader who has faithfully followed Lewis' 'dialectic of love' is once again able to share the life of the 'solid people' of the Christian community, which is the same, yet different. 'Narnia within Narnia', or Puritania transfigured, is the beginning of all good adventure, and we can say of the Christian in this world what Lewis says of the children in redeemed Narnia: 'All their life in this world and all their adventures in Narnia had only been the cover and the title page: now at last they were beginning Chapter One of the Great Story which no one on earth has read: which goes on forever: in which every chapter is better than the one before.'[69] This is just as in *The Great Divorce*, where the image to be retained is not simply that of an anticipation of eternal life, but also a description of the 'philosophy of the good life', a description of the true nature of the Christian life which is so to speak the glorious side of theology, the 'practick part' of religion, as Bunyan said, and of which John Smith said: 'Were I to define divinity, I should rather call it *a divine life* than *a divine science.*'[70] That is why Lewis' tales and even the visionary parts of his apologetics have themselves to be renounced, given up, because they lead us but to the porch of the church, and tomorrow is a 'Monday morning', even if it is a transfigured Monday-morning world.

11

HOW TO SAVE WESTERN CIVILISATION: C. S. LEWIS AS PROPHET

Peter Kreeft

Cars have windscreens as well as rear-view mirrors. So do civilisations. However, our rearward, Epimethian vision is far stronger than our forward, Promethian. We have more archivists than prophets. For archivists see through a micro-scope, sharply, but prophets see through a glass, darkly.

Yet even the little they see is of great importance to us, like the little that a driver sees when peering through a tiny hole of light in a muddy windscreen when the car is accelerating through thick fog over rocks – in other words, when the situation is like that of our civilisation.

The gift of prophecy, confined to a small number in Old Testament times, is offered to all Christians once the Holy Spirit, the One who makes and inspires prophets, is spread through the church and into the world in the new covenant (Acts 2:16–21). It is possible, therefore, to call C. S. Lewis a prophet without being absurd. Let us consult the writings of this most popular Christian author of our age with that hope in mind, and look for some Lewis-light on our civilisational teeter, we who stand poised on the brink of both spiritual and nuclear suicide.

I extract twelve major principles about history from Lewis:

five could be called a philosophy of history, four a description of history, and three a psychology of history. Then I apply these twelve principles to the issue of the future of humankind on this planet, and draw a single conclusion from them. Finally, from this conclusion I derive a number of immediately practical applications for our present lives.

A Philosophy of History

The first and most important principle of Lewis' philosophy of history is that he does not believe in the philosophy of history. In his 1954 Cambridge inaugural lecture, *'De Descriptione Temporum'*, he said:

> About everything that could be called 'the philosophy of history' I am a desperate sceptic. I know nothing of the future, not even whether there will be any future . . . I don't know whether the human tragi-comedy is now in Act I or Act V; whether our present disorders are those of infancy or of old age.[1]

In his volume on the sixteenth century in the *Oxford History of English Literature*, he wrote:

> Some think it is the historian's business to penetrate beyond . . . apparent confusion and heterogeneity, and to grasp in a simple intuition the 'spirit' or 'meaning' of his period. With some hesitation, and with much respect for the great men who have thought otherwise, I submit that this is exactly what we must refrain from doing. I cannot convince myself that such 'spirits' or 'meanings' have much more reality than the pictures we see in the fire . . . The 'canals' on Mars vanished when we got stronger lenses.[2]

And any reader of the above volume knows that Lewis had strong lenses.

Finally, from *Reflections on the Psalms*, here is the *reason* for Lewis' scepticism about the philosophy of history:

> Between different ages there is no impartial judge on earth, for no one stands outside the historical process; and, of course, no

one is so completely enslaved to it as those who take our own age to be not one more period but a final and permanent platform from which we can see all other ages objectively.[3]

The Christian religion is like the history of the human race: messy, unpredictable, surprising, lacking 'suspicious *a priori* lucidity', as Lewis puts it in *Miracles*:

> Christianity, faced with popular 'religion', is continually trouble- some . . . the real historian is similarly a nuisance when we want to romance about 'the old days' or 'the ancient Greeks and Romans.' The ascertained nature of any real thing is always at first a nuisance to our natural fantasies . . .[4]

'Don't confuse me with facts; I've made up my mind' is a far more prevalent attitude than we like to think.

But once we give up fantasising about history, we need not give up talking about it. Although our first Lewisian principle about the philosophy of history seems to exclude any further principles, it does not. It excludes only firm generalisations, dogmatic conclusions. Principles are not conclusions but starting-points, *principia*. When we *start* to approach history, we need principles as one of the two blades of our mental scissors, if they are to cut through the mass of historical paper. We also need a lower, empirical blade, lest we project our *a priori* principles on to the facts. Principles without facts are empty, but facts without principles are blind.

Principle Two could be called anti-historicism, or perhaps anti-Hegelianism. Before Hegel, nearly everyone agreed that truth, could we but know it, must be unchanging – at least truths about human nature and the laws of good and evil. Truths about our accidental qualities may change through history, but never the laws of our essence. As Lewis put it in *A Preface to Paradise Lost*, '. . . though the human heart is not unchanging (nay, changes almost out of recognition in the twinkling of an eye) the laws of causation are. When poisons become fashionable they do not cease to kill.'[5]

Modern man therefore continues to make the same essen- tial mistakes, is subject to the same addictions, sins the same sins, and reaps the same whirlwinds as his ancestors did. The only changes in the human essence were the fall and the redemption. Nothing else ever has or ever will change our very nature. No Nietzschean superman looms on the horizon. The 'rough beast' has already slouched towards Bethlehem to be born; there will be no others except false Messiahs until the end of time.

That is why Lewis is continually turning us from our search for 'contemporary relevance' to eternal relevance:

> The crisis of the present moment, like the nearest telegraph pole, will always loom largest. Isn't there a danger that our great, permanent, objective necessities – often more important – may get crowded out?

> While the moderns have been pressing forward to conquer new territories of consciousness, the old territory, in which alone man can live, has been left unguarded, and we are in danger of finding the enemy in our rear.[6]

That from *A Preface to Paradise Lost*. On the first page of *The Allegory of Love* Lewis gives the reason in principle why the study of the past is just as useful for an understanding of ourselves and our nature as a study of the present: 'Humanity does not pass through phases as a train passes through stations: being alive, it has the privilege of always moving yet never leaving anything behind. Whatever we have been, in some sort we are still.'[7] And from a letter written in 1931: 'I . . . find nothing obsolete. The silly things [the] great men say, were as silly then as they are now: the wise ones are as wise now as they were then.'[8]

Supposedly new fundamental ideas nearly always turn out to be old. Even technology is only sober and successful magic. The dream of 'man's conquest of nature' is only Prometheus and Faust secularised. Modernism is only the new Arianism. Determinism is only the new astrology. Kantianism is only the new Sophism in epistemology and the new Stoicism in ethics. The list is endless. The only radically new thing under the sun is the one Man who came from beyond the sun.

Principle Three is a negative one: a decisive disagreement with the prevailing philosophy of history, progressivism or universal evolutionism. Principle Two denied *essential* change in the human species; Principle Three denies accidental change for the better in the last few centuries – something which, unlike essential change, *could* have happened but didn't, according to Lewis. Like a rock standing against the nearly unanimous stream of progressivism, Lewis refuses to idealise the twentieth century. I think he would understand the prophet of Medjugorge who said that God gave the devil one century to do his worst work in, and the devil chose the twentieth.

Lewis loves to attack the cult of change for the sake of change, the exaltation of change and the demeaning of permanence, and the common rhetoric that goes with it. He asks, in 'The Funeral of a Great Myth':

> How has it come about that we use the highly emotive word 'stagnation' with all its malodorous and malarial overtones for what other ages would have called 'permanence'? Why does the word 'primitive' at once suggest to us clumsiness, inefficiency, barbarity? Where our ancestors talked of the primitive church or the primitive purity of our condition, they meant nothing [pejorative].[9]

His answer to the above question is found in 'The Poison of Subjectivism':

> I submit that what has imposed this climate of opinion so firmly on the human mind is a new archetypal image. It is the image of old machines being superseded by new and better ones. For in the world of machines the new most often really is better and the primitive really is clumsy . . .

> Our assumption that everything is provisional and soon to be superseded, that the attainment of goods we have never yet had, rather than the defence and conservation of those we have already, is the cardinal business of life would most shock and bewilder [our ancestors].[10]

Reason cuts through the fog of rhetoric to refute this myth:

Let us strip it of the illegitimate emotional power it derives from the word 'stagnation' with its suggestion of puddles and mantled pools. If water stands too long it stinks. To infer thence that whatever stands long must be unwholesome is to be the victim of metaphor. Space does not stink because it has preserved its three dimensions from the beginning. The square on the hypotenuse has not gone mouldy by continuing to equal the sum of the squares on the other two sides. Love is not dishonoured by constancy . . .[11]

The last point is the crucial one. It is in ethics that 'progressivism' is most deadly. Astonishingly, few modern minds see the simple and obvious point that an unchanging standard, far from being the enemy of progress, is the necessary condition for it: 'Does a permanent moral standard preclude progress? On the contrary, except on the supposition of a changeless standard, progress is impossible . . . [If] the terminus is as mobile as the train, how can the train progress toward it?'[12]

Lewis' Christianity gives him a much more radically progressive outlook than evolutionism can give, for Christianity calls on men to become not just better men, or even supermen, but to become Christs, to share in divine life – an infinitely greater transformation than any current secular fad.

Christian prophets, like Christ, are the true progressives, but not in the way of current liberalism, by 'keeping up with the world'. Lewis writes:

It sounds well to say that the true prophet is a revolutionary, going further and faster than the forward movement of the age, but the dictum bears little relation to experience. The prophets have *resisted* the current of their times . . . it would require a more than common effrontery of paradox to present Jeremiah as the nose on the face of the Zeitgeist.[13]

Lewis knows that in every field progress is made only by those who ignore the Zeitgeist and simply tell the truth. Thus he says in *The Problem of Pain*: 'I take a very low view of "climates of opinion". In his own subject every man knows that all discoveries are made and all errors corrected by those who ignore the "climates of opinion".[14]

Lewis gives a brilliant description in a single image of the 'evolution revolution', the revolutionary change the evolutionary world-view has effected, in *The Discarded Image*:

> In modern, that is, in evolutionary, thought Man stands at the top of a stair whose foot is lost in obscurity; in [medieval thought], he stands at the bottom of a stair whose top is invisible with light.

> [T]hat all perfect things are prior to all imperfect things . . . was common ground to nearly all ancient and medieval thinkers except the Epicureans . . . [T]he radical difference which this involves between their thought and the developmental or evolutionary concepts of our own period . . . leaves no area and no level of consciousness unaffected.[15]

Lewis' reason for rejecting the myth of universal progress is essentially Chesterton's observation that universal evolutionism seems credible only when you blink one eye; when you remember the fact that oaks come from acorns and forget the fact that acorns come from oaks; when you remember that big New York grew from little New Amsterdam and forget that little New Amsterdam came from big old Amsterdam; when you remember that the complex Saturn V and Apollo XII rockets came from Robert Goddard's simple little firecrackers but forget that Goddard's firecrackers came from Goddard's highly complex brain.

Lewis' *Principle Four* is another negation: the negation of the corollary of evolutionary progressivism that Lewis labels 'chronological snobbery' and defines in *Surprised by Joy* as 'the uncritical acceptance of the intellectual climate common to our own age and the assumption that whatever has gone out of date is on that account discredited'.[16] Reason erects a Stop sign to this prejudice:

> You must find why it went out of date. Was it ever refuted (and if so by whom, where, and how conclusively) or did it merely die away as fashions do? If the latter, this tells us nothing about its truth or falsehood. From seeing this, one passes to the realisation

that our own age is also 'a period,' and certainly has, like all periods, its own characteristic illusions. They are likeliest to lurk in those wide-spread assumptions which are so ingrained in the age that no one dares to attack or feels it necessary to defend them.[17]

(Lewis gives Owen Barfield credit for teaching him this all-important principle.)

In his essay on 'Historicism', Lewis calls chronological snobbery 'the vulgarest of all vulgar errors, that of idolizing as the goddess History what manlier ages belaboured as the strumpet Fortune'.[18]

Chronological snobbery is self-defeating, for 'the more "up-to-date" the look is, the sooner it will be dated'. In *An Experiment in Criticism* Lewis asks the avant-garde critic, 'If you take your stand on the "prevalent" view, how long do you suppose it will prevail? . . . All you can really say about my taste is that it is old-fashioned; yours will soon be the same.'[19]

Lewis freely confesses in a letter that 'In talking to me you must beware, because I am conscious of a partly pathological hostility to what is fashionable.'[20] He speaks of himself as 'a converted Pagan living among apostate Puritans'[21] and says (in *Surprised by Joy*): '. . . the key to my books is Donne's maxim, "The heresies that men leave are hated most." The things I assert most vigorously are those that I resisted long and accepted late.'[22]

Alan Watts finds in Lewis 'a certain ill-concealed glee in adopting an old-fashioned and unpopular position'.[23] But surely this is a good glee, for it is the joy of the underdog, the joy in winning a battle intrinsically worth winning, the joy of telling the truth to people who do not know it and need it.

There is more than personal proclivity behind Lewis' refusal to share modernity's 'chronological snobbery'. There is the very practical principle that 'it is not the remembered but the forgotten past that enslaves us', or, as Santayana put it, 'Those who do not learn from the past are condemned to repeat it.'

In the light of this principle, it is indeed disastrous timing to find ignorance of the past, in the form of chronological snobbery, arising within that particular generation of the species addicted to war which has discovered how to kill every living person on the planet; that it is this generation of the species with the death wish that has thrown away its history books and now believes in itself as the generation that will bring peace to the world.

Mention of war and killing brings us to *Principle Five*, which is the principle Malcolm Muggeridge has called the most unpopular of all the Christian dogmas and yet the only one empirically provable simply by reading the daily newspapers: the dogma of original sin.

It is this dogma which more than anything else distinguishes a conservative from a liberal. A conservative has been defined as a liberal who has just been mugged. In other words, conservatives believe in evil. They also believe in absolute moral standards. The two are interdependent, for if there are no moral absolutes, one man's evil is merely another man's good.

Rather than belabour the obvious with many quotations from Lewis on this point, let us remember only the whole masterly chapter in *The Problem of Pain* entitled 'Human Wickedness'.[24]

A Christian is not shocked by human wickedness, by the latest scandal to hit the press. For a Christian has seen Calvary. He would not be surprised to see Lucifer fall like lightning on New York as he fell on Sodom and Gomorrah. (Indeed, we may even think that if God spares New York he will owe an apology to Sodom.) A Christian expects to see the whole world dissolve in fervent heat, the stars fall from heaven, and the skies rolled back like a scroll; he is not unduly terrified by Hiroshima.

The God of Jesus Christ is a God of mercy and love and forgiveness, but he is also a God of justice and judgement. The very same authority that is virtually our only authority for believing that 'God is love' also clearly teaches that God is just, and that those who do not meet him clothed in his gift of salvation and grace must meet him naked, without a wedding garment. For all must meet him, since he is truth, and truth is universal and unavoidable. Mercy is truth clothed; judgement is truth naked.

Five historical principles, then: scepticism about the philosophy of history; denial of historicism and its belief in the malleability of human nature; denial of progressivism and universal evolutionism; denial of chronological snobbery; and denial of Enlightenment optimism and modern relativism and liberalism because of their denial of the reality of sin and judgement.

A Description of History

We now turn, more briefly, to four stages in Lewis' empirical description of our history: the pre-modern world, especially medieval Christendom; the Renaissance, or the Great Divide between the classical and the modern; the modern world; and the future.

The Pre-Modern World

First, what have we lost? Describing medieval Christendom as not merely a unified social order but a unified cosmos, Lewis writes in *The Discarded Image*: 'Marcus Aurelius wished that men would love the universe as a man can love his own city. I believe that something like this was really possible in the period I am discussing.'[25] For the medieval felt 'like a man being conducted through an immense cathedral, not like one lost in a shoreless sea'.[26]

Yet even as his head was in the clouds, his feet were on the ground – the proper place for both. Modern man, as G. K. Chesterton says, is simply upside down: nose to the ground, kicking up his feet in rebellion against the sky. Medieval man thought of himself (to use still another Chestertonian image) neither as a balloon flying loose in the sky (like our spiritualising orientalisers and Gnostics) nor as a mole burrowing in the earth (like our modern materialists) but as a tree, with roots firmly planted in the earth and branches reaching up into the heavens.

Lewis describes what a medieval boy learnt in school:

> farriery, forestry, archery, hawking, sowing, ditching, thatching, brewing, baking, weaving, and practical astronomy. This concrete knowledge, mixed with their law, rhetoric, theology, and mythology, bred an outlook very different from our own. High abstractions and rarified artifices jostled the earthiest particulars . . . They talked more readily than we about large universals such as death, change, fortune, friendship, or salvation; but also about pigs, loaves, boots, and boats. The mind darted more easily to and fro between that mental heaven and earth: the cloud of middle generalizations, hanging between the two, was then much smaller. Hence, as it seems to us, both the naïvety and the energy of their writing . . . They talk something like angels and something like sailors and stable-boys; never like civil servants or writers of leading articles.[27]

We moderns have lost the solid objectivity both of the high universals (especially truth and goodness) and of the low particulars, the concrete world. Both have been dissolved into a vague, abstract, ideological-political-sociological-psychological mid-range. *We* are the 'middle' ages.

The Great Divide

The great divide between medieval and modern has its origins in the forces that dissipated this medieval energy: philosophical nominalism and scepticism, clerical corruption, economic mercantilism, and biological plague. But it did not define itself until a new *summum bonum* appeared on the horizon. Francis Bacon announces the new age with the slogans 'knowledge for power' (rather than for its own sake) and 'man's conquest of nature' (rather than of himself).

Of the two great spiritual revolutions in the history of Western civilisation, the first from pre-Christian to Christian and the second from Christian to post-Christian, Lewis says:

> It appears to me that the second change is even more radical than the first (as divorce is more traumatic than marriage). Christians

and pagans had much more in common with each other than either has with a post-Christian. The gap between those who worship different gods is not so wide as that between those who worship and those who do not . . . the gap between Professor Ryle and, say, Dante is wider than that between Dante and Virgil.[28]

As Lewis sardonically says in the poem 'A Cliché Came Out of its Cage', the world is *not* 'going back to Paganism' ('Oh, bright Vision!') any more than a divorcee goes back to virginity.[29] For technology has replaced religion at the centre of our consciousness and our life. We have a new *summum bonum*.

The Modern World
The most important and enlightening single statement about our civilisation that I have ever read is this one from *The Abolition of Man*:

> There is something which unites magic and applied science while separating both from the 'wisdom' of earlier ages. For the wise men of old the cardinal problem had been how to conform the soul to reality, and the solution had been knowledge, self-discipline, and virtue. For magic and applied science alike the problem is how to subdue reality to the wishes of men [and] the solution is a technique . . .[30]

Aristotle rated technique, technical knowledge, *technē*, know-how, as third on the hierarchy of values, after (1) contemplation of the truth for its own sake and (2) practical knowledge, or knowledge for living, for acting. The modern world has simply turned this hierarchy exactly upside down, as it has turned man upside down.

Two other major changes are necessary corollaries of this change from contemplation to technique, from 'conforming the soul to reality' to 'conforming reality to the soul'. The first is a new conception of reality. For one does not try to conform God or the gods to the wishes of the human soul, but one tries to conform nature to those wishes. Thus naturalism replaces supernaturalism in metaphysics. At first this means only ignoring God, then denying God, finally (worst of all) both.

The second corollary is equally crucial. It is 'the poison of subjectivism', the belief that the Tao, moral values, are man-made.[31] This follows from naturalism, for if there is no God to originate values, man is the only other possible origin. But then values are only the rules of our games. If we made the rules, we can change them or break them. As Dostoyevsky puts it so succinctly, 'If God does not exist, everything is permissible.'[32] With God, all things are possible, but without God, all things are permissible.

Technologism, secularism, subjectivism: the unholy trinity of planks in the platform of man as God. A new potency, a new position, and a new positing. Potency to conquer nature by the sober magic of applied science – knowledge for power or potency rather than for truth or virtue. The new position of top dog on the cosmic totem pole, God having been lopped off or forgotten. And man positing values rather than humbly discovering and acknowledging them – thus an ethic of 'positive law' rather than 'natural law'.

Our civilisation is now well advanced in its new experiment with its new God. How has it turned out? Has it made us happy or good? Has it even made us honest with ourselves? W. H. Auden answers no to all three questions in his poem '1st September 1939':

> Faces along the bar
> Cling to their average day:
> The lights must never go out,
> The music must always play,
> All the conventions conspire
> To make this fort assume
> The furniture of home;
> Lest we should see where we are,
> Lost in a haunted wood,
> Children afraid of the night
> Who have never been happy or good.[33]

Even Freud admits this. In his most philosophical work, *Civilization and its Discontents*, he asks the simple but great question: If the gods were only the projections of our dreams, and if our dreams have now become true by our having become gods, 'masters and possessors of nature', then why aren't we happy?[34]

The twentieth century is the century of destruction, genocide, suicide, anxiety, and psychosis. Here is how Lewis' mouthpiece, Ransom, describes the modern world to the resuscitated Merlin in *That Hideous Strength*:

> However far you went you would find the machines, the crowded cities, the empty thrones, the false writings, the barren beds: men maddened with false promises and soured with true miseries, worshipping the iron works of their own hands, cut off from Earth their mother and from the Father in Heaven . . . The shadow of one dark wing is over all Tellus.[35]

The Pilgrim's Regress describes our 'progress' thus:

> Their labour-saving devices multiply drudgery,
> Their aphrodisiacs make them impotent,
> Their amusements bore them,
> Their rapid production of food leaves half of them starving,
> And their devices for saving time have banished leisure from
>   their country.[36]

The Future

Finally – the fourth stage of our descriptive analysis of our history according to Lewis – where are we going?

Lewis is sceptical of the philosophy of history, as we know, claims to have no crystal ball, and is highly suspicious of all who do. But he traces a movement, a single trend, from the past into the present, that can be projected into a future; a movement that is accelerating both in rapidity and intensity. The movement is, in a word, reductionism, 'that great movement of internalisation [subjectivisation] and that consequent aggrandisement of man and desiccation of the outer universe, in which the psychological history of the West has so largely consisted' (as *The Discarded Image* puts it).[37] It is the movement away from Hamlet's philosophy that

> There are more things in heaven and earth, Horatio,
> Than are dreamt of in your philosophy.[38]

As more and more things appear in our philosophy, our dreams, our consciousness, fewer and fewer are left in heaven and earth, in objective reality. Our history is the story of King Midas: 'Man with his new powers became rich like Midas but all that he touched had gone dead and cold.'[39]

Lewis described this process in his Preface to D. E. Harding's quirky, obscure and unsuccessful attempt to reverse that process in *The Hierarchy of Heaven and Earth*:

> We can observe a single one-way progression. At the outset the universe appears packed with will, intelligence, life and positive qualities; every tree is a nymph and every planet a god. Man himself is akin to the gods. The advance of knowledge gradually empties this rich and genial universe: first of its gods, then of its colours, smells, sounds and tastes, finally of solidity itself . . . As these items are taken from the world, they are transferred to the subjective side of the account: classified as our sensations, thoughts, images or emotions. The Subject becomes gorged, inflated, at the expense of the Object.[40]

A Psychology of History

We need now only three more principles – psychological ones this time – and we are ready to derive our prophetic conclusion.

A first is what Lewis calls the principle of 'First and Second Things'. Presupposing the Tao, the doctrine of objective values, this principle states that whenever one of two values is really greater than another, prior to another, if man upsets this hierarchy he loses *both* values. In other words, to sacrifice a 'First Thing' to a 'Second Thing' is to lose not only the 'First Thing' but the 'Second Thing' as well.

The principle is used extensively in *The Four Loves*,[41] but it is first defined in a 1942 essay in *Time and Tide* (reprinted as 'First and Second Things' in the collection of that name[42]) about the Nazis' ideological perversions of their own Teutonic mythology. The Nazi ideologues declared that henceforth Hagen rather than Siegfried should be regarded as the hero of the story of the Nibelungs (since the dark and crafty dwarf Hagen resembled Hitler more than the noble and generous Siegfried did). The lesson: if you subordinate high art to low politics, you pervert both. The contemporary application is that any civilisation, like ours, which ranks its own mere survival above any objective values to survive for, will not survive. If you have nothing worth dying for, you will die. If you have nothing worth living for except mere living, you will not live.

> To preserve civilization has been the great aim . . . Peace, a high standard of life, hygiene, transport, science and amusement – all these, which are what we usually mean by civilization, have been our ends . . . But . . . [what] if civilization has been imperilled precisely by the fact that we have all made civilization our *summum bonum*?[43]

Lewis ends the prophetic essay with these prophetic words:

> There is much rash idealization of past ages about, and I do not wish to encourage more of it. Our ancestors were cruel, lecherous, greedy and stupid, like ourselves. But while they cared for other things more than for civilization . . . was civilization often in serious danger of disappearing?
>
> At least the suggestion is worth a thought. To be sure, if it were true that civilization will never be safe till it is put second, that immediately raises the question, second to what? What is the first thing? The only reply I can offer here is that if we do not know, then the first, and only truly practical thing, is to set about finding out.[44]

A second psychological principle is so common throughout Lewis' writings, and is shared with so many other twentieth-century writers (George Orwell, Aldous Huxley, T. S. Eliot,

W. H. Auden, Ortega y Gasset, David Riesman, Spengler, Ernst Becker) that I need only mention it. It is the demon of collectivism, of mob psychology, of mass consciousness. The dark side of this comfortable conformism is the death-wish. Free, thinking individuals do not usually kill themselves, but lemmings, Nazis or Jim Jones' Jonestowners do.

Our third and final psychological principle is the deepest one of all because it stems from our deepest centre, our heart. It is the deepest thing in Lewis himself, according to his own admission. It is, of course, our old familiar friend *Sehnsucht*, 'Joy', the 'inconsolable longing', Augustine's 'restless heart'.

A corollary of the 'restless heart' is Aquinas' principle that 'No man can live without delight, and that is why a man deprived of spiritual joy goes over to carnal pleasures.'[45] 'Carnal pleasures' includes violence as well as lust, and it is worth investigating at this point, in the interests of prognostications of civilisational survival, how these two things are connected.

Modern man needs somehow to assure himself of his own reality. Ever since Descartes he has thought of himself as 'the ghost in the machine', and ever since his denial of the Tao he has thought of himself as a free-floating spirit with no roots in eternity. To find a substitute for God as the origin of his values, he looks to the new god 'society', *i.e.* the *Zeitgeist*, fashion. How can such a man prove he is real? How can a ghost live?

Two things no ghost can do: no ghost can murder and no ghost can rape. Entering the concrete, living reality of another human body, to kill or to copulate, to forcibly destroy or to forcibly create life, proves he is no ghost. Thus the unconscious takes its revenge; if no bright sacred mysteries anchor man's life, the dark mysteries arise. For both sex and death are great mysteries, and our unconscious still knows that, even if our brains are addled by pop psychology's demythologisation and trivialisation of sex into a mere pleasure-function and of death into just another natural process.

Denied good sex and good death, we necessarily turn to bad sex and bad death, lust and violence, rape and war. Denied Jehovah, we turn to Moloch, for man cannot live without gods. The battles on our earth always begin in the heavens. It is Moloch come again who has devoured twenty million unborn babies with the blessing of our Supreme Court of Justice. And when Moloch comes, can Lucifer be far behind? Is it not hypocritical to ask God to deliver us from the horrors of nuclear holocaust when we 'cause our sons and daughters to pass through the fire' of the great abortion holocaust? How can we hope to avoid hearing the terrible cry 'Lucifer has fallen' in our world if he has already fallen into our hearts?

The Future of Humankind

It is time to collect our wits and our principles, and to roll them into a ball to try to hit the pins of the future with them. We know in part and prophesy in part. We see our own future through a glass, darkly.

Our first principle, scepticism about the philosophy of history, cautions us against anything more than a guess and a warning on the basis of our other eleven principles.

Truth is unchanging. The principles of morality are unchanging. The human essence is unchanging. Therefore there is no hope of a new man, heaven on earth, Babel rebuilt, a Brave New World, or Superman. Man has always been violent and selfish, and will be until the end of time. 'The poor you will always have with you', we were reminded by the most realistic of teachers. 'There will be wars and rumours of wars' until the end, unless Christ was a fool or a liar; only the size of the weapons and the terror will change. To think our fallen race will suddenly acquire a wisdom and a sanity which we seldom had and never kept for long, only because of the threat of Mutually Assured Destruction, is indeed mad, and is a mutually assured destruction. Our second philosophical principle, the unchangingness of human nature, thus gives us little reason to hope.

We are *not* progressing, even within the limits of our essence and our powers, in wisdom and virtue. Modern man is not enlightened man but apostate man, and the Bible holds out little hope to apostates. Evolution may be true of the body, and even of the brain, but it is not true of the soul. Our third philosophical principle, the denial of progressivism, combined with Lewis' four-point description of our history as a slippery slope from medieval Christian fullness, through Renaissance hubris, to modern misery and nihilism – the Midas story – gives us little reason to hope. The previous point gave us little hope from our nature, this one gives us little hope from our history. Neither our unchanging essence nor our changing story looks like a progress.

'Ah, but we have left behind that old pessimism,' cries the modern mind. 'We are the people, and wisdom was born with us.' 'Alas,' replies Lewis, 'those who do not learn from history are condemned to repeat it.' The refusal of this chronological snobbery, our fourth principle, also gives us little hope.

We are still sinners, but a new kind of sinners: sinners who no longer believe in sin. That is the most dangerous kind. Our fifth principle, the denial of modernity's denial of original sin, also sounds hopeless; for if the patient denies his disease, he will not go to the doctor. If we reject the only One who ever even claimed to save us not only from ignorance or impotence but from sin, as our civilisation is increasingly doing, there is no alternative but to pay 'the wages of sin', which is death. We no longer have nuclear families or even nuclear selves, only nuclear bombs. The death within will surely spill out into a death without if we refuse the only One who can save from both deaths.

Our first psychological principle, about 'First and Second Things', reinforces our hopelessness, for throughout our civilisation, as in our individual lives, 'Second Things' are more and more replacing 'First Things'. We grow our toys and shrink our wisdom until the toys become enormous clubs wielded by tiny spoilt children. What happens when you give explosives to toddlers?

Our second pyschological principle, the demon of collectivism, simply assures us that 'We'll all go together when we go' in our global village.

And our third psychological principle, our dark and desperate search for lost joy and life and power, means we can't stop. We are addicts who are only pretending to be free. In reality, if we do not serve God we must serve a demon. For we must worship something, and any idol, any non-god worshipped as God, turns into a demon. Our new god, the 'conquest of nature', has turned into the demon of Lucifer's nuclear fire. Further, our collective Oedipus complex has wrought the death of God the Father and the rape of our mother, nature. Meanwhile, our chronological snobbery is so strong that we do not hear or heed even the wisdom of the old butter commercial: 'It's not nice to fool Mother Nature.' Nor is it safe. Nor, even, is it possible.

Have *Glasnost* and *Perestroika* and the remarkable events in Eastern Europe discredited and outdated the pessimism of this essay?

Yes – if our hope and fear both lie in politics. Yes – if the pleasant, soft totalitarianism of the mind is our hope and the unpleasant, hard totalitarianism of the state is our fear. Yes – if Western materialism is our hope and Eastern materialism is our fear. Yes – if spiritual suicide is less fearful than nuclear suicide. Yes – if the hopes and fears of all the years are met in Moscow, not in Bethlehem; in our relationship with Gorbachev, not God.

Conclusions

What, then, can we do? Are we simply doomed? Can we find any hope in Lewis, or even any advice for living in a doomed and hopeless world?

Indeed we can. Lewis would offer us at least these four pieces of advice, I think.

First, as a Christian he would remind us of what modern Christians have forgotten for the first time in Christian history: that we are strangers and aliens in this world, spies in enemy territory. Perhaps we can do nothing to save our country, our civilisation, or even our planet; but even if this is so, we must remember that 'this world is not my home, I'm just a-passing through', that our true country is heaven, and that the church, Christ's own mystical body, is heaven's impregnable and indestructible outpost on earth, and that this is our mother, our home, our city. Let us remember our only absolute *patria*, and not misplace our primary patriotism. We are guaranteed survival, success and salvation as the church, but not as the British, as Americans, as Westerners, or as this world.

Second, we must remember what the greatest power and the greatest task and the greatest success is. There is more power in one atom of Christ's body than in all the atom bombs in the universe. There is a greater glory in saving our sanity and our souls than in saving our civilisation. And there is a greater success in contributing one tiny link in a long chain which God will use to pull a single soul out of the pit of modern error, than in single-handedly perfecting and perpetuating the pit, in inventing success, satisfaction, security and survival for our civilisation. It is a greater thing to invent a single argument or a single deed of charity which would sway one soul to turn to God, than to invent a planet-wide system of successful Star Wars defence hardware.

For we can never forget that electrifying truth that Lewis loves to tell, that 'Nations, arts, cultures, civilisations . . . their life is to ours as the life of a gnat. But it is immortals whom we joke with, work with, marry, snub, and exploit – immortal horrors or everlasting splendours.'[46]

In the third place, Lewis is no doomsday determinist, for divine grace, forgiveness and hope of salvation are always held out to our choice, as a civilisation as well as individuals. All the prophets say this. They appeal to free choice. They blame the people for having made the wrong choice (assuming it was made freely, for one does not blame machines) and exhort them to change to the right choice, to turn, to repent (again assuming the freedom to do so). Lewis does the same. Here is his most prophetic passage of all about modern civilisation, from *Miracles*:

> All over the world, until quite recently, the direct insight of the mystics and the reasonings of the philosophers percolated to the mass of the people by authority and tradition; they could be received by those who were no great reasoners themselves in the concrete form of myth and ritual and the whole pattern of life. In the conditions produced by a century or so of Naturalism, plain men are being forced to bear burdens which plain men were never expected to bear before. We must get the truth for ourselves or go without it. There may be two explanations for this. It might be that humanity, in rebelling against tradition and authority, have made a ghastly mistake . . . On the other hand, it may be that the Power which rules our species is at this moment carrying out a daring experiment. Could it be intended that the whole mass of the people should now move forward and occupy for themselves those heights which were once reserved only for the sages? Is the distinction between wise and simple to disappear because all are now expected to become wise? If so, our present blunderings would be but growing pains.[47]

How hopeful! But also how sternly serious and demanding:

> But let us make no mistake about our necessities. If we are content to go back and become humble plain men obeying a tradition, well. If we are ready to climb and struggle on till we become sages ourselves, better still. But the man who will neither obey wisdom in others nor adventure for her himself is fatal.[48]

Finally, how can we work towards this hope for our civilisation? What can we *do* for the peace and survival that comes only through wisdom?

It is good to work for peace in whatever social and political ways really do work, whether this means working for disarmament or whether it means working for stronger armaments. We do not know with certainty which way will work best on the political level (though we nearly always claim we do). But we *do* know with certainty, because God himself has told us, what will work on the spiritual level, and we also know that that level cuts deeper and works at the roots. So to anyone who is concerned with peace and with the life and survival of our civilisation, here is a summary of what I have learnt from C. S. Lewis, what I think he would say today if he had only a single paragraph: 'Sodom and Gomorrah almost made it. If God had found but ten righteous men, he would have spared two whole cities. Abraham's intercession nearly saved Sodom, and did save Lot. We must be Abrahams. Charles Williams said that "the altar must often be built in one place so that the fire from heaven may come down at another". It is also true that the altar must be built and prayer and sacrifice made at one place so that the fire from hell may not come down at another. It can be done. The most important thing each of us can do to save the world from holocaust and from hell, from nuclear destruction and from spiritual destruction, is the most well-known, most unoriginal thing in the world: to love God with our whole heart and soul and mind and strength, and to love our neighbours as ourselves. You the individual can make a difference. You can be the straw that breaks the camel's back, the vote that wins the election. You can save the world.'

12

RESEARCHING C. S. LEWIS

Lyle W. Dorsett

Over a quarter of a century ago, towards the end of his life, C. S. Lewis predicted that no one would read his books after he had been dead five or six years. Lewis was a brilliant man with many talents, but he was no futurist. More than twenty-five years after his death nearly everything he wrote is in print. Much of his writing is available in several languages, and his works sell better today than during his lifetime.

Not only do his own writings sell extremely well, books about C. S. Lewis find a ready market too. Indeed, since his death almost sixty books have been written and edited on Lewis' life and work, hundreds of magazine and journal articles have appeared, and almost one hundred and fifty master's and doctoral dissertations have been prepared on this author.

The quantity and quality of serious research on C. S. Lewis increases each year. Most of it is being done in the United States, but there is growing interest in Canada, the United Kingdom, Australia, West Germany and Japan. Trickles of interest are welling up in other countries, usually in the wake of translations of Lewis' books in another language.

Sooner or later most serious Lewis scholars end up at the Marion E. Wade Center at Wheaton College, Wheaton, Illinois, twenty-five miles west of Chicago. The Wade Center houses a major research collection of writings by and about C. S. Lewis, and an ongoing programme is underway to collect everything Lewis wrote, both published and unpublished. The Center also attempts to acquire all of the related secondary sources, including unpublished theses and dissertations. Also, the staff is in the process of building a major video-oral history record of the reminiscences of Lewis' relatives, friends and associates. The Wade Center likewise subscribes to periodicals that focus on C. S. Lewis, and a large file of photographs is maintained.

The Wade Center's purpose is to collect, preserve and make available to researchers all writings related to C. S. Lewis and six other authors: Owen Barfield, G. K. Chesterton, George MacDonald, Dorothy L. Sayers, J. R. R. Tolkien and Charles Williams. These influenced or complemented Lewis' thinking in important ways; consequently their writings often shed light on the Oxford don's own thought.

The Center dates back to 1965, when the late Dr Clyde S. Kilby, then Professor of English Literature at Wheaton College, started an aggressive acquisitions and preservation programme. In 1974 the family and associates of Mr Marion E. Wade, founder of ServiceMaster Industries, established the Marion E. Wade Center in memory of this Christian businessman who was committed to the promulgation of the books and ideas of C. S. Lewis and like-minded authors.

Today the Wade Center includes over 25,000 letters, over 500 manuscripts, more than 10,000 books, thousands of clippings, articles and periodicals, hundreds of dissertations, and several hundred photographs. Of these written sources approximately 2400 letters are by Lewis, and over four thousand books by and about him are available, including rare first editions of most of his works. The Wade Center also houses nearly 2500 books from Lewis' personal library. Half of these bear his signature, underlinings, or annotations. Nearly three dozen oral-history tapes related to Lewis are available, as well as some interesting tapes that contain Lewis' own voice. Many museum pieces are also there, including the famous C. S. Lewis wardrobe (handmade by Lewis' grandfather, and from the Lewis family home in Belfast), and Lewis' writing desk.

The Wade Center also houses important related collections, such as the oral history, the books and the letters of his wife (Joy Davidman), and the books and letters of his brother (Warren Hamilton Lewis).

A substantial C. S. Lewis collection exists at the Bodleian Library, Oxford. This first-rate research library contains some original Lewis manuscripts. The Bodleian also holds copies or originals of all Lewis' letters, because years ago that library and the Wade Center agreed to exchange copies of every C. S. Lewis letter that they acquire. In this way researchers on one side of the Atlantic will not have to travel to the other side to see the letters. Although it does not attempt to collect all of the relevant secondary materials related to C. S. Lewis, the Bodleian is the place to begin for the researcher who resides in the United Kingdom.

One or two minor collections related to C. S. Lewis exist outside the Bodleian and the Wade Center. Four to five dozen of the books from Lewis' personal library are at the University of North Carolina, Chapel Hill. Most of these are annotated by Lewis. Also, Father Walter Hooper has some unpublished Lewis letters and manuscripts in his home in Oxford, and there are a few Lewis letters at the University of Texas, Austin, and at the University of North Carolina, Chapel Hill.

As interest in Lewis continues to grow, other universities will undoubtedly collect Lewisiana, but the centre of Lewis scholarship is likely to continue to be Wheaton, with the Bodleian serving as a strong secondary centre in the United Kingdom.

13

BIOGRAPHIES AND BIBLIOGRAPHIES ON C. S. LEWIS

Joe R. Christopher

Biographies

For the average reader of C. S. Lewis, where should he or she begin on the biographies of Lewis? (The bibliographies are fewer in number and will be discussed later.)

Since the Lewis enthusiast will probably read the *Letters of C. S. Lewis* anyway, the memoir by Lewis' brother which introduces that volume (New York: Harcourt, Brace & World; London: Geoffrey Bles, 1966; revised and enlarged, London: Collins Fount, 1988) will give a basic orientation to Lewis' life. Actually, W. H. Lewis – C. S. Lewis' brother – intended the volume to be something of a life of his brother, and wrote it with excerpts of Lewis' diary and many of his letters interspersed with his account; but it was edited into its present shape for the British publishers by Christopher Derrick – although W. H. Lewis was still listed as its sole editor in the book as originally published.

Anyone who wants to read more by W. H. Lewis about his brother should turn to *Brothers and Friends: The Diaries of Major Warren Hamilton Lewis*, edited by Clyde S. Kilby and Marjorie Lamp Mead (San Francisco: Harper & Row, 1982).

As the subtitle suggests, it has long excerpts from W. H. Lewis' diary. It reprints a full account of the brothers' walking tour of 1–6 January 1934, and has a number of briefer accounts of meetings of the Inklings, C. S. Lewis' literary circle (comprising Lewis, J. R. R. Tolkien and Charles Wlliams, in particular), in the 1940s. There are several more walking tours of the 1930s described in the full diary, and one can only hope that eventually they too will be edited and published.

Now then, what about the standard biographies? The first full-scale biography is, probably, still the best. This is *C. S. Lewis: A Biography*, by Roger Lancelyn Green and Walter Hooper (New York: Harcourt Brace Jovanovich; London: Collins, 1974; revised, London: Centenary Press, 1989). Green was a friend of Lewis and a good scholar on popular literature in his own right. Lewis had him read and comment on the manuscripts of the Narnian books before they were published, so his chapter on the writing of the Chronicles of Narnia in this book is invaluable. Delightful is Green's first-hand account of the trip of Lewis and his wife to Greece. About Walter Hooper, who wrote chapters 4, 5, 8, 9, and part of 10, there is some controversy. Anyone who wants to do scholarship on Lewis should read Kathryn Lindskoog's book *The C. S. Lewis Hoax* (Portland: Multnomah Press, 1988), and her small newsletter, *The Lewis Legacy*, and make up his or her own mind what to believe about Hooper. (There has not yet been a full answer from Hooper's side.) For the casual reader, however, there is nothing wrong with the essential facts about Lewis' life that are given in this biography.

The other basic biography out at present is *Jack: C. S. Lewis and His Times*, by George Sayer (San Francisco: Harper & Row; London: Macmillan, 1988). This is an excellent book, marred only by some brief repetitions of content in the early chapters and by a few, minor factual errors (for example, an essay on Lewis' early narrative poem *Dymer* is attributed to Marjorie Mack, but her name is Marjorie *Milne* – or at least it was when she wrote the essay – and Sayer does not note that Lewis dedicated *Dymer* to her). But the flaws in this book are minor, and it has all the feel of a biography which will be valuable for a long time. Sayer, like Green, knew Lewis well; furthermore, he is explicit about Lewis' early sexuality and other personal matters in a way that Green and Hooper's biography does not try to be.

Two other biographies should be mentioned. The first – *Clive Staples Lewis: A Dramatic Life*, by William Griffin (San Francisco: Harper & Row, 1986), published in Britain as *C. S. Lewis: The Authentic Voice* (Oxford: Lion, 1988) – is an odd sort of popular biography, being factual in quotations but otherwise rather dramatised (as the title promises). It runs, with some flashbacks, from 1927 to Lewis' death in 1963. Since it goes through Lewis' life, trivial incident set down alongside significant, its lack of discrimination gets tiring, but for popular reading it is a pleasant book to dip into. Collins, Lewis' current British publisher, has announced that A. N. Wilson has been commissioned to write a 'definitive' biography – it will have been published before this collection appears, and the American publication should be about the same time or slightly after the British.[1] (This account has omitted two minor biographies of Lewis – one aimed at teenagers – but neither had much that was original to offer.)

There are two pictorial biographies that a reader may want to *look* at. The better is *C. S. Lewis: Images of his World*, by Douglas Gilbert and Clyde S. Kilby (Grand Rapids: Wm. B. Eerdmans, 1973). Gilbert is a professional photographer, and many of the pictures are in colour. The other is *Through Joy and Beyond: A Pictorial Biography of C. S. Lewis*, by Walter Hooper (New York: Macmillan, 1982). A few of the photographs are a bit fuzzy, since Hooper is not a professional and he uses a number of his own photos; but the book contains a large number of other black-and-white pictures and has some brief reminiscences by Owen Barfield, one of Lewis's longtime friends; Pauline Baynes, the illustrator of the Narnia books; and others, which are valuable. (There is a third pictorial biography, but it is very inaccurate in its facts.)

Finally, three partial biographies should be mentioned. Humphrey Carpenter's *The Inklings: C. S. Lewis, J. R. R. Tolkien, Charles Williams, and Their Friends* (London: Allen & Unwin, 1978; Boston: Houghton Mifflin, 1979) is the basic account of Lewis' literary group; it is also valuable to the student of Lewis in that it does not take so laudatory a view of Lewis himself as the Green and Hooper biography does. Anyone who wants to know more about the Tolkien-Lewis friendship should also read Carpenter's *J. R. R. Tolkien: A Biography* (Boston: Houghton Mifflin; London: Allen & Unwin, 1977).

Another partial biography is *And God Stepped In*, by Lyle W. Dorsett (New York: Macmillan, 1983; London: Marshall Pickering, 1987). This biography of Joy Davidman is significant since Lewis married Davidman late in his life (he married her twice, as a matter of fact), and Dorsett spends over a third of his book on the Lewis-Davidman romance and marriage. Since Davidman was a divorced American (with her previous husband still alive), Jewish by background though not by practice, and a one-time atheist and communist, she made an unexpected marriage partner for Lewis – although he too was a one-time atheist. Particularly those readers who saw the British TV film on Lewis and Davidman, *Shadowlands*, will find this account interesting for comparison's sake. (The film, scripted by William Nicholson and directed by Norman Stone, had Joss Ackland as Lewis and Claire Bloom as Davidman.) It is a pity that Joy Davidman's own account of her marriage to Lewis has disappeared: the manuscript is mentioned once in an unpublished passage in W. H. Lewis' diary. Perhaps, after most of those reading these pages are long dead, it will show up at an auction at a high price!

The third partial biography is actually an autobiography by one of Joy Davidman's sons by her first husband – *Lenten Lands*, by Douglas H. Gresham (New York: Macmillan, 1988; London: Collins, 1989). Gresham was seven years old when he, his brother, and his divorced mother left for

England in 1953; in 1956 Lewis and Davidman married (in their first, civil marriage), and, of course, by late 1963 both Lewis and Davidman were dead. Gresham describes those years well, from his perspective (he has a different explanation than that of the main biographies for Davidman's temporary remission from cancer), and his account of Lewis' grief after Davidman's death is stronger than that in the other books. About fifteen out of the twenty-three chapters are a description of those years in England.

Bibliographies

Bibliographies are divided into two types – primary, what Lewis himself wrote, and secondary, what has been written about him. Oddly enough, despite all the collections of material by Lewis published since his death, not all his writings are yet available in book form. Also, even a dedicated Lewisphile – unless he or she *owns* the fifty-odd books by Lewis – may have some trouble tracking down a particular work by Lewis. That is where the primary bibliography comes in. The basic listing of Lewis' writings is by Walter Hooper, 'A Bibliography of the Writings of C. S. Lewis: Revised and Enlarged'; it is published at the back of *C. S. Lewis at the Breakfast Table and Other Reminiscences*, edited by James T. Como (New York: Macmillan, 1979; London: Collins, 1980). The problems with Hooper's account of his relationship to Lewis (alluded to earlier, in the biographical section of this essay) do not affect this bibliography; but the scholarly will want to note that Lindskoog's book raises questions about the authenticity of some minor works, such as 'The Dark Tower', which since his death have been published as if by Lewis. (Again, a reader of Lindskoog will have to make up his or her own mind about the matter.[2]) At any rate, the works printed in Lewis' lifetime are not in question – and they are the majority of those listed in Hooper's bibliography.

There are two basic problems about Hooper's checklist.

The first is simply that it is about ten years old, and the second is that it is cumbersome to use if a reader is trying to find which essays are in what collection. The essay contents are not listed with the book titles, but the index of titles gives the essays with cross-references *by number* to where they appear. Some day a book-length primary bibliography will appear with full information at a reader's fingertips, but it has not yet been published. (One has been announced – it is listed in *Books in Print* – but the publisher has indicated that the book is presently on hold, perhaps for revisions, perhaps for completion. At any rate, Hooper has the basic information.)

Hooper's bibliography has been updated, but the information will be difficult for the casual reader to find. It was compiled by Stephen Thorson and Jerry Daniel and published in *CSL: The Bulletin of the New York C. S. Lewis Society* as 'Bibliographic Notes': 'Published Drawings by C. S. Lewis', 14:8/164 (June 1983), pp. 6–7; 'Published Holographs', 14:10/166 (August 1983), pp. 6–7; [Supplements to Section E (Poems) in Hooper's revised bibliography], 17:9/201 (July 1986), pp. 5–6; [Supplements to Section D (Essays, Pamphlets and Miscellaneous Pieces)], 17:10/202 (August 1986), pp. 6–8; [Supplements to Section G (Published Letters) and Section H (Books Containing Numerous Small Extracts of Lewis' Unpublished Writings)], 18:1/205 (November 1986), pp. 15–18, and 18:2/206 (December 1986, pp. 6–7; and [Supplements to Sections A (Books) and B (Short Stories)], 18:5/209 (March 1987), pp. 6–7. If one's library cannot find *CSL* for an interlibrary loan, it is possible, at some cost for time and Xeroxing, to obtain copies from the Wade Center, Wheaton College, Wheaton, Illinois.

On secondary sources, the basic book is *C. S. Lewis: An Annotated Checklist of Writings about Him and His Works*, compiled and annotated by Joe R. Christopher and Joan K. Ostling (Kent, Ohio: Kent State University Press, 1974). It would be helped by a running headline, to indicate what section and subsection a reader is looking at; but it remains a useful, if also cumbersome, volume. Unfortunately, it too

shares with Hooper's bibliography the problem of being out
of date. Here there is no simple answer to what to check for in
supplements. A reader has to check standard guides: *MLA
International Bibliography of Books and Articles on the Modern Languages and Literature* for literary criticism (this
annual compilation actually begins its title with the year being
covered); *Readers' Guide to Periodical Literature* for popular
writings on Lewis; and *Religion Index One: Periodicals* or
Religious and Theological Abstracts for religious commentary
– with various others as suggested by librarians. *CSL* pub-
lishes a 'Book Notes' section, which sometimes includes
journal articles also ('Book Notes' is often written by Richard
Hodgens); *Mythlore* has had for about ten years an 'Inklings
Bibliography' compiled and annotated by Joe R. Christopher
(about a third on Lewis), currently being reorganised into a
three-person contribution, and has a book review section
under the direction of Nancy-Lou Patterson; *The Lamp-post
of the Southern California C. S. Lewis Society* also carries
book reviews; and the annotated checklist in the back of
Christianity and Literature sometimes catches Christian-
oriented items missed elsewhere. All one can say is: good
hunting! A sequel to the Christopher and Ostling checklist is
to be desired, but one does not seem to be forthcoming very
soon.

On the other hand, most general readers do not need to
bury themselves in secondary materials – particularly articles.
A book such as Joe R. Christopher's *C. S. Lewis* (Boston:
Twayne Publishers, 1987) lists most of the books about Lewis
at the back – forty-seven of them! – in an annotated listing,
and that is probably enough for anyone to struggle with.

NOTES

In order to avoid frequent and unnecessary repetition of details, references to works by C. S. Lewis in the notes that follow are generally to the 'basic' title of each work, and normally contain English publication details of the more recent, and more easily available, editions. Fuller publication details are given in the Select Bibliography.

Introduction

1 C. S. Lewis, *The Pilgrim's Regress* (London: Collins Fount, 1977).
2 Charles Gore (ed.), *Lux Mundi: A Series of Studies in the Religion of the Incarnation* (London: John Murray, 1889).
3 See C. S. Lewis, '*De Descriptione Temporum*', *Selected Literary Essays* (Cambridge: Cambridge University Press, 1969), pp. 1–14.
4 See C. S. Lewis, *Out of the Silent Planet* (London: Pan Books, 1952); *Voyage to Venus (Perelandra)* (London: Pan Books, 1953); *That Hideous Strength* (London: Pan Books, 1983).
5 C. S. Lewis, *The Discarded Image* (Cambridge: Cambridge University Press, 1964).
6 C. S. Lewis, *The Screwtape Letters* (London: Collins Fount, 1977).

1 Reflections on C. S. Lewis, Apologetics, and the Moral Tradition

1 C. S. Lewis, *Surprised by Joy* (London: Collins Fount, 1977).
2 C. S. Lewis, *The Lion, the Witch and the Wardrobe* (London: Collins Lions, 1980). For a full list of The Chronicles of Narnia, see Chapter 6, note 1.
3 C. S. Lewis, *Miracles* (London: Collins Fount, 1977).
4 C. S. Lewis, *The Problem of Pain* (London: Collins Fount, 1977).
5 C. S. Lewis, *Mere Christianity* (London: Collins Fount, 1977).
6 J. Beversluis, *C. S. Lewis and the Search for Rational Religion* (Grand Rapids, MI: Wm B. Eerdmans, 1985).
7 C. S. Lewis, *The Abolition of Man* (London: Collins Fount, 1978).
8 Alasdair MacIntyre, *After Virtue: A Study in Moral Theory* (London: Duckworth, ^{2}1985).

224   A CHRISTIAN FOR ALL CHRISTIANS

9   Alasdair MacIntyre, *Whose Justice? Which Rationality?* (London: Duckworth, 1988).
10 Basil Mitchell, *The Justification of Religious Belief* (London: Macmillan, 1973; rpr. New York: Oxford University Press, 1981).
11 Basil Mitchell, *Morality: Religious and Secular. The Dilemma of the Traditional Conscience* (Oxford: Oxford University Press, 1980).
12 John Macmurray, *Persons in Relation* (London: Faber & Faber, 1961).
13 Thomas S. Kuhn, *The Structure of Scientific Revolutions* (Chicago: Chicago University Press, ^{2}1970).
14 C. S. Lewis, '*De Descriptione Temporum*', *Selected Literary Essays* (Cambridge: Cambridge University Press, 1969), pp. 1–14.

2   Did C. S. Lewis Lose his Faith?

1   The television play *Shadowlands*, which featured Joss Ackland as C. S. Lewis and Claire Bloom as Joy Davidman, was written by William Nicholson and directed by Norman Stone. It was first broadcast in 1985, and is available as a BBC video.
2   Brian Sibley's book *Shadowlands* (London: Hodder & Stoughton, 1985), which was a television tie-in, paints a different and somewhat more satisfactory picture.
3   John Beversluis, *C. S. Lewis and the Search for Rational Religion* (Grand Rapids, MI: Wm B. Eerdmans, 1985).
4   John Beversluis, 'Beyond the Double Bolted Door', *Christian History* 4/3 (1985), pp. 28–31.
5   Humphrey Carpenter, *The Inklings: C. S. Lewis, J. R. R. Tolkien, Charles Williams, and their friends* (London: Allen & Unwin, 1978). Subsequent quotations from Carpenter's *The Inklings* are taken from the Unwin Paperbacks edition of 1981 and follow the page numbering of that volume.
6   Carpenter, *The Inklings*, pp. 216–17.
7   Richard B. Cunningham, *C. S. Lewis: Defender of the Faith* (Philadelphia: Westminster Press, 1967).
8   See Chapter 10, 'Specimen', of Beversluis, *C. S. Lewis and the Search for Rational Religion*, pp. 162–7.
9   C. S. Lewis, *Mere Christianity* (London: Collins Fount, 1977), pp. 120, 121–2.
10 C. S. Lewis, *Voyage to Venus (Perelandra)* (London: Pan Books, 1953), p. 9. *Voyage to Venus* was first published in 1943 by John Lane (the Bodley Head) under the title *Perelandra*.
11 C. S. Lewis, *A Grief Observed* (London: Faber & Faber, 1961). *A Grief Observed* originally appeared under the pseudonym N. W. Clerk.
12 Unpublished letter to Sister Madelva, 19 March 1963.

13   C. S. Lewis, *Letters to Malcolm: Chiefly on Prayer* (London: Geoffrey Bles, 1964) was Lewis' last book and was published shortly after his death. Subsequent quotations are taken from the Collins Fount edition of 1977, which appeared under the title *Prayer: Letters to Malcolm.*

14   C. S. Lewis, *Till We Have Faces* (London: Geoffrey Bles, 1956). The book was first issued as a Collins Fount Paperback in 1978.

15   W. H. Lewis (ed.), *The Letters of C. S. Lewis* (New York: Harcourt, Brace & World, 1966; London: Geoffrey Bles, 1966). Lewis' Letters have now been reissued in the following revised and enlarged edition: Walter Hooper (ed.), *Letters of C. S. Lewis: Edited, with a Memoir by W. H. Lewis* (London: Collins Fount, 1988).

16   Clyde S. Kilby (ed.), *Letters to an American Lady* (Grand Rapids, MI: Wm B. Eerdmans, 1967).

17   Walter Hooper (ed.), *They Stand Together: The Letters of C. S. Lewis to Arthur Greeves (1914–1963)* (New York: Macmillan, 1979; London: Collins, 1979).

18   Letter to Arthur Greeves, 22 May 1961, in Hooper (ed.), *They Stand Together*, p. 558.

19   The interview is in the records at the Marion E. Wade Center, Wheaton, Illinois.

20   In a videotaped interview with Douglas Gresham at the Marion E. Wade Center, Illinois.

21   Letter to Sister Penelope, 5 June 1951, in Hooper (ed.), *Letters of C. S. Lewis*, p. 410.

22   Richard L. Purtill, *C. S. Lewis's Case for the Christian Faith* (San Francisco: Harper & Row, 1981).

23   Richard L. Purtill, *International Philosophical Quarterly* 26/2 (1986).

24   T. V. Morris, *Faith and Philosophy* 5/3 (1988), pp. 319–22. Professor Morris' reference to his 'own first book, a critique of a very popular evangelical apologist' is to T. V. Morris, *Francis Schaeffer's Apologetic: A Critique* (Moody Press, 1976; reprinted Grand Rapids, MI: Baker Book House, 1987).

25   C. S. Lewis, *Miracles: A Preliminary Study* (London: Geoffrey Bles, 1947). The book was subsequently revised and appeared in a second edition in 1960. Subsequent quotations are taken from the Collins Fount Paperbacks edition of 1977.

26   Lewis, *Mere Christianity*, p. 6.

27   See Chapter 13, 'On Probability', of C. S. Lewis, *Miracles* (London: Collins Fount, 1977), pp. 104–11.

28   See C. S. Lewis, 'The Humanitarian Theory of Punishment' in *First and Second Things* (London: Collins Fount, 1985), pp. 96–114.

29   C. S. Lewis, 'The Founding of the Oxford Socratic Club' in *Timeless at Heart* (London: Collins Fount, 1987), pp. 80, 82.

30   Purtill, *C. S. Lewis's Case for the Christian Faith*, pp. 23–4.

226   A CHRISTIAN FOR ALL CHRISTIANS

31 G. E. M. Anscombe and P. T. Geach, *Three Philosophers* (Oxford: Basil Blackwell, 1961), pp. 109–25.
32 *The Socratic Digest* 4 (1948), pp. 15–16. (Reproduced in Lewis, *Timeless at Heart*, pp. 103–4.)
33 *ibid.* (Reproduced in Lewis, *Timeless at Heart*, p. 104.)
34 George Sayer, *Jack: C. S. Lewis and his Times* (New York: Harper & Row, 1988; London: Macmillan, 1988), pp. 186–7.
35 G. E. M. Anscombe, *Collected Philosophical Papers* (Cambridge: Cambridge University Press, 1981), vol. 2.
36 Carpenter, *The Inklings*, pp. 216–17.
37 C. S. Lewis, *The Problem of Pain* (London: Geoffrey Bles, 1940). This book is also available in the Collins Fount edition of 1977.
38 Austin Farrer, 'The Christian Apologist' in Jocelyn Gibb (ed.), *Light on C. S. Lewis* (London: Geoffrey Bles, 1965), p. 40.
39 'On Obstinacy in Belief' first appeared in *The Socratic Digest* in 1955. It is now available in C. S. Lewis, *Screwtape Proposes a Toast and other pieces* (London: Collins Fount, 1977), pp. 59–74.
40 Lewis, 'On Obstinacy in Belief', *Screwtape Proposes a Toast*, pp. 62–6.
41 Beversluis, 'Beyond the Double Bolted Door', p. 29.
42 Roger Lancelyn Green and Walter Hooper, *C. S. Lewis: A Biography* (London: Collins Fount, 1979), p. 232.
43 C. S. Lewis, *Prayer: Letters to Malcolm* (London: Collins Fount, 1977), pp. 123–4.
44 See, for example, Richard Swinburne, *The Concept of Miracle* (London: Macmillan, 1970); *The Coherence of Theism* (Oxford: Oxford University Press, 1977); *The Existence of God* (Oxford: Oxford University Press, 1979); *Faith and Reason* (Oxford: Oxford University Press, 1981); *The Evolution of the Soul* (Oxford: Oxford University Press, 1986); *Responsibility and Atonement* (Oxford: Oxford University Press, 1989).
45 John Lucas, *The Freedom of the Will* (Oxford: Oxford University Press, 1970); *Freedom and Grace* (London: SPCK, 1976); *The Future: An Essay on God, Temporality and Truth* (Oxford: Basil Blackwell, 1989).
46 Lewis, *Prayer: Letters to Malcolm*, pp. 118–19.
47 Lewis, 'On Obstinacy in Belief', *Screwtape Proposes a Toast*, pp. 73–4.

3 Under the Russian Cross
1 The word 'anonymous' being a humorous oblique reference to Karl Rahner's famous notion of the 'anonymous Christian'.
2 C. S. Lewis, 'On the Reading of Old Books' in *First and Second Things* (London: Collins Fount, 1985), pp. 25–33.

3 In my book *Enemy Territory: The Christian Struggle for the Modern World* (London: Hodder & Stoughton/C. S. Lewis Centre, 1987), p. 45.

4 See C. S. Lewis, *The Lion, the Witch and the Wardrobe* (London: Collins Lions, 1980), chapters 13–15.

5 *cf.* Augustine's comment: 'The devil jumped for joy when Christ died; and by the very death of Christ the devil was overcome: he took, as it were, the bait in the mousetrap. He rejoiced at the death, thinking himself death's commander. But that which caused his joy dangled the bait before him. The Lord's cross was the devil's mousetrap; the bait which caught him was the death of the Lord' (Sermon 261.1, quoted in Henry Bettenson (ed.), *The Later Christian Fathers* (Oxford: Oxford University Press, 1977), p. 222).

6 *cf.* Gregory's *oratio catechetica (magna)* – his '(Great) Catechetical Oration': 'In order that the exchange for us might be easily accepted by him who sought for it, the divine nature was concealed under the veil of our human nature so that, as with a greedy fish, the hook of divinity might be swallowed along with the bait of flesh' (quoted in Bettenson (ed.), *Later Christian Fathers*, p. 142).

7 See Walker, *Enemy Territory*, chapters 1 and 2. See also Charles Taliaferro, 'A Narnian Theory of the Atonement', *Scottish Journal of Theology* 41 (1988), pp. 75–92.

8 See *The Philokalia*, 3 vols., trans. G. E. H. Palmer, *et al.* (London: Faber & Faber, 1981–4).

9 In recorded conversation, Oxford, August 1987. All subsequent quotations from Mrs Zernov are from this conversation. I wish to thank Mr Jacob Osborne for his help with this recording.

10 For example: C. S. Lewis, *Fern-Seed and Elephants and other essays on Christianity* (London: Collins Fount, 1977), pp. 11–25.

11 C. S. Lewis, *Prayer: Letters to Malcolm* (London: Collins Fount, 1977), p. 12.

12 As Walter Hooper has told me, it is no great secret that Major Lewis was in fact drunk. His absence is confirmed by J. R. R. Tolkien in one of his letters, dated 26 November 1963, which briefly describes Lewis' funeral, and the people who were present at it (see Humphrey Carpenter (ed.), *The Letters of J. R. R. Tolkien* (London: Allen & Unwin, 1981), p. 341).

4 The Christian Influence of G. K. Chesterton on C. S. Lewis

1 C. S. Lewis, *Surprised by Joy* (London: Collins Fount, 1977).

2 G. K. Chesterton, *The Everlasting Man* (London: Hodder & Stoughton, 1925).

3 G. K. Chesterton, *Chaucer* (London: Faber & Faber, 1932).

4   Thomas Carlyle, 'Signs of the Times', *Edinburgh Review* XLIX (June 1829).
5   From the encyclical *De Condicione Opificum* (*'Rerum Novarum'*, 15 May 1891, popularly known and published as *The Worker's Charter*.
6   George MacDonald, *The Princess and the Goblin* (Strahan, 1872).
7   G. K. Chesterton, 'Introduction' to Greville MacDonald, *George MacDonald and His Wife* (London: Allen & Unwin, 1924).
8   G. K. Chesterton, *Autobiography* (London: Hamish Hamilton, 1986), pp. 92–4. (The *Autobiography* was first published in 1936 by Hutchinson & Co.)
9   From G. K. Chesterton, *The Wild Knight and Other Poems* (London: Dent, 1900). Included in the *Collected Poems*.
10 T. S. Eliot, 'The Hollow Men', *Collected Poems 1909–1962* (London: Faber & Faber, 1974), p. 92.
11 From a BBC radio talk broadcast in March 1936, printed in *The Listener*, 18 March 1936, and collected in the book of essays of the same title, *The Great Minimum* (Darwen Finlayson, 1964).
12 C. S. Lewis (ed.), *George MacDonald: An Anthology* (London: Geoffrey Bles, 1946). The selections from MacDonald's works are almost all from the three volumes of *Unspoken Sermons*.
13 G. K. Chesterton, *Orthodoxy* (London: John Lane, 1908).
14 From the report on Chesterton's 'The Future of Religion', an address given to the Heretics Club, Cambridge University, November 1911, in the *Cambridge Daily News*, 18 November 1911. The talk was later reprinted as a separate pamphlet.
15 Chesterton, *Autobiography*, p. 325.
16 Chesterton, *Autobiography*, p. 159.
17 Lewis, *Surprised by Joy*, pp. 153–4.
18 G. K. Chesterton, *The Napoleon of Notting Hill* (London: John Lane, 1904); *What's Wrong With the World* (London: Cassell, 1910); *Eugenics and Other Evils* (London: Cassell, 1922); *William Cobbett* (London: Hodder & Stoughton, 1925); *The Outline of Sanity* (London: Methuen, 1926).
19 This refers to 'The Manchester School', a philosophy of utilitarian economics, strongly opposed to trade unions, minimum wages, *etc*. It was closely associated with Richard Cobden, MP (1804–65).
20 From a letter written by Chesterton during a controversy between himself and Hilaire Belloc in opposition to George Bernard Shaw and H. G. Wells, in *The New Age*, a journal edited by A. R. Orage. The letter appeared in the issue of 4 January 1908. It has not been collected.
21 Dr Johnson (1709–84) is another figure of great influence, revered by both Lewis and Chesterton and frequently quoted by them.
22 Michael D. Aeschliman, *The Restitution of Man: C. S. Lewis and the Case Against Scientism*, Foreword by Malcolm Muggeridge (Grand

Rapids, MI: Wm B. Eerdmans, 1983), pp. 3–4, 5. Aeschliman's book is a brief (94pp.) and brilliant study, and is of great importance to readers of both Lewis and Chesterton.

23 C. S. Lewis, 'Willing Slaves of the Welfare State', *The Observer*, Sunday 20 July 1958, p. 6. This was one of a series of articles by well-known writers on their answers to the questions 'Is man progressing today?' and 'Is progress even possible?' It is collected in C. S. Lewis, *Timeless At Heart* (London: Collins Fount, 1987), pp. 118–24.

24 C. S. Lewis, quoting a friend and applying it also to himself, in C. S. Lewis, with E. M. Tillyard, *The Personal Heresy: A Controversy* (Oxford: Oxford University Press, 1939), p. 49.

25 G. K. Chesterton's long epic poem, *The Ballad of the White Horse* (London: Methuen, 1911), included in the *Collected Poems*. A separate illustrated edition was issued by the same publisher in 1928.

26 C. S. Lewis, 'Notes on the Way', *The Spectator*, 9 November 1946. Not collected.

5 A Peculiar Debt

1 C. S. Lewis, 'Preface' in C. S. Lewis (ed.), *Essays Presented to Charles Williams* (Oxford: Oxford University Press, 1947; Grand Rapids, MI: Wm B. Eerdmans, 1977), p. xiv.

2 *ibid.*

3 Charles Williams, *The Place of the Lion* (1931; London: Faber & Faber, 1965).

4 Nevill Coghill, 'The Approach to English' in Jocelyn Gibb (ed.), *Light on C. S. Lewis* (London: Geoffrey Bles, 1965), p. 62. *Surprised by Joy*, to which Coghill refers, was published in 1955 by Geoffrey Bles and reissued in 1977 by Collins Fount Paperbacks.

5 Erik Routley, 'A Prophet' in James T. Como (ed.), *C. S. Lewis at the Breakfast Table and Other Reminiscences* (London: Collins, 1980), p. 33.

6 *ibid.*, p. 35.

7 Austin Farrer, 'In His Image' in Como (ed.), *C. S. Lewis at the Breakfast Table*, p. 244.

8 Coghill, 'The Approach to English', p. 63.

9 C. S. Lewis, *A Preface to Paradise Lost* (1942; Oxford: Oxford University Press, 1960).

10 *ibid.*, p. v.

11 Charles Williams, *Taliessin Through Logres* (Oxford: Oxford University Press, 1938).

12 Charles Williams, *The Region of the Summer Stars* (London: Editions Poetry, 1944).

13 See C. S. Lewis, *Arthurian Torso* (Oxford: Oxford University Press, 1948), which contained 'the posthumous fragment of "The Figure of Arthur" by Charles Williams and "A Commentary on the Arthurian Poems of Charles Williams" by C. S. Lewis'.

14 Roger Lancelyn Green and Walter Hooper, *C. S. Lewis: A Biography* (London: Collins, 1974), p. 184.

15 Austin Farrer, 'The Christian Apologist' in Gibb (ed.), *Light on C. S. Lewis*, p. 224.

16 I think this is as true of the late essays as it is of the early essays. He faced rationalists, radical biblical critics and liberalising theologians with equal courage and assurance.

17 C. S. Lewis, *Letters to Malcolm: Chiefly on Prayer* (London: Geoffrey Bles, 1964). All references in the text and in the Notes of this essay are to the Collins Fount Paperbacks edition, *Prayer: Letters to Malcolm* (London: Collins Fount, 1977).

18 *ibid.*, pp. 23, 75, 92.

19 Coghill, 'The Approach to English', p. 60.

20 Farrer, 'The Christian Apologist', p. 40.

21 Lewis (ed.), *Essays Presented to Charles Williams*, p. xiii.

22 Lewis, *A Preface to Paradise Lost*, pp. 131 and 97.

23 C. S. Lewis, *The Screwtape Letters* (1942; London: Collins Fount, 1977).

24 C. S. Lewis, *Screwtape Proposes a Toast and other pieces* (London: Collins Fount, 1977).

25 Lewis, *The Screwtape Letters*, pp. 114–15.

26 *ibid.*, p. 112.

27 *ibid.*, p. 160.

28 Charles Williams, *He Came Down From Heaven* (London: Heinemann, 1938).

29 *ibid.*, p. 19.

30 C. S. Lewis, 'The Fall of Man', *The Problem of Pain* (1940; London: Collins Fontana, 1957), pp. 57–76.

31 Lewis, *Prayer: Letters to Malcolm*, p. 106.

32 Williams, *He Came Down From Heaven*, pp. 40 and 42.

33 Lewis, *Prayer: Letters to Malcolm*, pp. 23, 75, 92 are where the aphorism (in its various forms) appears. The mention of Williams' name is on p. 117.

34 Williams, *He Came Down From Heaven*, p. 2.

35 Lewis, *Prayer: Letters to Malcolm*, p. 121.

36 C. S. Lewis, *That Hideous Strength* (1945; London: Pan Books, 1983). All references in the text and in the Notes of this essay are to the Pan edition.

37 Lancelyn Green and Hooper, *C. S. Lewis: A Biography*, p. 174.

38 C. S. Lewis, *Out of the Silent Planet* (1938; London: Pan Books, 1952).

39   C. S. Lewis, *Voyage to Venus (Perelandra)* (1943; London: Pan Books, 1953).
40   Lewis, *That Hideous Strength*, p. 83.
41   Williams, *The Place of the Lion*, p. 31.
42   Lewis, *That Hideous Strength*, pp. 320–42.
43   *The Figure of Arthur* was published in Lewis' *Arthurian Torso*, which also contained Lewis' 'A Commentary on the Arthurian Poems of Charles Williams'.
44   Lewis, *That Hideous Strength*, p. 194.
45   C. S. Lewis, *Till We Have Faces* (1956; London: Collins Fount, 1978).
46   Charles Williams, 'The Way of Exchange' in Anne Ridler (ed.), *The Image of the City and Other Essays* (Oxford: Oxford University Press, 1958), p. 150.
47   Coghill, 'The Approach to English', p. 63.
48   Lewis, *Till We Have Faces*, pp. 311, 316, 319.

6   Journeys into Fantasy

1   The Chronicles of Narnia comprise (in reading order): *The Magician's Nephew* (1955; London: Collins Lions, 1980); *The Lion, the Witch and the Wardrobe* (1950; London: Collins Lions, 1980); *The Horse and His Boy* (1954; London: Collins Lions, 1980); *Prince Caspian* (1951; London: Collins Lions, 1980); *The Voyage of the Dawn Treader* (1952; London: Collins Lions, 1980); *The Silver Chair* (1953; London: Collins Lions, 1980); *The Last Battle* (1956; London: Collins Lions, 1980).
2   C. S. Lewis, *The Screwtape Letters* (London: Collins Fount, 1977).
3   C. S. Lewis, *The Great Divorce* (London: Collins Fount, 1977).
4   C. S. Lewis, *Till We Have Faces* (London: Collins Fount, 1978).
5   C. S. Lewis, *Out of the Silent Planet* (1938; London: Pan Books, 1952).
6   C. S. Lewis, *Voyage to Venus (Perelandra)* (1943; London: Pan Books, 1953). All quotations cited in the Notes to this essay are taken from the Pan edition, although the title given in the text of the essay is *Perelandra*.
7   C. S. Lewis, *That Hideous Strength* (1945; London: Pan Books, 1983).
8   C. S. Lewis, *Surprised by Joy* (London: Collins Fount, 1977), p. 34.
9   H. G. Wells, *The First Men in the Moon* (1901; London: Collins, 1973).
10   David Lindsay, *A Voyage to Arcturus* (London: Methuen, 1920; London: Sphere Books, 1980).
11   C. S. Lewis, 'Unreal Estates' in *Of This and Other Worlds* (London: Collins Fount, 1984), p. 183.
12   C. S. Lewis to Charles A. Brady, 29 October 1944, in *Letters of C. S. Lewis: Edited, with a memoir, by W. H. Lewis*, revised and enlarged edition, ed. Walter Hooper (London: Collins Fount, 1988), p. 375.
13   C. S. Lewis to Ruth Pitter, 4 January 1941, in the Bodleian Library, Oxford, quoted in Muriel Graham, *L'oeuvre romanesque de C. S.*

Lewis, unpublished PhD thesis, Université de Paris III-Sorbonne Nouvelle, 1973, p. 155.

14 David Lindsay, *The Devil's Tor* (1932).
15 C. S. Lewis, 'On Science Fiction' in *Of This and Other Worlds*, p. 94.
16 C. S. Lewis, 'On Stories' in *Of This and Other Worlds*, p. 43.
17 Lewis, 'Unreal Estates', p. 183.
18 For what follows, see also Bernard Sellin, *The Life and Works of David Lindsay* (Cambridge: Cambridge University Press, 1981).
19 David Lindsay, *The Haunted Woman* (1922).
20 Lindsay, *A Voyage to Arcturus*, pp. 286–7.
21 Lewis, 'On Stories', p. 29.
22 *ibid.*, pp. 32–3
23 *ibid.*, p. 33.
24 *ibid.*, p. 35.
25 *ibid.*, p. 35.
26 *ibid.*, pp. 35–6.
27 *ibid.*, p. 43.
28 Roger Lancelyn Green, *Into Other Worlds. Space-Flight in Fiction from Lucian to Lewis* (London: A. Schuman, 1957).
29 Lewis, 'On Science Fiction', in *Of This and Other Worlds*, pp. 80–96.
30 *ibid.*, p. 86.
31 Hélène Tuzet, *Le cosmos et l'imagination* (Paris: J. Corti, 1965).
32 *ibid.*, p. 207.
33 George MacDonald, *Phantastes* (1858).
34 Lewis, *Voyage to Venus (Perelandra)*, p. 149.
35 David Lindsay, *A Voyage to Arcturus*, pp. 59–60.
36 C. S. Lewis, 'The Dark Tower' in *The Dark Tower and Other Stories* (London: Collins Fount, 1983), p. 33.
37 Lindsay, *A Voyage to Arcturus*, p. 45.
38 Lewis, *Voyage to Venus (Perelandra)*, p. 32.
39 Lewis, 'The Dark Tower', p. 29.
40 Gunnar Urang, *Shadows of Heaven: Religion and Fantasy in the Fiction of C. S. Lewis, Charles Williams and J. R. R. Tolkien* (London: SCM Press, 1971), p. 5.
41 David Lindsay, *The Witch* (1947).
42 George MacDonald, *Lilith* (London: Chatto & Windus, 1895).
43 Lewis, *Surprised by Joy*, pp. 144–6.
44 C. S. Lewis (ed.), 'Introduction' to *George MacDonald: An Anthology* (London: Geoffrey Bles, 1946).
45 J. B. Pick, C. Wilson and E. H. Visiak, *The Strange Genius of David Lindsay* (London: John Baker, 1970), p. 98.
46 Lewis, 'On Science Fiction', p. 93.

7 Elusive Birds and Narrative Nets

1 John Warwick Montgomery, 'The Chronicles of Narnia and the Adolescent Reader', *Journal of Religious Education* 54 (Sept–Oct 1959), p. 423, quoting Frank M. Gardner, 'The Carnegie Medal Award for 1956', *Library Association Record* 59 (May 1957), p. 168.

2 D. E. Myers, 'The Compleat Anglican: Spiritual Style in the Chronicles of Narnia', *Anglican Theological Review* 66 (April 1984), p. 148.

The publication details of the Chronicles of Narnia are, in chronological order, as follows: *The Lion, the Witch and the Wardrobe* (London: Geoffrey Bles, 1950); *Prince Caspian* (London: Geoffrey Bles, 1951); *The Voyage of the Dawn Treader* (London: Geoffrey Bles, 1952); *The Silver Chair* (London: Geoffrey Bles, 1953); *The Horse and His Boy* (London: Geoffrey Bles, 1954); *The Magician's Nephew* (London: The Bodley Head, 1955); *The Last Battle* (London: The Bodley Head, 1956).

In reading order the sequence is: *The Magician's Nephew*; *The Lion, the Witch and the Wardrobe*; *The Horse and His Boy*; *Prince Caspian*; *The Voyage of the Dawn Treader*; *The Silver Chair*; and *The Last Battle*.

The Chronicles of Narnia have been reprinted by Collins Lions (1980), and all subsequent references in the Notes that follow (with the exception of Note 7) are to the Collins Lions editions.

3 See C. S. Lewis, *Of This and Other Worlds* (London: Collins Fount, 1984): 'On Three Ways of Writing for Children' (1952), pp. 56–70; 'Sometimes Fairy Stories May Say Best What's to be Said' (1956), pp. 71–5; 'On Juvenile Tastes' (1958), pp. 75–8; and 'It All Began with a Picture . . .' (1960), pp. 78–9.

4 C. S. Lewis, 'On Stories' in *Of This and Other Worlds*, pp. 25–45.

5 *ibid.*, pp. 38–9.

6 Lewis, *The Voyage of the Dawn Treader*, p. 7.

7 C. S. Lewis, *The Voyage of the Dawn Treader* (New York: Macmillan, 1952), p. 5. The reading of the Macmillan edition fits both the situation and Eustace's subsequent development as a character better than the reading of the Bles/Collins Lions edition, 'as he was far too stupid to make anything up himself' (p. 10).

8 Lewis, *The Voyage of the Dawn Treader*, p. 70.

9 Lewis, 'On Stories', pp. 28–9.

10 *ibid.*, p. 42.

11 *ibid.*

12 *ibid.*

13 *ibid.*, p. 27.

14 *ibid.*, p. 28.

15 Lewis, *The Voyage of the Dawn Treader*, p. 139.

16 Lewis, 'On Stories', p. 29.

234   A CHRISTIAN FOR ALL CHRISTIANS

17 C. S. Lewis, 'On Science Fiction' in *Of This and Other Worlds*, pp. 80–96.
18 C. S. Lewis, *Out of the Silent Planet* (London: Pan Books, 1952).
19 C. S. Lewis, *Voyage to Venus (Perelandra)* (London: Pan Books, 1953).
20 'If you want to plunge into . . . the very quiddity of some Narnian countryside, you must go to what Lewis considered the loveliest spot he had ever seen. It is in the Carlingford Mountains of southern Ireland', Walter Hooper, quoted in Douglas Gilbert and Clyde S. Kilby, *C. S. Lewis: Images of His World* (Grand Rapids, MI: Wm B. Eerdmans, 1973), p. 143.
21 Lewis, *The Lion, the Witch and the Wardrobe*, pp. 14–15.
22 *ibid.*, ch. 2, 'What Lucy found there'.
23 *ibid.*, p. 53.
24 See Walter Hooper's Preface to Kathryn Ann Lindskoog, *The Lion of Judah in Never-Never Land* (Grand Rapids, MI: Wm B. Eerdmans, 1973), p. 14.
25 Lewis, *The Lion, the Witch and the Wardrobe*, p. 70.
26 Lewis, 'On Stories', p. 37.
27 *ibid.*, p. 38.
28 Lewis, 'On Science Fiction', p. 90.
29 *ibid.*, p. 93.
30 Lewis, *The Magician's Nephew*, pp. 93–4.
31 Lewis, *The Voyage of the Dawn Treader*, p. 159.
32 Lewis, 'On Stories', p. 39.
33 Lewis, *The Last Battle*, pp. 46–8.
34 *ibid.*, pp. 167, 169.
35 *ibid.*, p. 161.
36 C. S. Lewis, *The Great Divorce: A Dream* (London: Geoffrey Bles, 1946), p. 9.
37 C. S. Lewis, 'Equality' (1943), in *Present Concerns* (London: Collins Fount, 1986), p. 18.
38 *ibid.*, p. 19.
39 *ibid.*, p. 20.
40 C. S. Lewis, 'Rejoinder to Dr Pittenger' in *Timeless at Heart* (London: Collins Fount, 1987), p. 114.
41 Lewis, 'On Stories', p. 37.
42 Lewis, *The Lion, the Witch and the Wardrobe*, p. 75.
43 Lewis, *The Voyage of the Dawn Treader*, pp. 186–7.
44 *ibid.*, p. 188.
45 C. S. Lewis, *Miracles* (London: Collins Fount, 1977).
46 C. S. Lewis, *Mere Christianity* (London: Collins Fount, 1977).
47 Lewis, 'On Stories', p. 40.
48 For example: 'Peter deserves the role of the Apostle Paul . . . Lucy is

much like John, the disciple whom Jesus loved . . . For a long time [Edmund] seems to be Judas . . . but he does come round in the end, rather in the fashion of the Apostle Peter', Paul A. Karkainen, *Narnia Explored* (Old Tappen, NJ: Fleming H. Revel Co., 1979), pp. 15–16.

49 Lewis, 'On Stories', p. 44.
50 *ibid.*, p. 45.

8 C. S. Lewis the Myth-Maker

1 C. S. Lewis, *Voyage to Venus (Perelandra)* (London: Pan Books, 1953), p. 131. The original (1943) title was *Perelandra*. All quotations in the text and the Notes are taken from the Pan edition. *Perelandra* is used throughout the text of this essay; *Voyage to Venus (Perelandra)* is used throughout these Notes.

2 William Shakespeare, *A Midsummer Night's Dream*, 5.1.2–3.

3 *ibid.*, 4.1.196–7.

4 Walter Hooper (ed.), *They Stand Together: The Letters of C. S. Lewis to Arthur Greeves (1914–1963)* (London: Collins, 1979), p. 427. Lewis is reporting a crucial conversation with J. R. R. Tolkien and Hugo Dyson on the night of 19 September 1931.

5 C. S. Lewis, 'Myth Became Fact' in *God in the Dock* (London: Collins Fount, 1979), pp. 43–4.

6 See C. S. Lewis, *Mere Christianity* (London: Collins Fount, 1977), p. 51; 'Religion Without Dogma?' in *Timeless at Heart* (London: Collins Fount, 1987), pp. 86–8.

7 Lewis, 'Myth Became Fact', p. 44. See also C. S. Lewis, *Miracles* (London: Collins Fount, 1977), p. 138, n. 1: 'The story of Christ demands . . . an imaginative response.'

8 Lewis, *Mere Christianity*, p. 55.

9 Hooper (ed.), *They Stand Together*, p. 428.

10 See, for example, C. S. Lewis, *The Pilgrim's Regress* (London: Collins Fount, 1977), p. 217: 'mythology . . . is but truth, not fact'.

11 Notably Rudolf Bultmann, 'New Testament and Mythology: The Mythological Element in the Message of the New Testament and the Problem of its Re-interpretation' in H. W. Bartsch (ed.), *Kerygma and Myth: A Theological Debate*, trans. R. H. Fuller (London: SPCK, 1953), pp. 1–44.

12 *e.g.*, John Knox, *Myth and Truth* (London: Kingsgate Press, 1964), pp. 51–64.

13 See, for example, W. Pannenberg, 'Kerygma and History' in *Basic Questions in Theology*, trans. G. H. Kehm (London: SCM Press, 1970), vol. 1, pp. 81–95.

14 So, for example, David Tracy, *The Analogical Imagination: Christian Theology and the Culture of Pluralism* (London: SCM Press, 1981).

15 Lewis, *Voyage to Venus (Perelandra)*, p. 92.

16 C. S. Lewis, 'Forms of Things Unknown' in *The Dark Tower and Other Stories* (London: Collins Fount, 1983), pp. 124–32.
17 Shakespeare, *A Midsummer Night's Dream*, 5.1.
18 C. S. Lewis, 'Sometimes Fairy Stories May Say Best What's to be Said' in *Of This and Other Worlds* (London: Collins Fount, 1984), pp. 72–3.
19 C. S. Lewis to Sister Penelope, 9 August 1939, cited in *Of This and Other Worlds*, p. 19.
20 C. S. Lewis, *Out of the Silent Planet* (London: Pan Books, 1952).
21 Lewis, *Voyage to Venus (Perelandra)*, pp. 110, 131–2, 134, 136, 140, 168.
22 *ibid.*, p. 55.
23 C. S. Lewis, *That Hideous Strength* (London: Pan Books, 1983).
24 *ibid.*, p. 55.
25 *e.g.*, Deuteronomy 32:8; Psalm 82; Ephesians 6:10–12. For an exposition of this biblical theme, see G. B. Caird, *Principalities and Powers* (Oxford: Clarendon Press, 1956).
26 Lewis, *Out of the Silent Planet*, p. 178; *cf.* C. S. Lewis, *The Allegory of Love* (Oxford: Oxford University Press, 1936), p. 362.
27 Lewis, *Voyage to Venus (Perelandra)*, pp. 182–3.
28 For the foregoing, see Romans 8:19–23; Psalm 8; Isaiah 11:6–9; Job 5:22–3; Hebrews 2:5–9; 1 Corinthians 15:42–5; 2 Corinthians 5:17.
29 Galatians 4:1–7; *cf.* Galatians 3:19. Lewis, *Voyage to Venus (Perelandra)*, p. 182.
30 Lewis, *That Hideous Strength*, p. 285.
31 C. S. Lewis, 'On Stories' in *Of This and Other Worlds*, p. 36.
32 C. S. Lewis, 'Is Theology Poetry?' in *Screwtape Proposes a Toast and other pieces* (London: Collins Fount, 1977), p. 44.
33 Lewis, *That Hideous Strength*, p. 287.
34 *ibid.*, p. 288.
35 *ibid.*, p. 289.
36 Lewis, 'Is Theology Poetry?', p. 46.
37 Lewis, *Out of the Silent Planet*, pp. 83, 84.
38 C. S. Lewis, *The Lion, the Witch and the Wardrobe* (London: Collins Lions, 1980), p. 37.
39 Lewis, *Voyage to Venus (Perelandra)*, p. 61.
40 *ibid.*
41 *ibid.*, p. 198.
42 *ibid.*, pp. 132.
43 *ibid.*
44 *ibid.*
45 *ibid.*
46 *ibid.*, p. 201.
47 Paul Tillich, *Systematic Theology* (Welwyn: James Nisbet, 1957), vol. 2, pp. 84–5.

48 Lewis, *Mere Christianity*, p. 139.
49 Lewis, *Out of the Silent Planet*, pp. 78, 99.
50 Lewis, *Voyage to Venus (Perelandra)*, p. 195.
51 Genesis 3:15. Charles Williams uses the 'dolorous stroke' of Balin as an image for the fall in 'Lamorak and the Queen Morgause of Orkney', *Taliessen Through Logres* (Oxford: Oxford University Press, 1969), pp. 39–41. For Lewis' use of the Arthurian myth in this novel, see Charles Moorman, *Arthurian Triptych* (University of California Press, 1960), pp. 116ff.
52 Lewis, *That Hideous Strength*, p. 291.
53 Lewis, *Voyage to Venus (Perelandra)*, p. 204, cf. p. 135.
54 C. S. Lewis, *The Voyage of the Dawn Treader* (London: Collins Lions, 1980), p. 188.
55 C. S. Lewis, *The Last Battle* (London: Collins Lions, 1980), p. 132.
56 C. S. Lewis, 'The Dark Tower' in *The Dark Tower and Other Stories*, pp. 17–91.
57 C. S. Lewis, *The Magician's Nephew* (London: Collins Lions, 1980).
58 Lewis, *The Lion, the Witch and the Wardrobe*, p. 75.
59 C. S. Lewis, *Prince Caspian* (London: Collins Lions, 1980), pp. 136–8, 168–9.
60 Lewis, *The Voyage of the Dawn Treader*, chapter 14.
61 Lewis, *The Lion, the Witch and the Wardrobe*, pp. 97–101.
62 Lewis, *The Voyage of the Dawn Treader*, p. 187.
63 Lewis, 'Myth Became Fact', p. 43.
64 Lewis, *The Lion, the Witch and the Wardrobe*, p. 148. Lewis allows the same openness of meaning in his doctrinal treatment of the atonement, in *Mere Christianity*, pp. 53–8.
65 C. S. Lewis, *The Silver Chair* (London: Collins Lions, 1980), pp. 187–8.
66 Lewis, *The Magician's Nephew*, p. 108.
67 Lewis, *The Last Battle*, chs 12–14.
68 Lewis, *The Voyage of the Dawn Treader*.
69 Lewis, *The Lion, the Witch and the Wardrobe*, p. 166.
70 C. S. Lewis, *Prince Caspian* (London: Geoffrey Bles, 1951), p. 125.
71 C. S. Lewis, *The Horse and His Boy* (London: Collins Lions, 1980), p. 128.
72 Lewis, *The Last Battle*, ch. 13.
73 On this, see Lionel Adey, *C. S. Lewis's 'Great War' with Owen Barfield* (University of Victoria, 1978), pp. 83–91.
74 Lewis, *Prince Caspian*, p. 125.
75 Lewis, *The Horse and His Boy*, pp. 130, 158.
76 Lewis, *The Last Battle*, p. 155.
77 *ibid.*, p. 171.
78 *ibid.*, p. 170.

238   A CHRISTIAN FOR ALL CHRISTIANS

C. S. Lewis, *Till We Have Faces* (London: Collins Fount, 1978), p. 302.
80 C. S. Lewis to Clyde Kilby, 10 February 1957, in Walter Hooper (ed.), *Letters of C. S. Lewis: Edited, with a Memoir by W. H. Lewis* (London: Collins Fount, 1988), p. 462.
81 See Lewis, *Till We Have Faces*, p. 57.
82 *ibid.*, pp. 318–19.
83 Salvation as divinisation was a central theme of the *De Incarnatione* of Athanasius, to a translation of which Lewis wrote an Introduction (London: Geoffrey Bles, 1944).
84 C. S. Lewis, *The Four Loves* (London: Collins Fontana, 1963), p. 95.
85 *e.g.*, Jurgen Moltmann, *The Trinity and the Kingdom of God: The Doctrine of God*, trans. Margaret Kohl (London: SCM Press, 1981), pp. 52–60.
86 Lewis, *Till We Have Faces*, p. 253.
87 *ibid.*, p. 305.
88 *ibid.*, p. 306.
89 *ibid.*, p. 287.
90 C. S. Lewis, *Prayer: Letters to Malcolm* (London: Collins Fount, 1977), pp. 22–3.
91 Lewis, *Till We Have Faces*, p. 319; *cf.* Job 42:1–6.
92 *ibid.*, p. 315; *cf.* Jeremiah 31:31–4; Ezekiel 36:26–7.
93 2 Corinthians 3:16–18, RSV; *cf.* John 1:16–18.
94 Lewis, *Till We Have Faces*, p. 182.
95 *ibid.*
96 Lewis, *The Lion, the Witch and the Wardrobe*, ch. 15.
97 Lewis summarises this idea in *Arthurian Torso* (Oxford: Oxford University Press, 1948; repr. 1969), p. 123.
98 Peter J. Schakel, *Reason and Imagination in C. S. Lewis* (Grand Rapids, MI: Wm B. Eerdmans, 1984), pp. 161–2.

9 C. S. Lewis and Idealism

The Lewis Papers and Journals in the Wade Collection at Wheaton College, Illinois, are referred to in the following Notes as LP and LJ respectively, and references to these sources are given in brackets by volume and page numbers.
1 C. S. Lewis, *Spirits in Bondage: A Cycle of Lyrics* (London: William Heinemann, 1919), published under the pseudonym Clive Hamilton.
2 C. S. Lewis to Albert Lewis, 14 August 1925, in Walter Hooper (ed.), *Letters of C. S. Lewis: Edited, with a Memoir by W. H. Lewis* (London: Collins Fount, 1988), p. 211.
3 C. S. Lewis, *The Pilgrim's Regress* (London: Collins Fount, 1977), p. 9. *The Pilgrim's Regress* was first published in London by Geoffrey Bles in 1933.

4   C. S. Lewis to Arthur Greeves, 2 December 1918, in Walter Hooper (ed.), *They Stand Together: The Letters of C. S. Lewis to Arthur Greeves (1914–1963)* (London: Collins, 1979), p. 239.
5   C. S. Lewis to Arthur Greeves, 12 September 1918, in Hooper (ed.), *They Stand Together*, p. 230.
6   C. S. Lewis, *Surprised by Joy* (London: Collins Fount, 1977), p. 168.
7   James Patrick, *The Magdalen Metaphysicals: Idealism and Orthodoxy at Oxford, 1901–1945* (Macon, GA: Mercer University Press, 1985), p. 114; LJ, 1, 23 June 1922; 9, 10 March 1924 (8: 148, 196–198); see also Hooper (ed.), *Letters of C. S. Lewis*, pp. 163–4, 191–2.
8   Patrick, *Magdalen Metaphysicals*, p. 116; C. S. Lewis to Albert Lewis, undated, 1925 (LP 8:225); 14 March; 6, 14, 26 May; 3 June 1924 (LP 8:202, 224, 229, 236); see also C. S. Lewis to Albert Lewis, 11 May 1924, in Hooper (ed.), *Letters of C. S. Lewis*, pp. 193–4.
9   Lewis, *Surprised by Joy*, p. 168.
10 *ibid.*, pp. 170–2.
11 Patrick, *Magdalen Metaphysicals*, pp. 35, 93.
12 H. J. Paton, 'Fifty Years of Philosophy' in H. D. Lewis (ed.), *Contemporary British Philosophy*, Third Series (London: Allen & Unwin, 1956), p. 340.
13 Patrick, *Magdalen Metaphysicals*, pp. 59–64.
14 See Hooper (ed.), *They Stand Together*, p. 10; Lewis, *Surprised by Joy*, pp. 52–3.
15 Lewis, *Surprised by Joy*, pp. 141–4 (the quotation is from p. 142).
16 Lewis, *Surprised by Joy*, p. 163; see also C. S. Lewis to Arthur Greeves, 22 April 1923, in Hooper (ed.), *They Stand Together*, pp. 292–3, where the man is identified as Dr John Askins.
17 C. S. Lewis letter to Albert Lewis, March 1924 (8:198); LJ, 12 May 1924 (8:228).
18 See C. S. Lewis, *Prayer: Letters to Malcolm* (London: Collins Fount, 1977), pp. 75–7. Originally published as *Letters to Malcolm: Chiefly on Prayer* (London: Geoffrey Bles, 1964), this was Lewis' last book and was published shortly after his death. All subsequent quotations are taken from the Collins Fount Paperbacks edition of 1977, which appeared under the title *Prayer: Letters to Malcolm*.
19 Lewis, *Surprised by Joy*, p. 119.
20 *ibid.*, p. 178. A copy of the philosophy lectures of 1924 is in the Wade Collection.
21 See Lewis' essay 'On the Reading of Old Books' in *First and Second Things* (London: Collins Fount, 1985), pp. 25–33. The essays collected in *First and Second Things* also appeared in Lewis' *God in the Dock: Essays on Theology and Ethics* (Grand Rapids, MI: Wm B. Eerdmans, 1970) and in his *Undeceptions* (London: Geoffrey Bles, 1971). All

subsequent quotations from the essay 'On the Reading of Old Books' are taken from the Collins Fount Paperbacks edition of *First and Second Things*.

22 C. S. Lewis, *That Hideous Strength* (London: Pan Books, 1983), p. 299. *That Hideous Strength* was first published by John Lane (the Bodley Head) in 1945.

23 C. S. Lewis, 'Religion Without Dogma?' in *Timeless at Heart* (London: Collins Fount, 1987), pp. 102–4.

24 See Herbert Warren to C. S. Lewis, 4 November 1922, J. A. Smith Papers, III:3, Magdalen College Archives; Patrick, *Magdalen Metaphysicals*, p. 115.

25 See C. S. Lewis, *The Abolition of Man* (1943; London: Collins Fount, 1978); 'On Ethics' in *Christian Reflections* (1967; London: Collins Fount, 1981), pp. 65–79.

26 C. S. Lewis, *The Allegory of Love* (Oxford: Oxford University Press, 1936), p. vii.

27 Lewis, *Surprised by Joy*, p. 178.

28 Lewis, *Pilgrim's Regress*, pp. 89–92.

29 *ibid.*, pp. 7–10; see also C. S. Lewis, *Narrative Poems* (London: Geoffrey Bles, 1969), pp. 4–5.

30 Lewis, *Allegory of Love*, p. 48.

31 C. S. Lewis, J. A. Smith and Clement C. J. Webb, the public representatives at Oxford of the persisting idealism of Green and Bradley, mistrusted neo-scholasticism and disliked its representatives. See Patrick, *Magdalen Metaphysicals*, pp. 140–2.

32 Christopher Derrick, *C. S. Lewis and the Church of Rome* (San Francisco: St Ignatius Press, 1981), pp. 31–2.

33 Lewis, *Allegory of Love*, p. 323.

34 *ibid.*, p. 323.

35 *ibid.*, pp. 44–5.

36 Derrick, *Lewis and the Church of Rome*, p. 29.

37 Lewis, *Prayer: Letters to Malcolm*, pp. 46–7, 93.

38 *ibid.*, p. 75.

39 *ibid.*, p. 76.

40 C. S. Lewis, *Mere Christianity* (London: Collins Fount, 1977), pp. 92–101. The comment about the imposition of monogamy on Muslims occurs on p. 99.

41 Humphrey Carpenter (ed.), *The Letters of J. R. R. Tolkien* (London: Allen & Unwin, 1981), pp. 59–62.

42 Lewis, *Allegory of Love*, p. 46.

43 Lewis, *Prayer: Letters to Malcolm*, pp. 105–6.

44 C. S. Lewis, 'Myth Became Fact' in *God in the Dock* (London: Collins Fount, 1979), pp. 39–45.

45 Lewis, *Prayer: Letters to Malcolm*, p. 104.

46 C. S. Lewis, *Letters to Children*, eds. Lyle W. Dorsett and Marjorie Lamp Mead (New York: Macmillan, 1985), p. 52.
47 *e.g.* C. S. Lewis, *Voyage to Venus (Perelandra)* (London: Pan Books, 1953), p. 55.
48 The Fathers of the second and third centuries faced this criticism and, with the exception of Origen, argued that there must be some identity between the body of the saints in this life and the resurrected life belonging to the new creation. St Justin Martyr, St Irenaeus, St Athenagoras and St Methodius wrote treatises on the resurrection, making this argument.
49 Lewis, *Prayer: Letters to Malcolm*, p. 121.
50 *ibid.*, p. 76.
51 Lewis, *Mere Christianity*, pp. 11–12.
52 Lewis, *Allegory of Love*, p. 323.
53 C. S. Lewis, *Miracles: A Preliminary Study* (London: Geoffrey Bles, 1947) contained the original argument that naturalism is always self-refuting. The debate with G. E. M. Anscombe took place in 1948. *Miracles* was subsequently revised and appeared in a second edition (1960) which attempted to avoid Anscombe's earlier criticisms. There is an account of the debate in Humphrey Carpenter, *The Inklings* (London: Allen & Unwin, 1978), pp. 216–17 and Anscombe has herself commented on the debate in her collected papers. See also the essay 'Did C. S. Lewis Lose his Faith?' by Richard L. Purtill, pp. 27–62 of this book.
54 Derrick, *Lewis and the Church of Rome*, p. 213.
55 *cf.* Hooper (ed.), *Letters of C. S. Lewis*, p. 444.
56 Lewis, *Voyage to Venus*, chapter 7; see also n. 47.
57 C. S. Lewis, *The Screwtape Letters* (London: Collins Fount, 1977).

10 'Look Out! It's Alive!'
1 C. S. Lewis, 'Dogma and the Universe' in *God in the Dock* (London: Collins Fount, 1979), p. 33.
2 C. S. Lewis, *Mere Christianity* (London: Collins Fount, 1977), p. 55.
3 C. S. Lewis, 'Christian Apologetics' in *Timeless at Heart* (London: Collins Fount, 1987), p. 14.
4 C. S. Lewis, *The Problem of Pain* (London: Collins Fount, 1977), p. 12.
5 R. C. Moberley, 'The Incarnation as the Basis of Dogma' in Charles Gore (ed.), *Lux Mundi: A Series of Studies in the Religion of the Incarnation* (1889; London: John Murray, [15]1904), p. 158.
6 Lewis, 'Christian Apologetics', p. 15.
7 Lewis, *The Problem of Pain*, p. 125.
8 Lewis, *Mere Christianity*, pp. 53–4.
9 C. S. Lewis, 'Is Theism Important?' in *Timeless at Heart*, p. 107.

10 C. S. Lewis, *The Pilgrim's Regress* (London: Collins Fount, 1977), p. 219.
11 Aubrey Moore, 'The Christian Doctrine of God' in Gore (ed.), *Lux Mundi*, p. 49.
12 C. S. Lewis, 'Learning in War-Time' in *Fern-seed and Elephants and Other Essays on Christianity* (London: Collins Fount, 1977), p. 31.
13 Lewis, *Mere Christianity*, p. 61.
14 See the chapter entitled 'The New Men' in Lewis, *Mere Christianity*, pp. 181–9.
15 *ibid.*, p. 159.
16 C. S. Lewis, *Miracles* (London: Collins Fount, 1977), pp. 90–1.
17 *ibid.*, p. 91.
18 *ibid.*, p. 95.
19 C. S. Lewis, *Voyage to Venus (Perelandra)* (London: Pan Books, 1953), p. 28. (References in the text are simply to *Perelandra*; quotations in the text, and references to them in these Notes, are from the 1953 Pan Books edition, *Voyage to Venus (Perelandra)*.)
20 C. S. Lewis, *Out of the Silent Planet* (London: Pan Books, 1952), pp. 62, 152–3.
21 C. S. Lewis, *That Hideous Strength* (London: Pan Books, 1983), p. 322.
22 C. S. Lewis, *The Lion, the Witch and the Wardrobe* (London: Collins Lions, 1980), p. 74.
23 C. S. Lewis, *Surprised by Joy* (London: Collins Fount, 1977), p. 20.
24 *ibid.*, p. 20.
25 *ibid.*, p. 62.
26 C. S. Lewis, 'The Weight of Glory' in *Screwtape Proposes a Toast* (London: Collins Fount, 1977), pp. 94–110.
27 C. S. Lewis, *Till We Have Faces* (London: Collins Fount, 1978).
28 *cf.* C. S. Lewis with E. M. Tillyard, *The Personal Heresy: A Controversy* (London: Oxford University Press, 1939), pp. 1–30.
29 *cf.* C. S. Lewis, 'Meditation in a Toolshed' in *First and Second Things* (London: Collins Fount, 1985), pp. 50–4.
30 C. S. Lewis, 'What Chaucer did to *Il Filostrato*' in *Selected Literary Essays* (Cambridge: Cambridge University Press, 1969), p. 44.
31 C. S. Lewis, 'Myth Became Fact' in *God in the Dock*, p. 43.
32 *ibid.*, p. 41.
33 Lewis, 'Hero and Leander' in *Selected Literary Essays*, p. 67.
34 This is not exactly to mean that Lewis is aiming at 'medievalising' us as Chaucer 'medievalised' Boccaccio: beyond the 'discarded image' of the Old Model there is the whole continent of outer reality, of the universal world to which, according to Lewis' own form of Platonism, we truly belong.
35 *cf.* Lewis and Tillyard, *The Personal Heresy*, pp. 1–30.

36 *cf.* Lewis, *Voyage to Venus (Perelandra)*, p. 27.
37 Lewis, *The Pilgrim's Regress*, p. 15.
38 Lewis, *Surprised by Joy*, p. 190.
39 C. S. Lewis, 'On the Reading of Old Books' in *First and Second Things*, p. 29.
40 C. S. Lewis, *The Great Divorce* (London: Collins Fount, 1977), p. 41.
41 Lewis, *Mere Christianity*, pp. 11–12.
42 C. S. Lewis, *The Silver Chair* (London: Collins Lions, 1980), p. 27.
43 *cf.* C. S. Lewis, 'On Obstinacy in Belief' in *Screwtape Proposes a Toast*, pp. 59–74.
44 *cf.* Lewis, *Miracles*, p. 46, for a wholly different use of the word.
45 *cf.* Lewis, *That Hideous Strength*, ch. 13, 'They Have Pulled Down Deep Heaven on Their Heads', part 1, pp. 271–4.
46 Lewis, *The Pilgrim's Regress*, p. 15.
47 *ibid.*, p. 20.
48 Charles Gore, *The Incarnation of the Son of God, being The Bampton Lectures for the Year 1891* (London: John Murray, 1891), p. 185.
49 *ibid.*
50 *cf.* Christopher Derrick, *C. S. Lewis and the Church of Rome: A Study in Proto-Ecumenism* (San Francisco: Ignatius Press, 1981), pp. 73ff. for a discussion of this subject.
51 Lewis, *The Pilgrim's Regress*, p. 18.
52 C. S. Lewis, *Reflections on the Psalms* (London: Collins Fount, 1977), p. 95.
53 Lewis, *The Pilgrim's Regress*, pp. 128–31.
54 C. S. Lewis, 'Is Theology Poetry?' in *Screwtape Proposes a Toast*, p. 41.
55 Lewis, 'Myth Became Fact', p. 45.
56 Gore, *The Incarnation of the Son of God*, p. 188.
57 C. S. Lewis, *The Allegory of Love* (Oxford: Oxford University Press, 1936).
58 C. S. Lewis, *Letters to Malcolm: Chiefly on Prayer* (London: Geoffrey Bles, 1964). *Letters to Malcolm* was later reissued as *Prayer: Letters to Malcolm* (London: Collins Fount, 1977).
59 Lewis, *Mere Christianity*, p. 6.
60 John Bunyan, *The Pilgrim's Progress*, ed. with an introduction by Roger Sharrock (Harmondsworth: Penguin Books, 1987), p. 195.
61 C. S. Lewis, *The Abolition of Man* (London: Collins Fount, 1978), ch. 1.
62 Lewis, *That Hideous Strength*, p. 185.
63 Lewis, *The Abolition of Man*, p. 13.
64 C. S. Lewis, 'On the Transmission of Christianity' in *First and Second Things*, p. 67.
65 Lewis, *Out of the Silent Planet*, p. 180.

66 Lewis, *Miracles*, p. 95.
67 C. S. Lewis, 'Fern-seed and Elephants' in *Fern-Seed and Elephants*, p. 107.
68 Lewis, *The Pilgrim's Regress*, p. 219.
69 C. S. Lewis, *The Last Battle* (London: Collins Lions, 1980), p. 172.
70 John Smith, quoted in Moore, 'The Christian Doctrine of God' in Gore (ed.), *Lux Mundi*, p. 65.

11   How to Save Western Civilisation

1   C. S. Lewis, *'De Descriptione Temporum'*, in *Selected Literary Essays* (Cambridge: Cambridge University Press, 1969), p. 3.
2   C. S. Lewis, *English Literature in the Sixteenth Century Excluding Drama* (Oxford: Oxford University Press, 1973), pp. 63–4.
3   C. S. Lewis, *Reflections on the Psalms* (London: Collins Fount, 1977), p. 102.
4   C. S. Lewis, *Miracles* (London: Collins Fount, 1977), pp. 90–1.
5   C. S. Lewis, *A Preface to Paradise Lost* (Oxford: Oxford University Press, 1960), p. 57.
6   *ibid.*
7   C. S. Lewis, *The Allegory of Love* (Oxford: Oxford University Press, 1936), p. 1.
8   Walter Hooper (ed.), *Letters of C. S. Lewis: Edited, with a Memoir by W. H. Lewis* (London: Collins Fount, 1988), p. 294.
9   C. S. Lewis, 'The Funeral of a Great Myth' in *Christian Reflections* (London: Collins Fount, 1981).
10 C. S. Lewis, 'The Poison of Subjectivism' in *Christian Reflections*.
11 *ibid.*, p. 102.
12 *ibid.*, p. 103.
13 *ibid.*
14 C. S. Lewis, *The Problem of Pain* (London: Collins Fount, 1977), p. 122.
15 C. S. Lewis, *The Discarded Image* (Cambridge: Cambridge University Press, 1964), pp. 74–5, 85.
16 C. S. Lewis, *Surprised by Joy* (London: Collins Fount, 1977), p. 167.
17 *ibid.*, p. 167.
18 C. S. Lewis, 'Historicism' in *Christian Reflections*, p. 134.
19 C. S. Lewis, *An Experiment in Criticism* (Cambridge: Cambridge University Press, 1961), pp. 105–6.
20 Hooper (ed.), *Letters of C. S. Lewis*, p. 343.
21 Lewis, *Surprised by Joy*, p. 60.
22 *ibid.*, p.170.
23 Alan Watts, *Behold the Spirit* (New York: Vintage Books, 1971), p. 186.

24 Lewis, Chapter 4, 'Human Wickedness', *The Problem of Pain*, pp. 43–56.
25 Lewis, *The Discarded Image*, p. 203.
26 *ibid.*, p. 100.
27 Lewis, *English Literature in the Sixteenth Century*, p. 62.
28 see *ibid.*, pp. 13–14.
29 C. S. Lewis, 'A Cliché Came Out of its Cage', *Poems* (London: Geoffrey Bles, 1964), p. 3.
30 C. S. Lewis, *The Abolition of Man* (London: Collins Fount, 1978), p. 46.
31 For 'the poison of subjectivism', see pp. 194–5. For a discussion of the Tao, see Chapter 2, 'The Way', and the Appendix, 'Illustrations of the Tao', of Lewis' *The Abolition of Man*, pp. 21–33 and pp. 49–59 respectively.
32 Fyodor Dostoyevsky, *The Brothers Karamazov*, tr. and introduced David Magarshack (Harmondsworth: Penguin Books, 1982), p. 309.
33 W. H. Auden, '1st September 1939', quoted from John Hayward (ed.), *The Penguin Book of English Verse* (Harmondsworth: Penguin Books, 1956), p. 454.
34 Sigmund Freud, *Civilization and Its Discontents* (1930), vol. 21 of *The Standard Edition of the Compete Psychological Works of Sigmund Freud*, ed. James Strachey (London: Hogarth Press, 1953–74). For a discussion of *Civilization and Its Discontents* see also Robert Bocock, *Freud and Modern Society* (Walton-on-Thames: Thomas Nelson, 1976), chapter 6, 'Instincts and Society', pp. 103–27.
35 C. S. Lewis, *That Hideous Strength* (London: Pan Books, 1983), p. 293.
36 C. S. Lewis, *The Pilgrim's Regress* (London: Collins Fount, 1977).
37 Lewis, *The Discarded Image*, p. 42.
38 William Shakespeare, *Hamlet* 1.5.166–7.
39 Lewis, *English Literature in the Sixteenth Century*, p. 4.
40 C. S. Lewis, 'The Empty Universe' in *Present Concerns* (London: Collins Fount, 1986), p. 81. 'The Empty Universe' is Walter Hooper's title for Lewis' Preface to D. E. Harding, *The Hierarchy of Heaven and Earth* (London: Faber & Faber, 1952).
41 See C. S. Lewis, *The Four Loves* (London: Collins Fount, 1963).
42 See C. S. Lewis, 'First and Second Things' in *First and Second Things* (London: Collins Fount, 1985), pp. 19–24.
43 *ibid.*, p. 23.
44 *ibid.*, pp. 23–4.
45 Thomas Aquinas, *Summa Theologica* 1–11, 4, 1, ad 3.
46 C. S. Lewis, 'The Weight of Glory' in *Screwtape Proposes a Toast and other pieces*, p. 109.

47 Lewis, *Miracles*, p. 46.
48 *ibid.*, pp. 46–7.

13 Biographies and Bibliographies on C. S. Lewis

1 Editors' note: As Joe Christopher expected, A. N. Wilson, *C. S. Lewis: A Biography* (London: Collins, 1990) appeared while *A Christian for All Christians* was in the press.
2 Editors' note: Speaking for ourselves, we are quite convinced that 'The Dark Tower' is a genuine Lewis story (though badly written).

SELECT BIBLIOGRAPHY

The works cited here are those referred to in the text and the Notes. For further bibliographical material on C. S. Lewis, see Joe Christopher's essay 'Biographies and Bibliographies on C. S. Lewis' (pp. 216–22).

Works by C. S. Lewis
Spirits in Bondage: A Cycle of Lyrics (London: William Heinemann, 1919), published under the pseudonym Clive Hamilton
The Pilgrim's Regress: An Allegorical Apology for Christianity, Reason and Romanticism (London: J. M. Dent, 1933; London: Collins Fount, 1977)
The Allegory of Love: A Study in Medieval Tradition (Oxford: Oxford University Press, 1936)
Out of the Silent Planet (London: John Lane (the Bodley Head), 1938; London: Pan Books, 1952)
The Personal Heresy: A Controversy, with E. M. Tillyard (Oxford: Oxford University Press, 1939)
The Problem of Pain (London: Geoffrey Bles, 1940; London: Collins Fount, 1977)
The Screwtape Letters (London: Geoffrey Bles, 1942; London: Collins Fount, 1977)
A Preface to Paradise Lost (Oxford: Oxford University Press, 1942, 1960)
Perelandra (London: John Lane (the Bodley Head), 1943); reprinted as *Voyage to Venus (Perelandra)* (London: Pan Books, 1953)
The Abolition of Man; or Reflections on Education with Special Reference to the Teaching of English in the Upper Forms of Schools (Oxford: Oxford University Press, 1943; London: Geoffrey Bles, 1946; London: Collins Fount, 1978)

That Hideous Strength: A Modern Fairy-Tale for Grown-Ups (London: John Lane (the Bodley Head), 1945; London: Pan Books, 1983)

The Great Divorce: A Dream (London: Geoffrey Bles, 1946; London: Collins Fount, 1977)

George MacDonald: An Anthology, ed. C. S. Lewis (London: Geoffrey Bles, 1946)

Essays Presented to Charles Williams, ed. C. S. Lewis (Oxford: Oxford University Press, 1947; Grand Rapids, MI: Wm B. Eerdmans, 1977)

Miracles: A Preliminary Study (London: Geoffrey Bles, 1947; London: Collins Fount, 1977)

Arthurian Torso: Containing the Posthumous Fragment of the Figure of Arthur by Charles Williams and A Commentary on the Arthurian Poems of Charles Williams by C. S. Lewis (Oxford: Oxford University Press, 1948)

The Lion, the Witch and the Wardrobe (London: Geoffrey Bles, 1950; London: Collins Lions, 1980)

Prince Caspian: The Return to Narnia (London: Geoffrey Bles, 1951; London: Collins Lions, 1980)

Mere Christianity (London: Geoffrey Bles, 1952; London: Collins Fount, 1977)

The Voyage of the Dawn Treader (London: Geoffrey Bles, 1952; London: Collins Lions, 1980)

The Silver Chair (London: Geoffrey Bles, 1953; London: Collins Lions, 1980)

The Horse and His Boy (London: Geoffrey Bles, 1954; London: Collins Lions, 1980)

English Literature in the Sixteenth Century Excluding Drama (Oxford: Oxford University Press, 1954)

The Magician's Nephew (London: The Bodley Head, 1955; London: Collins Lions, 1980)

Surprised by Joy: The Shape of My Early Life (London: Geoffrey Bles, 1955; London: Collins Fount, 1977)

The Last Battle (London: The Bodley Head, 1956; London: Collins Lions, 1980)

Till We Have Faces: A Myth Retold (London: Geoffrey Bles, 1956; London: Collins Fount, 1978)

Reflections on the Psalms (London: Geoffrey Bles, 1958; London: Collins Fount, 1977)

The Four Loves (London: Geoffrey Bles, 1960; London: Collins Fontana, 1963)

A Grief Observed (London: Faber & Faber, 1961); originally published under the pseudonym N. W. Clerk

An Experiment in Criticism (Cambridge: Cambridge University Press, 1961)

Letters to Malcolm: Chiefly on Prayer (London: Geoffrey Bles, 1964); reissued as *Prayer: Letters to Malcolm* (London: Collins Fount, 1977)

The Discarded Image: An Introduction to Medieval and Renaissance Literature (Cambridge: Cambridge University Press, 1964)

Poems, ed. Walter Hooper (London: Geoffrey Bles, 1964)

Screwtape Proposes a Toast and other pieces (London: Fontana, 1965; London: Collins Fount, 1977)

Christian Reflections, ed. Walter Hooper (London: Geoffrey Bles, 1967; London: Collins Fount, 1981)

Narrative Poems, ed. Walter Hooper (London: Geoffrey Bles, 1969)

Selected Literary Essays, ed. Walter Hooper (Cambridge: Cambridge University Press, 1969)

Fern-Seed and Elephants and Other Essays on Christianity, ed. Walter Hooper (London: Collins Fontana, 1975)

The Dark Tower and Other Stories, ed. Walter Hooper (London: Collins, 1977; Collins Fount, 1983)

God in the Dock: Essays on Theology, ed. Walter Hooper (London: Collins Fount, 1979)

Of This and Other Worlds, ed. Walter Hooper (London: Collins, 1982; Collins Fount, 1984)

First and Second Things: Essays on Theology and Ethics, ed. Walter Hooper (London: Collins Fount, 1985)

Present Concerns, ed. Walter Hooper (London: Collins Fount, 1986)

Timeless at Heart, ed. Walter Hooper (London: Collins Fount, 1987)

Letters

Letters to an American Lady, ed. Clyde S. Kilby (Grand Rapids, MI: Wm B. Eerdmans, 1967)

They Stand Together: The Letters of C. S. Lewis to Arthur Greeves

(1914–1963), ed. Walter Hooper (New York: Macmillan, 1979; London: Collins, 1979)
Letters to Children, eds. Lyle W. Dorsett and Marjorie Lamp Mead (New York: Macmillan, 1985)
Letters of C. S. Lewis: Edited, with a Memoir by W. H. Lewis, Revised and Enlarged Edition, ed. Walter Hooper (London: Collins Fount, 1988)

Works about C. S. Lewis and his Writings
Lionel Adey, *C. S. Lewis's 'Great War' with Owen Barfield* (University of Victoria, 1978)
Michael D. Aeschliman, *The Restitution of Man: C. S. Lewis and the Case Against Scientism* (Grand Rapids, MI: Wm B. Eerdmans, 1983)
John Beversluis, *C. S. Lewis and the Search for Rational Religion* (Grand Rapids, MI: Wm B. Eerdmans, 1985)
John Beversluis, 'Beyond the Double Bolted Door', *Christian History* 4/3 (1985), pp. 28–31
Humphrey Carpenter, *The Inklings: C. S. Lewis, J. R. R. Tolkien, Charles Williams, and their friends* (London: Allen & Unwin, 1978)
Humphrey Carpenter (ed.), *The Letters of J. R. R. Tolkien* (London: Allen & Unwin, 1981)
James T. Como (ed.), *C. S. Lewis at the Breakfast Table and Other Reminiscences* (London: Collins, 1980)
Richard B. Cunningham, *C. S. Lewis: Defender of the Faith* (Philadelphia: Westminster Press, 1967)
Christopher Derrick, *C. S. Lewis and the Church of Rome: A Study in Proto-Ecumenism* (San Francisco: Ignatius Press, 1981)
Jocelyn Gibb (ed.), *Light on C. S. Lewis* (London: Geoffrey Bles, 1965)
Douglas Gilbert and Clyde S. Kilby, *C. S. Lewis: Images of His World* (Grand Rapids, MI: Wm B. Eerdmans, 1973)
Muriel Graham, *L'oeuvre romanesque de C. S. Lewis*, unpublished PhD thesis, Université de Paris III-Sorbonne Nouvelle, 1973
Roger Lancelyn Green, *Into Other Worlds. Space-Flight in Fiction from Lucian to Lewis* (London: A. Schuman, 1957)
Roger Lancelyn Green and Walter Hooper, *C. S. Lewis: A Biography* (London: Collins Fount, 1979)
Douglas Gresham, *Lenten Lands* (London: Collins, 1989)

Paul A. Karkainen, *Narnia Explored* (Old Tappen, NJ: Fleming H. Revel Co., 1979)

Kathryn Ann Lindskoog, *The Lion of Judah in Never-Never Land* (Grand Rapids, MI: Wm B. Eerdmans, 1973)

John Warwick Montgomery, 'The Chronicles of Narnia and the Adolescent Reader', *Journal of Religious Education* 54 (Sept–Oct 1959)

D. E. Myers, 'The Compleat Anglican: Spiritual Style in the Chronicles of Narnia', *Anglican Theological Review* 66 (April 1984)

James Patrick, *The Magdalen Metaphysicals: Idealism and Orthodoxy at Oxford, 1901–1945* (Macon, GA: Mercer University Press, 1985)

Richard L. Purtill, *C. S. Lewis's Case for the Christian Faith* (San Francisco: Harper & Row, 1981)

George Sayer, *Jack: C. S. Lewis and his Times* (New York: Harper & Row, 1988; London: Macmillan, 1988)

Peter J. Schakel, *Reason and Imagination in C. S. Lewis: A Study of 'Till We Have Faces'* (Grand Rapids, MI: Wm B. Eerdmans, 1984)

Brian Sibley, *Shadowlands: The Story of C. S. Lewis and Joy Davidman* (London: Hodder & Stoughton, 1985)

Charles Taliaferro, 'A Narnian Theory of the Atonement', *Scottish Journal of Theology* 41 (1988), pp. 75–92

Hélène Tuzet, *Le cosmos et l'imagination* (Paris: J. Corti, 1965)

Gunnar Urang, *Shadows of Heaven: Religion and Fantasy in the Fiction of C. S. Lewis, Charles Williams and J. R. R. Tolkien* (London: SCM Press, 1971)

A. N. Wilson, *C. S. Lewis: A Biography* (London: Collins, 1990)

NOTES ON CONTRIBUTORS

Joe R. Christopher is a professor of English at Tarleton State University, Stephenville, Texas. He is the co-compiler, with Joan K. Ostling, of *C. S. Lewis: An Annotated Checklist about Him and His Works* (Kent, OH: Kent State University Press, 1974), and the author of *C. S. Lewis* (Boston: Twayne Publishers, 1987). He is the author of many essays and notes on C. S. Lewis, as well as a variety of other works. He is a member of the Episcopal Church, and is active at the local level ('a lector, a one-time layreader, thrice a vestryperson, and once a senior warden, *etc.*').

Lyle W. Dorsett is Professor of History and Director of the Marion E. Wade Center at Wheaton College, Illinois. He is the author of *And God Came In: The Extraordinary Story of Joy Davidman, Her Life and Marriage to C. S. Lewis* (New York: Macmillan, 1983; London: Marshall Pickering, 1987), the editor of *The Essential C. S. Lewis* (New York: Macmillan, 1988), and the co-editor, with Marjorie Lamp Mead, of *C. S. Lewis' Letters to Children* (New York: Macmillan; London: Collins, 1985)

Paul S. Fiddes is the Principal of Regent's Park College in the University of Oxford, and specialises in teaching Christian doctrine. He is ordained as a minister in the Baptist Union of Great Britain. He is the author of *The Creative Suffering of God* (Oxford: Oxford University Press, 1988), and *Past Event and Present Salvation: The Christian Idea of Atonement* (London: Darton, Longman & Todd, 1989). His latest book, on the relationship between theology and literature, entitled *Freedom and Limit*, is due to be published by Macmillan in 1990.

Brian Horne is Lecturer in Christian Doctrine and History at King's College, London. He is the author of *A World to Gain* (London: Darton, Longman & Todd, 1983), the co-editor of *Seven. An Anglo-American Literary Review*, and a member of the Doctrine Commission of the Church of England.

Peter Kreeft is Professor of Philosophy, Boston College, Massachusetts, and the author of seventeen books, including *C. S. Lewis* (Christendom College Press, 1979), *Heaven, the Heart's Deepest Longing* (Ignatius Press) and *Love is Stronger Than Death* (San Francisco: Harper & Row, 1987).

Aidan Mackey is a Roman Catholic writer and researcher, with a particular interest in G. K. Chesterton. He has had a long career as a teacher, and is currently the administrator of the Top Meadow Trust, which aims 'to purchase Chesterton's home, Top Meadow, Beaconsfield, and to establish there a centre for the study of his work and thought'.

Basil Mitchell, now retired, was Nolloth Professor of the Christian Religion, Oxford. He is the author of *The Justification of Religious Belief* (London: Macmillan, 1973) and *Morality: Religious and Secular* (Oxford: Clarendon Press, 1980).

James Patrick is Provost of The College of Saint Thomas More in Fort Worth, Texas, and is the author of *The Magdalen Metaphysicals: Idealism and Orthodoxy at Oxford, 1901–1945* (Macon, GA: Mercer University Press, 1985). He is a Roman Catholic theologian who lectures and writes on English Christian intellectuals of the nineteenth and twentieth centuries: C. S. Lewis, G. K. Chesterton, Charles Williams, and R. G. Collingwood.

Richard L. Purtill is Professor of Philosophy at Western Washington University, Bellingham, Washington. He is the author of many works, including *Thinking About Religion: A Philosophical Introduction to Religion* (Englewood Cliffs, NJ: Prentice-Hall, 1978) and *C. S. Lewis's Case for the Christian Faith* (San Francisco: Harper & Row, 1981).

Peter J. Schakel is a Peter C. and Emajean Cook Professor of English at Hope College, Holland, Michigan. The author of *The Poetry of Jonathan Swift* (Madison: University of Wisconsin Press, 1978), *Reading with the Heart: The Way into Narnia* (Grand Rapids, MI: Wm B. Eerdmans, 1987), and *Reason and Imagination in C. S. Lewis: A Study of 'Till We Have Faces'* (Grand Rapids, MI: Wm B. Eerdmans, 1984), he is also the editor of *The Longing for a Form: Essays on the Fiction of C. S. Lewis* (Kent, OH: Kent State University Press, 1977), and a co-editor of a forthcoming collection of essays, *Word and Story in C. S. Lewis* (Columbia: University of Missouri Press). He is a member of, and an active layperson in, the Third Reformed Church, Holland, a congregation in the Reformed Church of America.

Bernard Sellin is Professor of English Language and Literature at the University of Brest, France. He is the author of *The Life and Works of David Lindsay* (Cambridge: Cambridge University Press, 1981), and has also edited *L'Ecosse* (Rennes: Institut culturel de Bretagne, 1986) and *Pays de Galles, Ecosse, Irlande* (Brest: CRBC, 1987). His study of *The Novels of Robin Jenkins* is now being revised for publication.

Jacques Sys is a Roman Catholic scholar with a particular interest in C. S. Lewis' thought. He teaches in the Department of English Studies, Université de Lille III, France. His doctorate was on the subject of time and history in the works of C. S. Lewis, and he is the author of several essays on Lewis.

Andrew Walker is the Director of the C. S. Lewis Centre. He is a sociologist, a lay theologian in the Orthodox tradition, the author of *Restoring the Kingdom* (London: Hodder & Stoughton, [2]1988), *Enemy Territory: The Christian Struggle for the Modern World* (London: Hodder & Stoughton, 1987), and is the editor of *Different Gospels: Christian Orthodoxy and Modern Theologies* (London: Hodder & Stoughton, 1988).